SO-AUO-535

Is the Left Brain Always Right?

A GUIDE TO WHOLE CHILD DEVELOPMENT

by

Clare Cherry
Douglas Godwin
Jesse Staples

Photographs by Sam Cherry

Fearon Teacher Aids
Belmont, California

Anatomical Illustrations: Tom Rolain

Book and Cover Design: Bonnie Grover

Copyright © 1989 by Fearon Teacher Aids, 500 Harbor Boulevard, Belmont, California 94002. All rights reserved. No part of this book may be reproduced by any means, transmitted, or translated into a machine language without written permission from the publisher.

ISBN 0-8224-3911-5

Printed in the United States of America
1. 9 8 7 6 5 4 3 2

To all of our right-hemisphere–dominant friends who don't take what we say for granted, but keep searching for new possibilities

Contents

Preface

THIS BOOK is an exploration of the asymmetry of the human brain and of the types of developmental experiences that lend themselves to that asymmetry. For the past 25 years, new discoveries in the fields of neurology and psychology have provided fresh insights into the behavior of young children. Breakthroughs in the study of the brain and the central nervous system are providing new sensitivity regarding human development that has stimulated our interest in the different functions of the two brain hemispheres. The authors have each had experiences—in and out of the classroom—that have led us to wonder why Suzie can't seem to adjust to the group or why Andy can't stay with one task for what seems to us a reasonable amount of time. Our search for these answers has led us to write this book.

Several concerns repeatedly arose in our discussions. First, we did not want this book to be another "bandwagon." Whenever something new comes along, there is a temptation to latch onto it because of its popularity. In doing so, it is easy to make premature statements and claims based on insufficient evidence, such as the many simplistic stereotypes regarding "right brain" and "left brain" traits that have become popular but that cannot be supported by any substantial body of research. We have attempted to avoid such oversimplifications because we are aware that the reader will rely in part on our interpretation of the research. We have therefore taken a conservative stance on which findings provide sufficient evidence to be considered valid.

Second, we wanted to give the reader information that relates as closely as possible to the original work of the researcher. We have, where possible, gone to the neurological and psychological research itself and to the research summaries conducted by other researchers in those fields. We felt it was from this base that we could gather the information and the activities that would have the greatest impact on the developing child.

Third, we deliberated and debated about what information concerning the functions of the brain the reader needs in order to better understand and work with children, what aspects of the new findings would be of greatest interest, and in what form and at what technical level that information would be of most value. Our conclusions led us to provide a condensed overview of the anatomy of the brain and of some of the more significant brain theories, with a more detailed treatment of the theories related to hemispheric function. Much of our discussion of child development is based on the work of the late Dr. Newell C. Kephart when he was a psychology professor at Purdue University, Indiana, executive director of the Achievement Center for Children (sponsored by the U.S. Children's Bureau) in Lafayette, Indiana, and director of the Glen Haven, Colorado, Achievement Camp for Children. We believe that Kephart's work, as well as that of Dr. Miriam L. Bender, who worked with Kephart at Purdue, provides a valid guide to wholesome, balanced perceptual-motor development. We also depend heavily on the work of Dr. Jean Ayres, professor emeritus of the University of Southern California, as well as on Piaget's work in the cognitive field.

Fourth, on the basis of our own combined experiences, we created an assessment guide to help readers determine dominance factors in the children with whom they are involved. And finally, we translated our conclusions into meaningful classroom activities designed to enhance total development, including that of the functions of both right and left hemispheres of the brain. We rely heavily on both movement and sensorimotor experiences because they are the most developmentally appropriate for preschool and primary-grade children. Because development continues through age 11, however, we have also included more complex variations of the basic activities.

We urge the reader to look at this work not as something to get through during a school semester or year but rather as an ongoing supplement to other activities promoting the natural growth and development of all young children. The activities are not sacred. Feel free to add to them, subtract from them, or otherwise modify them in whatever way best meets your own teaching style, your classroom environment, and the needs of the children in your life.

We wish to thank
- the students in the early childhood graduate classes at Texas A & M University for their many hours of dialogue with Doug,
- Jesse's students and fellow teachers at Lytle Creek and Urbita schools in San Bernardino, especially Sharon Sedrowski and Janice Down, as well as Gwen and Boyd Johnson at the Diagnostic Education Success Center in Redlands, California,
- Jesse's mentors, Dr. Clara Lee Edgar and Betty Kesterson, and Lois Roberts, Lou Denti, and Dr. Wayne Rubel for their encouragement,
- Clare's co-workers at Congregation Emanu El Nursery and Elementary School in San Bernardino for their willingness to try out the various activities and for lending us their students for the delightful photographs taken by Clare's partner and husband, Sam Cherry,
- Jean Warren and Dick and Liz Wilmes for their inspiration, Sunny Wallick for her interest, Lois Ledbetter for her critiques, Barbara Armentrout and Ina Tabibian at David S. Lake Publishers for their editorial support, and
- all our other friends and colleagues, especially our cooperative and patient families, who have helped us through to this conclusion.

CLARE CHERRY
DOUG GODWIN
JESSE STAPLES

SECTION I

Whole Child Development

CHAPTER 1

Is the Left Brain Always Right?

*F*rom 7 A.M., parents had been bringing children into the
private school and rushing off to their various responsibilities
throughout the city. By 10 A.M., the entire center of seven
preschool and kindergarten classes had become a wondrous
and beautiful ballet in which developing children were
weaving in and out of activities and experiences. Here were
2-year-olds crawling in and out under the furniture. Here
were 3-year-olds busy giving shots, applying bandages, and
making sick dolls well in the "hospital" that their teachers
had set up for them.

In the play telephone booth, Bobby was busy calling home
to his mother. Nearby, Jennifer was deeply engrossed in a
pegboard activity. Across the hall, the 4 year olds were
working puzzles, putting various building toys together, and
taking turns on the balance beam. A colorful array of paints
were put out on a table. Brushes—fat, thin, long-handled,
and short—were dipped into the sparkling colors and swished
about over the large triangular-shaped papers that had been
put out for use. Ho, Johnnie, and Lupe were playing with
unit blocks that they had made into a "train." They were now
extending it into the hallway. Jean and Eduardo were
creating a marvelous sunburst design with the large mosaic
tiles spread out on the floor. And in the kindergarten room
next door, similar activities were going on. Painting, puzzles,

mosaics. Three children were sprawled around a large circular paper on the floor, drawing birthday greetings for one of their classmates. There were trees, flowers, and airplanes. There were dots, lines, shapes, and spaces—as an enticing example of creative cooperation as one would hope to find in kindergarten. Pedro and Swen were cleaning out the hamster cage, and Joan, Marea, and Leah were restructuring the playhouse area. Ruthie and Richard were at the snack table spreading peanut butter on their celery sticks and counting 20 raisins as the "menu" instructed. The entire room, as the rest of the school, was abuzz with the happy sound of active minds.

Just then, Ms. Stone, the director, walked in with a visitor. She introduced the teacher, saying, "Joan, I want you to meet Mrs. Rosco. She has a 5-year-old who is ready for kindergarten. I'll leave you to explain your program." The director left, leaving the dubious Mrs. Rosco behind. As Joan began enthusiastically describing the learning activities that were taking place, Mrs. Rosco just shook her head. She had her own questions: "But when do they learn?" "Surely these children won't be ready for the first grade next year, will they?" "How do you stand the noise?" As Joan tried to explain, Mrs. Rosco said, "I think it's nice for children to go to school so they can learn to sit still and be quiet, don't you?" Finally, "Well, I don't think this is really the kind of place for my son. He knows the alphabet already, and he can count to 50. I sure don't want him to just waste time playing. I want to send him to a kindergarten where he can start learning something." And she gradually edged her way out of the room and subsequently out of the building, muttering to herself as she went. She was just too overwhelmed by all the excitement of this marvelous right-hemisphere-oriented environment and its developmentally oriented curriculum. Failing to see the value of children using their own bodily movements freely and using their inherent creative abilities *in the self-pacing of their own experiences, Mrs. Rosco was one of that vast category of well-meaning, intelligent individuals who are tied in to traditional, formal, and often outdated educational systems.*

That very same day, Mary W., the new kindergarten teacher at the public school down the street, was having a comparable experience. She had worked hard to make her classroom a delightful place. Her students had become deeply involved in the imaginative games and manipulative activities she had presented. They had asked important questions in pursuit of the many ideas she had introduced. Her bulletin boards had stimulated stories created by the children, and a number of parents had expressed excitement with the new vocabulary they were bringing home. Mary had capitalized on planting beans and building ant farms to develop a number of thinking skills. She felt warm inside every time she entered the classroom and realized how electrifying the environment was. She was confident that she would indeed be a successful teacher.

When the principal called her into the office, she was certain that it was to praise her for the outstanding learning environment she had created. Instead, she heard, "Ms. W., I know you're a new teacher, so I haven't wanted to interfere with your plans. I wanted to give you a chance to get oriented to the school and to the idea of having your own classroom. But I realize I've let things get out of hand. Now here are some workbooks I ordered for you. I've arranged to have your tables replaced by individual desk chairs—that way, the children can be kept in their seats more. Now I want you to start getting them ready for the first grade. They're old enough to stop playing around so much and to start learning something. For example, this is the spelling book. . . ." As he went on and on, Mary's heart gave a few jumps, her stomach felt as though it were going to cave in, the back of her neck became tense and hot, and all her enthusiasm for her job became a memory. With head bowed and feet dragging, she went back to her room, looked around at that right-brained world, and shouted, "IS THE LEFT BRAIN ALWAYS RIGHT?"

YOU WOULD THINK SO if you examine the number of times scenarios such as the ones above take place in both private and public educational institutions. The traditional educational systems are based on left-hemisphere processing skills. These systems are reluctant to allow for change, in spite of new insights into how the mind works and how learning occurs. The system is so ingrained with what has taken place in the past in education and with what might be taking place in the future in education that it leaves little room for the important factor of what is taking place at the moment. Teaching methods have become ingrained in linear, analytical, predetermined expectations that per-petuate themselves in the world of academia. The goal is the "degree" rather than the amount of learning that is acquired. The goal is "class-room management" rather than the joy of learning. The goal is meeting the expectations of next year's teacher rather than responding to the inspiration and curiosity of the moment.

There have always been gifted teachers who related to their students in humane and meaningful ways, thus bringing out the best in the children. But these teachers are often forced to return to more tradi-tional methods, regardless of the rate of success they may be having. Needing their jobs and their paychecks, they frequently succumb to the establishment. As new recruits enter the teaching field, the credentialing system forces them into objective thinking. Those whose sensibilities introduce elements of subjectiveness and affectiveness risk being called incompetent or at least eccentric.

Back to Basics

In spite of the establishment, increasing numbers of teachers have learned to expand their teaching to the farthest reaches of the mind. As they take into consideration the newer models of lateral and vertical thinking, we continually hear from the establishment the frightened countering cry of "back to basics." It is certainly an important part of education to concentrate on reading, writing, and mathematics. These are solid left-brain-hemisphere skills steeped in tradition without which students would not be able to participate in higher academic pursuits nor achieve success in the everyday world of business. Their usefulness for making this a better world, however, cannot be realized unless they are balanced with an equal amount of right-hemisphere activities, such as imagination, holistic and visionary thinking, imagery, and sensitivity to others and to new and intuitive ideas. Mathematical computations become important, for example, only after the architect has imagined and visualized the expansion of a suspended dome large enough to cover an athletic field. Only when the forces of both hemispheres respond to each other in an informative and integrative manner that includes the lower brain functions as well will we find ourselves on the way to the realization of our full potential.

A Two-sided World

We live in a two-sided world in which nature gives us balance and harmony. Light is balanced by dark, and dim is balanced by bright. Large is balanced by small, and big is balanced by little. We have hot and cold, hard and soft, smooth and rough. We have long and short, fat and thin, stiff and flexible, and shiny and dull. We have dry air balanced by moist air. We have still air balanced by wind. As we look at the natural world, we find balance everywhere.

We could reverse all the foregoing pairs and they would still be balanced. Because each half of the pair is the opposite of the other, the pair is asymmetrical.

If both sides of a balance are identical, then we have symmetry. If a system is balanced but one side differs from the other in content, appearance, or kind, then we have asymmetry. Figure 1.1 is symmetrically balanced. Figure 1.2 is also balanced, but it is asymmetrically balanced.

As with other things in the natural world, the two sides of our body are alike. Or are they? When we look at photographs of ourselves, we

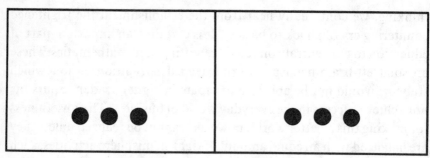

FIGURE 1.1. SYMMETRICAL BALANCE

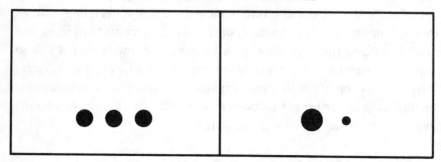

FIGURE 1.2. ASYMMETRICAL BALANCE

look symmetrical, as in Photo 1.1. But if we cut the photo in half and put each half together with a mirror image, we have two different likenesses, as in Photos 1.2 and 1.3.

One side is usually thinner than the other. The eyes may slant differently; the eyebrows may be of different shapes or thicknesses. If a full figure were shown, the limbs on one composite would undoubtedly be of slightly different size than those of the other. In most people, the parts and functions of the right side of the body are predominant—not as the result of use, but from the moment of birth. For example, the skin of an infant is more sensitive on the right side than on the left. The fingertips of the right hand and the sole of the right foot have more ridges than their left counterparts. The bone mass of the right hand is greater than that of the left. The same is true of the right side of the pelvic bones and of other parts of the body. Some parts and functions of the body are more predominant on the left side, however. For example, the ridges on the left palm are more numerous than on the right—as opposed to the ridges on the fingers. The femur bone of the

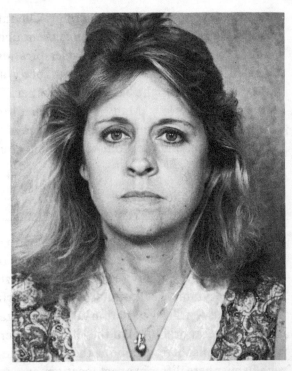

PHOTO 1.1

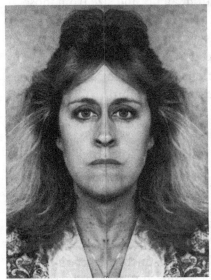

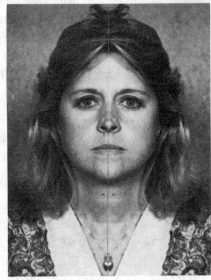

PHOTO 1.2.
COMPOSITE OF RIGHT HALVES

PHOTO 1.3.
COMPOSITE OF LEFT HALVES

left arm is larger than that of the right. The rate of skeletal growth is greater on the left side and, strangely enough, so is the amount of sodium emitted through the skin by perspiration. Even the organs that we have in duplicate throughout our body are asymmetrical. One kidney is lower down the back than the other. The right lung is usually heavier than the left. Many other such differences can be found throughout the body, although some organs, such as the heart, the liver, the spleen, and the stomach, have no counterpart.

The Two-sided Brain

Like much of the body, the brain appears to be symmetrical. To the casual observer, its two cerebral hemispheres seem identical. In actuality, however, many sections differ in size, shape, or placement from their asymmetrical counterparts. The surfaces of the two sides of the brain show striking variation in the organization of the cortex. The outer side (temporal lobe) of the left hemisphere is larger than that of the right hemisphere. Many of the walnutlike contours (fissures) of each hemisphere differ in exact location, angle, and size from those of the corresponding areas of the other. Microscopically, the hemispheres are also asymmetrical in such details as cell size, "packing density" of cells, and distribution of types of cells. Even chemically, the hemispheres differ. There is a strong difference between the brains of males and females. This difference is present before birth (Ornstein and Thompson, 1984, pg. 170).

Relationship of the Brain to the Body

In most people, the right hemisphere controls the left side of the body and the left hemisphere controls the right side. Both hemispheres receive messages from the body, however. In acting on those messages, each hemisphere controls the activity of the opposite side. As the newborn slowly gains control of the body, one hemisphere becomes more efficient than the other in acting on incoming stimuli. As this efficiency increases, that hemisphere assumes a dominant role in the child's physical behavior. By definition, dominance is the tendency for one hemisphere to process a particular type of information and to control response behavior based on that information. If the left hemisphere becomes dominant in physical activities, the child then becomes right-handed; the opposite occurs if the right hemisphere becomes dominant. In some cases hemisphere dominance does not become complete, resulting in a degree of ambidextrous traits.

Communication between the Hemispheres

Though each hemisphere processes information somewhat different-ly, there is a constant exchange of information and joint processing of thought and activity through a bridge, called the corpus callosum, that extends between the hemispheres. Through this cluster of connecting nerve fibers, constant coordination takes place as each hemisphere makes its contributions to the thought and behavior of the child. In the mature brain, the only way that memory, perceptions, or impulses to perform fine motor-coordination tasks can reach both hemispheres is to pass through some of the billions of fibers of the corpus callosum. Just as the size and shape of any other part of the body vary among individuals, so do the size and shape of the corpus callosum. Those of males differ from those of females; those of left-handed people differ from those of right-handed people; those of people of one profession differ from those of another profession (Trevarthen, 1987 pg. 109). Also, there are differences according to cognitive skill; this seems to indicate that people differ in mental abilities because the anatomy of their cerebral hemispheres differs. Even though people's brains may have slight anatomical and functional differences, developmental patterns and thought-processing patterns of the brain are common to all. Although the corpus callosum is in place even before birth, much rearranging and adjustment, including additional myelination (the gradual insulation of a neural axon with a fatty substance called myelin), takes place during the first two years of life. Consequently, until age 2, infants and toddlers function primarily as though they had only a right hemisphere, and they respond better to those functions processed by the right hemisphere than to those processed by the left.

Contributions of Each Hemisphere to Thought

Given the asymmetrical physical differences of the hemispheres, it is not surprising that each deals with information in different ways. The chart, "Asymmetry in Hemispheric Functions," lists some of the ways in which these differences are processed.

Normal people do not have only half a brain, however, and they do not have two brains. They have a single brain made up of two parts that function best when their natural integrative mechanisms are intensified. The two hemispheres are of equal importance, one balancing the other, and each contributing in its own way to the development of the whole child.

Creativity

Note that creativity is not included in the chart of asymmetrical brain functions. The authors believe that to produce a truly creative act, idea, or product takes the intuitive, spontaneous, holistic, visuo-spatial, originative, metaphoric, and sensory functions of the right hemisphere balanced by the logical, organizational, and linear skills of the left hemisphere. Ideas and concepts produced by the right hemisphere alone are frequently nonfunctional until they can be tempered with the skills of the left hemisphere. Creativity is the process of making a change in the world—however minute. Children, through their exploratory and originative ideas, frequently make "new" discoveries that, when joined with left-hemisphere balance and awareness, can become harmonious creative works (see also pg. 133).

Whole Child Development

Balance can be achieved only by "whole child" development. This means that we develop not only the left or the right hemisphere but the whole brain, which must be a partner to itself. Whole child development means that we develop not only the brain but the physical self as well. Whole child development means we develop not by bits and pieces, nor

ASYMMETRY IN HEMISPHERIC FUNCTIONS

Left Hemisphere	**Right Hemisphere**
Analytic Analyzes the data	Intuitive Responds to the data intuitively
Logical Uses logic in handling information	Spontaneous Handles information spontaneously
Temporal Is aware of time: past, present, and future	Atemporal Processes information without consideration of time
Sequential Deals with events and actions sequentially	Random Deals with events and actions randomly
Orderly Organizes information	Diffuse Diffuses information
Systematic and Formal Deals with information and objects in a variety of systematic ways	Casual and Informal Deals with information and objects according to the need of the moment
Linear Reduces whole to parts and reassembles parts to whole	Holistic Sees only the gestalt (wholeness) of information and objects
Verbal Processes language into meaningful communication: receptive and expressive	Nonverbal Responds to tones, body language, and touch
Compositional Writes music scientifically	Responsive Responds to tones and sounds
Computational Uses mathematics and computations	Visuo-spatial Perceives shapes and patterns; intuitively estimates
Practical Concerned with cause and effect	Originative Concerned with ideas and theories
Abstract Has abstract-oriented cognitive functions	Sensory Has sensory-oriented cognitive functions
Factual Uses facts	Visual Uses imagery
Concrete Explicit, precise	Metaphoric Symbolic, representational

do we assist in developing only bits and pieces of a person; we develop the whole person.

A special problem arises, however. As we examine the items in the list for hemispheric preferences (pg. 13) and relate them to the focus of educational curricula, where do we find the greater emphasis? And as we recount the games some teachers play in the name of education, which hemisphere is favored? The answer causes us to reexamine the dilemma facing our kindergarten teacher, Mary W.: Is the left brain always right? But if all activities focused mostly on the right hemisphere, would the child be any better off? The answers to these questions are perhaps the answers to the following questions, which are the focus of this book.

• What kinds of information about the brain would best help us in our day-to-day planning for and working with young children?

• How does whole child development take place and how does it progress?

• What are the thinking and learning patterns of young children?

• What can be done when a child's thought patterns become too one-sided?

• What kinds of activities develop the whole child, providing a balance and integration between the right and left hemispheres of the brain?

Summary

Traditional educational systems are based on left-hemisphere processing skills, although there are always gifted teachers who reach out to those who function best through the right hemisphere. The recent "back to basics" trend has put greater emphasis on reading, writing, and mathematics and has devalued much of the imagination, visionary thinking, imagery, and related skills of the right hemisphere. We live in a two-sided world, however, and the brain, like the rest of the body and much else in the natural world, is bilaterally asymmetrical. We don't have two brains, and we don't have half a brain. Rather, we have a two-sided brain that functions most productively when both sides are able to develop their partnership and work in unison, each complementing the other, and each having valuable contributions to make. The functions of each hemisphere are complementary to the functions of the other. Integration of their functions serves to bring balance into children's lives.

For Further Study

1. There has been much recent research on the functions of the two hemispheres of the brain. Look up a journal article on the subject and write a summary of it.
2. Observe a prekindergarten classroom. Note how many activities are geared toward right-hemisphere processes and how many toward those of the left.
3. Do the same in a third-grade classroom.
4. Why is it important to promote creative thinking? What research defends the process of creativity?

References

Ornstein, Robert E., and Richard F. Thompson. 1984. *The Amazing Brain.* Boston: Houghton Mifflin.

Trevarthen, Colwyn. 1987. "Brain Development." In *Oxford Companion to the Mind,* ed. Richard L. Gregory. New York: Oxford University Press.

CHAPTER 2

Psychological Models of the Brain

It's a delightful spring day, and the children in Mr. Gary's class are working on mosaics for Mother's Day gifts. Brian and Paul are busily getting started, sitting next to each other at a small table. Paul says, "Whatcha doing that for?" Brian replies, "Well, when you make mosaic, first you have to get all the pieces you're gonna use and put them in little piles and know where you're gonna put it." Paul disagrees, saying, "No. No. It's better if you put it on just like that. See? You just sprinkle it on and let it look purty. See that?" He sprinkles several colors of small rocks all over his board, on which he had already spread wide bands of glue. Brian, nervous, says, "No. See? It won't come out the way it's s'posed to be. You have to have one color here and one color there and then it looks right." But Paul persists. "No! No! Let me show you. You see. You shake it," he says as he sprinkles glitter over the rocks. "See how good it looks. That's good. It looks good." Brian shouts, "No! That doesn't look good to me. It gets on the floor and the teacher won't like it and he'll be mad and 'sides, it doesn't even look right."

THIS EPISODE is a typical example of how people who favor the right-hemisphere functions differ from those who favor those of the left. Brian is very organized and precise in everything he does. He plans ahead, follows the rules, and always tries to stay within known parameters. He has carefully sketched out a drawing of a tree, and with great precision, he assembles brown rocks for the tree trunk, and green rocks for the top of the tree. He uses his glue bottle with care, putting on only a few drops at a time because "the teacher said so." He keeps wiping the glue off his hands so "it can't be messy." As he observes Paul's actions, he gets so upset that he finally puts his hands up to his head and says, "I can't stand it." Paul, however, is having a marvelous experience. He is operating on pure intuition. He has an innate sense of color balance and harmony and a good understanding of the use of space. With a great deal of imagination, he creates an abstract design by sensing what will look pleasing to the eye rather than by any kind of planning. He's absorbed in the process of handling the various colors, gambling with the outcome of how he puts them on—not haphazardly, as it may appear, but with a carefree manner indicative of sheer joy in what he is producing.

Each of these boys is doing the right thing. Creative experiences should fit one's own style of operation. As in this example, materials should be given to children, and they should be allowed to use them in their own way. But, by the same token, each would probably benefit from a few of the qualities of the other. Brian would benefit from allowing his imagination a little more freedom, for imagination unused becomes stagnant. Paul would benefit from a little planning, thus better enabling him to utilize his artistic skills for a truly creative product.

As we observe Paul and Brian, we search for tools that will best help us understand what we are observing. We have therefore selected a popular model used by researchers to study the brain: the examination of the asymmetrical nature of its hemispheres. The term used for this process is "hemisphericity."

Hemisphericity: The Asymmetrical Processes

As previously stated, it has been known for some time that each hemisphere controls the opposite side of the body and that the left hemisphere of most people is dominant, controlling both speech and the right side of the body. Paul-Pierre Broca, a French surgeon and anthropologist, discovered the relationship to the right side of the body in 1861, when he noted that people with injuries to their left hemisphere either lost their speech or had it seriously affected. Subsequent studies began to show that the right hemisphere specializes in spatial awareness.

The greatest gains in understanding the functions of the two hemispheres came from the work of Roger Sperry and his colleagues (Sperry, Gazzaniga, and Bogen, 1969). From their early work in the 1930s, the surgical procedure of severing the corpus callosum was developed to reduce or stop seizures in extreme cases of epilepsy. The procedure allowed the patient to live a normal life, but communication between the hemispheres was no longer possible. By observing people whose corpus callosum had been severed, Sperry and others were able to examine more specifically the functions of each hemisphere. Some of their findings are listed in Chapter 1 (pg. 13).

It appears that from the early stages of in utero development of the brain, each hemisphere begins to be "wired" in its own way. Signs of asymmetry manifest themselves in the preschool years, when, some studies show, some asymmetrical strategies parallel the strategies used by adults. Overall, the traits and the resulting knowledge of the left hemisphere are more easily measured than those of the right, because language is housed in the left hemisphere. The traits and knowledge of the right hemisphere, while equally important to human behavior, are less easily detected and measured, because they are not expressed through spoken language. For example, a person who plays the piano by ear cannot explain the relationship between the sounds but is able to produce them over and over again, often in intricate ways. Brandwein (1971) calls these intuitive traits "operations," which are found in the right hemisphere and therefore do not lend themselves to language and left-hemisphere logic. He considers an operation to be a right-brain concept. Young children have been shown to produce many operational concepts for which they have little or no explanation.

The Nature of Psychological Dominance

Although much is still to be learned, it has been clearly established that both hemispheres are active and contribute to any given task; one hemisphere does not take a break while the other takes over. The contribution of each hemisphere, however, is related to the cognitive processes that are unique to it.

Both hemispheres seem to have a capacity for many of the same cognitive functions, though each carries them out in its own unique way. Due to the unique makeup of each hemisphere, however, each becomes more efficient than the other in carrying out certain functions. In those particular cognitive functions, the hemisphere is said to be dominant. Dominance therefore results when processes unique to a hemisphere are active or, in case of dual capacity, when one hemisphere takes charge of the process.

A child who uses cognitive strategies of the right hemisphere to approach a task is said to be right-brained for that task. A child who organizes his or her world with many more cognitive strategies from the right hemisphere is called a right-brained child. In the case of the two boys we have been observing, Brian displays left-brain tendencies because his behavior reflects many functions for which the left hemisphere is noted. The opposite is true for Paul. Each boy approaches the world in his own unique way.

Implications for Educators

There are a couple of cautions to be aware of if we are to effectively apply the concepts of hemisphericity to our work with young children. First, the catch phrases "right brain" and "left brain" are oversimplifications. They are not completely accurate and tend to close our eyes to alternate behaviors displayed by a given child. Because both hemispheres are involved in a given function, with one perhaps playing the dominant role, the best we can say is that for that function, the child shows right-brain or left-brain tendencies. For other tasks, the child will utilize strategies from the other hemisphere or even integrated strategies, which means that the child can utilize strategies from either hemisphere in order to achieve a task. By avoiding labels, we can observe each child for unique characteristics. By being exact in our evaluation of each behavior, we can plan more effectively for and with the children.

The second caution is that dominance is not a sign of mental problems or malfunctions. Many children show a high frequency of dominance of one hemisphere. T. G. Bever (1983) describes three possible causes:

1. Physiology of the brain
   - Sally is human, so each hemisphere performs in a human way.
   - Right-brain tendencies run in Bill's family; he may well have inherited the tendencies.
2. Experience in the world
   - Most of Johnny's school activities require left-brain processing, so this hemisphere dominates most of his habits.
3. Choice of the child
   - Carmiel chooses imagery over language in remembering where she puts the doll.

The presence of these variables in brain dominance means that children are pliable and their mental processes are enriched by planned experiences in their environment.

In addressing asymmetry in young children, the authors have set the following three goals:

1. *To enhance each child's capacity to use hemisphere strengths.* For children who favor imagery, we wish to enrich its depth and breadth (see pgs. 125–29). We want to provide them with a variety of opportunities to use it and to translate it into personally meaningful products. For children who are orderly and precise, we want to provide opportunities to expand their organizational skills and utilize them in classroom activities. Each child then can contribute his or her special strengths to the needs and activities of the group.

2. *To increase each child's capacity to use new processes in the less dominant hemisphere.* For Sammy, whose only organizational scheme is to "keep everything within the county lines at all times," games that favor placement values or cleanup strategies that use silhouette or color markings to show where things go can be

helpful. Carla's consistent "one-piece-at-a-time" approach to putting scattered rice back into the converted water table might be balanced with two-handed painting or blowing bubbles (pgs. 158–60 and pgs. 210–12).

3. *To give each child opportunities to use strategies from both hemispheres to address given situations.* Such integration provides for a multiplicity of mental strategies for problem solving. For example, one time Donny may remember where he placed his lunch pail through a mental image of where he put it. Another time, he might decide to identify a hiding place for buried treasure by taking six steps north of the corner of the house and eight steps toward the gatepost. Through application of a variety of approaches to given tasks, children create a rich repertoire of mental skills in both hemispheres.

The Triune Brain

Lois and David are in the playhouse area. Lois says, "Let's make pancakes. You get the bowl." David gets a bowl and puts it on the play sink. Sally pretends to pour something in. David says, "You got to have eggs." He pretends to crack an imaginary egg and add it to the imaginary mixture. Sally stirs it very slowly. She says, "I'll make it very smooth." David grabs the spoon out of her hand, takes hold of the bowl, and, beating the imaginary mixture vigorously, he says, "See, this is how you do it." Lois says, "We have to get the frying pan ready. Light the fire." David says, "If we don't eat soon I'm gonna starve to death. I'm hungry." He runs out of the playhouse area to the snack table. He grabs a piece of cinnamon toast out of Jackie's hand, puts it to his nose and says, "This smells good." He then takes a big bite out of it.

The teacher says, "How dare you take someone's food like that! You know we all have to wait for our turn." David throws the rest of the toast on the floor, looks at the angry

*face of the teacher and the confused face of Jackie, and he
runs out of the room. He sits down on the floor in the
hallway and begins to cry. In a few moments, he stops
crying, walks abashedly into the room, and starts explaining
to the teacher how he smelled the cinnamon and it made him
hungry.*

This episode is perhaps best explained by the triune brain model, one
of the ways that has been developed for studying the brain (Figure 2.1).
This model views the brain as actually being three brains, representing
the evolution of human beings from fish. This phylogenetic model
superimposes three separate brains over one another and incorporates
them into a multiple-function operating system. The theory, developed
by Paul D. MacLean (1978), is somewhat oversimplified. The hierarchy
of human development is much more complex than a vertical relation-

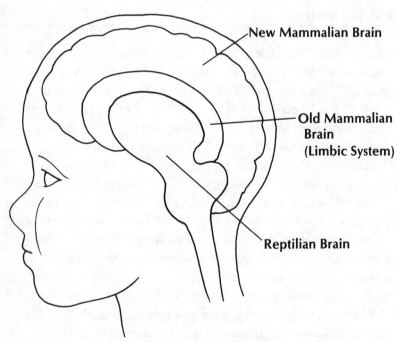

FIGURE 2.1. THE TRIUNE BRAIN

ship between the three parts of the triune brain. This theory does give us an important point of view, however, on the process of our development. The three parts are the following:

1. *The Reptilian Brain.* So-called because it is similar to that found in all reptiles, including those of prehistoric times that roamed the earth for hundreds of millions of years, the reptilian brain constitutes the upper part of our brain stem, including the reticular activating system, the midbrain, the basal ganglia, and most of the hypothalamus. It governs our preservation-of-life and survival instincts, as well as most of our sensory input.

    In the scenario above, the reptilian brain comes into play in David's fear of the consequences of his actions, which caused him to run out of the room.

2. *The Old Mammalian Brain.* Encircling the reptilian brain is the limbic system (Figure 3.4), which is called the old mammalian brain. It controls our hormonal activity. It deals with our emotions and much of our learning and memory functions and also controls our autonomic nervous system, which governs certain unconscious body activities, such as breathing and heartbeat.

    The limbic system comes into play in the scenario in several ways: (a) The olfactory stimuli from the cinnamon toast overwhelmed David's ability to use reason to alleviate his hunger; (b) crying released his emotional tension enough so that he was able to calm down and reconsider his actions; (c) the teacher's anger was an automatic response to the crisis.

3. *The New Mammalian Brain (Neocortex).* This is the cerebrum (Figure 3.4), which is fairly well developed in primates, but especially in humans. This is the thinking part of the brain, by far the largest and most active part. It is able to employ both lower sections, thus extending its powers and possibilities. This part of the brain, of course, is the center for intellectual activity through which so many of our functions take place.

    The cerebral cortex was the part of the brain that enabled the children to plan how to make pancakes. This effort involved recall, sequence, procedure, and following through with a plan. Also, the conversation about eating alerted David to the reaction he was getting from the old mammalian brain regarding hunger.

Implications for Educators

Traditionally, education is geared largely toward the analytical and problem-solving functions of the cerebral cortex, without much regard for the use of the total brain. The model of the triune brain, however, indicates that the integrative teaching techniques proposed by the authors are not to be overlooked. Lozanov (1978) suggests that when the affective system is taken into consideration, learning is enhanced. Here is an example.

Tom, age 7, was feeling very hurt because his best friend, Jim, spent the entire recess ignoring him and playing excitedly with Jose, a new student in class. During the ensuing arithmetic lesson, Tom daydreamed, doodled, and was generally withdrawn. Ms. Ruth, his teacher, had observed his dilemma on the playground. She cared enough to walk over to Tom and say, "I would like you and Jim to help me with the new bulletin board right after lunch." Tom immediately relaxed, bent over his arithmetic book, and quickly completed the assignment.

It has been shown that students experience learning at multiple levels at all times (Numella & Rosengren, 1986). Deep emotions within the old mammalian brain can block out reason and insight. Our goal must be to develop a balance between the older brains and the new, allowing for emotional reactions and helping children learn to be aware of, and thus in control of, their reactions, rather than being controlled by them.

The Sensorimotor or Association Cortex Model

*K*yung and Samantha are playing on the stationary
balance beam in the play yard. "I can do this easy. Watch
me," says Samantha as she carefully mounts the beam. It
had been raining the night before and she knows that it will
be slippery. With her eyes glued to the base of the beam just
ahead of her, she slowly places one foot in front of the other.
Four steps later, she slips off. Kyung says, "Now let me try."
He manages five steps before he slips. Realizing the challenge
of a slippery surface, Samantha says, "You hold my hand
while I walk. Then I'll hold your hand for you." The plan
works and both children succeed in traversing the entire
beam with each other's help.

The sensorimotor model of the brain provides insight into the
dynamics of this episode. Also called the association cortex model, it
maps the sensory and motor cortex of the brain, attributing each specific
area to the specific part of the body that area controls. Embedded in the
gray matter of the cerebral cortex, weaving in and out of the folds and
curves, are two parallel bands: one of motor neurons that control every
move a person voluntarily makes and the other of sensory neurons
ready to receive and react to sensory stimuli from throughout the body.

Implications for Educators

In the case of Kyung and Samantha, each was carefully monitoring,
through visual input, stimuli that would guide the motor activity
needed to achieve their immediate goal. Integrating motor activity
from the legs and upper body with balance stimuli from the vestibular
system (Figure 3.8) and with figure-ground input from the visual
system, they were able to partially coordinate these inputs enough to
take several steps successfully. When the challenge was beyond them,

they helped each other through additional sensory input in the form of tactile support, which aids kinesthesia (see pg. 200), brought about by the touch of the hand. Here the model shows us the neuro-integration of systems into a given sequence of behavior.

Since all information received is processed through sensorimotor systems, strong programs of sensorimotor activity should be included in all learning environments for young children.

The Holonomic Brain

The bulletin board has big yellow circles on it, cut out of a variety of materials, including construction paper, corrugated paper, poster board, colored newsprint, felt, and tissue paper. On top of and in between many of the big circles are smaller circles in shades of blue, green, lavender, orange, and pink. Holly is mesmerized by the vividness of the colors. Slowly she begins to run her hands over some of the forms. As she rubs her fingers back and forth over a 6-inch light orange circle, she suddenly says, "Ohhh!" For the past three weeks, Holly had been struggling to recognize the many shapes the teacher had shown them. Now her face lights up. She calls her teacher over and says knowingly, "Look, look, Ms. Anne. That's just like the face on my Cabbage Patch doll." Puzzled, her teacher asks, "How are they alike?" "They're circles, see? They're circles."

This example of a successful experience with memory is effectively explained by the model of the holonomic brain. Bob Samples refers to the holonomic mind in his book *Openmind/Wholemind* (1987), which suggests teaching techniques geared toward whole child development. Using the holographic model developed by Karl Pribram (1969) and the cell assembly model of D. O. Hebb (1964) as well as his own research and findings, Samples focuses on the connections between neurons in the central and peripheral nervous systems. He is concerned with how new experiences relate to memory of similar experiences. This model focuses on neurotransmitters, which are the chemicals that cause neurons to fire in a given sequence. Telephone switchboards and computer programs have been used as metaphors representing the processes associating neurochemical action with behaviors. Hebb (1964) argues that similar experiences result in a network of cell assemblies that comprise the stuff from which memory is made. Jerison (1982) calls this process "chunking," meaning forming a chunk of brain memory. Thus we can recall our Social Security number more easily by breaking it up into chunks of two or three numbers instead of trying to memorize a string of nine numbers. These chunks of memory allow for such generalized responses as elaboration, recognition, and anticipation of situations. For example, Susie recognizes a circle from generalized previous experiences with similar circles, which had been embedded in chunks of memory even though, until the episode described above, she had not tied those chunks together. Because memory is apparently distributed throughout the brain—rather than in any one particular spot as previously thought—it can surface in other locations when one part of the brain is injured.

Implications for Educators

Information is not stored as memory in a specific location in the brain, but rather bits and pieces of information about a particular event, idea, or thing are stored throughout the brain. New experiences may evoke one bit or the whole pattern of one type of information. Thus, it is important that children constantly have new multisensory experiences, presented in a variety of ways, in order to build their recall and memory. Because different techniques will trigger the storage and the recall of memory differently in different individuals, it is imperative that many approaches be used.

The Interplay of Human Development

As children use their sensory and reflexive skills to develop their motor skills, perceptions begin to form. As their motor-perceptual and perceptual-motor skills increase, conceptualization takes place. During all the steps of development, the processes of cognition within the cerebral cortex are occurring, and gradually the two hemispheres develop their separate interests. All the aspects of a child's development result from the interplay among all the parts of the body, including the muscular and skeletal systems, the nervous systems (including the brain), and the sensory organs, as well as the psychological self that is developing along with the physical self. These important developmental interplays occur as the various systems of the body communicate with one another and with the outside environment. To understand their workings, we need to gain a basic understanding of the brain and the central nervous system. By exploring the anatomy of the central nervous system, we lay the foundation for an understanding of the relationship between the brain and total development. With this information, what we know about human development becomes logical.

Summary

A number of psychological models can be used to study the brain. One is the hemispheric model, which examines the asymmetrical process through which each hemisphere of the brain functions differently. There are three goals in addressing asymmetry in young children: (1) to enhance their capacity to use the strengths of their dominant hemisphere, (2) to increase their capacity to utilize new processes in their less dominant hemisphere, and (3) to learn to integrate the two hemispheres, using strategies from both in given situations. The triune brain model emphasizes the integrative techniques proposed by the authors, along with the importance of affective education. The sensori-motor or association model is based on the strong role of sensorimotor activity in the processing of all information received by the brain. The holonomic brain model focuses on the functions of the neuro-transmitters, which are the chemicals that cause brain activity to occur and are responsible for memory. All these models are important, just as are all the aspects of development that result from the interplay among all the parts of the body, including all the parts of the brain.

For Further Study

1. Many other brain models exist, especially those that describe the function of the mind. Investigate some of those that have been reported on in various books on the brain and write a summary of one that you feel is valid.
2. How has the work of Roger Sperry influenced our knowledge of the differences between the two hemispheres of the brain?
3. Much recent research has focused on the chemicals of the brain. Look up a journal article on the subject and write a summary of it.
4. Observe a preschool class for one hour. Keep a record of the various episodes of emotional (limbic system) action you observe. Give two examples.
5. Observe a second-, third-, or fourth-grade class for two hours. Note the frequency of evidence of creative thinking. Give two examples.

References

Bever, T. G., 1983. "Cerebral Lateralization, Cognitive Asymmetry, and Human Consciousness." In *Cognitive Processing in the Right Hemisphere*, ed. Ellen Perceman. New York: Academic Press.

Brandwein, Paul H. 1971. "Essence of Curriculum." Keynote address, National Conference of the Association of School Curriculum Development, in Austin, Texas.

Hebb, D. O. 1964. *Organization of Behavior*. New York: Wiley.

Jerison, H. J. 1982. "The Evolution of Consciousness." In *Mind and Brain: The Many-faceted Problems*, ed. J. Eccles. Washington, DC: Paragon House.

Lozanov, G. 1978. *Suggestology and Outlines of Suggestopedy*. New York: Gordon and Breach.

MacLean, Paul D. 1978. "A Mind of Three Minds: Educating the Triune Brain." In *Education and the Brain: Seventy-Seventh Yearbook Part II, of the National Society for the Study of Education*, ed. J. Chall and A. Mirsky. Chicago: University of Chicago Press.

Numella, Renate M., and Tennes M. Rosengren. 1986. "The Triune Brain: A New Paradigm for Education." *Journal of Humanistic Education and Development* 24, pgs. 98–103.

Pribram, Karl. 1969. "The Four Rs of Remembering." In *On the Biology of Learning*, ed. K. H. Pribram. New York: Harcourt Brace.

Samples, Bob. 1987. *Openmind/Wholemind*. Rolling Hills Estates, CA: Jalmar Press.

Sperry, Roger W., M. S. Gazzaniga, and J. E. Bogen. 1969. "Interhemispheric Relationships: The Neocortical Commissures—Syndromes of Hemispheric Disconnection." In *Handbook of Clinical Neurology*, Vol. 4. Amsterdam: Elsevier-North Holland.

CHAPTER 3

The Anatomy of the Central Nervous System

You are wiping off a table in preparation for a morning snack. You glance over at 4-year-old Andrea, who has been busy for the last ten minutes creating a house out of clay for her clay turtle. You become fascinated with her concentration and determination. Her house is a shell, and it breaks in two when she picks it up. You watch as she carefully fights back her tears, examines the two pieces, and then fits them together. She cautiously uses her thumbs and fingers to fuse the edges together. Then, hesitating to pick it up again, she reaches under with her fingers and checks the crack from the inside. Her facial expressions change with each new discovery as she manipulates the miniature dome based on touch alone. Suddenly a question comes to your mind: How is this perceptive prekindergartner able to merge touch with seeing with manipulation, blending them into a harmony of skills to achieve such a delicate task? How does she so creatively blend her right-hemisphere awareness of shape and form with her left-hemisphere analysis of how to mend the cracked area?

The Foundations of the Central Nervous System

The central nervous system is composed of the brain, its cranial nerves, the spinal cord, and the spinal nerves. It is assisted by the peripheral nervous system, which includes

1. the somatic nervous system, which controls the skeletal muscle contractions, and
2. the autonomic nervous system, which produces cardiac and smooth muscle contractions that control heartbeat and breathing; it also controls certain glandular secretions.

These systems work in harmony, governing our thoughts and our actions as we progress through life.

Our concern will be primarily the brain, which we can best understand by reviewing its components and their separate functions. These components, working in unison with each other, allow Andrea to monitor her world and to learn to respond effectively to it.

Our Wiring System

The Neuron—A Specialized Cell for Thinking

The neuron, commonly known as a nerve cell, is an extremely complicated unit. It not only generates its own electricity, but it also manufactures the sodium and potassium needed to speed the electrical impulse along. Different kinds of neurons carry out different assignments throughout the body, but the way each produces a nerve impulse is basically the same. All neurons are composed of three basic parts: the cell body, the axon, and the dendrites (Figure 3.1). They might be compared to the root system of a growing plant, with the seed being the cell body, and the stem and its branches being the axon and dendrites.

1. *The cell body.* This is the heart of the cell and contains a nucleus

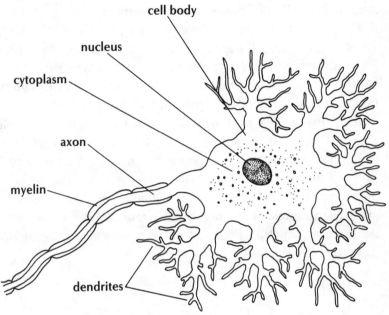

FIGURE 3.1. NEURON

surrounded by cytoplasm. It is the headquarters of the neuron and it supervises the neuron's smaller parts.

2. *Dendrites.* Around the cell body are a number of thick nerve fibers that spread out in many directions and that divide into many thin whiskery branches called dendrites, the ends of which branch out further into thousands of little sprouts. These sprouts form synapses, through which signals are transmitted from one neuron to another. The synapses are actually little gaps between the sprouts of one neuron and those of another. The signals are produced through chemical neurotransmitters that send electrical impulses between the neurons. When the signal is received, other electrical impulses are triggered to send it on to other neurons. Pool (1987) points out that a single neuron may have anywhere from 1,000 to 10,000 contacts with other neurons and their cell bodies. Every neuron is, in fact, a tiny electrical power plant, a miniature chemical factory, and a busy message center.

3. *Axons.* The cell body sends out its most important signals to the dendrites of other neurons through a long fiber called an axon. Axons vary in length depending on the function of the neuron. Some are several feet long. For example, the axons that control the toes extend from the motor portion of the brain through the body down to the bottom portion of the spinal column.

4. *Myelin sheath.* The axon of a neuron is covered with a myelin sheath. This is insulation much like that of electrical wires. It is a white, fatty substance that wraps itself around the axon in rolls. Myelin allows impulses to travel faster through the axon. Myelination occurs with use. It is estimated that millions of neurons can be involved in a single experience; thus the more experiences we have, the more myelination occurs, and the more quickly signals will travel through the brain.

Nerves

Nerves, made up of neurons, complete the wiring system of the body. A nerve is round, glistening, and flexible. It can be short and slender or long and thick. It can be a single neuron with a single long fiber or it can be a bundle of fibers. Most nerves split off into smaller and smaller branches on their course to outer parts of the body.

The Motor and Sensory Pathways

The millions of nerves that function throughout the body find their ultimate control in two special locations on the cerebral cortex. Along the rear of the frontal lobe, running across it from center to side, is a strip of nerve cells called the motor cortex (see Figure 3.2). This is the highest level of conscious control for the motor activity carried out in numerous areas of the central nervous system.

Running parallel to this band of motor neurons and along the front of the parietal lobe is a strip of nerve cells called the sensory cortex (see Figure 3.2). This band provides the highest form of interpretation of all sensory input that comes to it from the lower areas of the central nervous system.

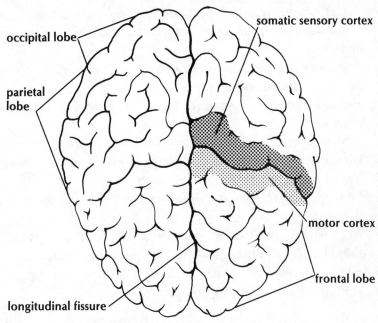

FIGURE 3.2. CEREBRUM, TOP VIEW

Sharing a common fissure, these two parallel bands serve in harmony with each other to control sensorimotor activity throughout the body.

The Cranial Nerves

Twelve pairs of cranial nerves form the major connections for our bodily functions. One of each pair serves the left side of the body and the other serves the right side. These nerves are connected in an orderly system from the base of the brain up through various parts of the brain stem and the cerebrum. They are usually known by the following numbering system:

I. Olfactory nerve, which processes smells
II. Optic nerve, which processes sight
III. Oculomotor nerve, which controls several eye muscles and the reaction of the pupils
IV. Trochlear nerve, which is connected to the eye muscles

  V. Trigeminal nerve, which processes sensations from various parts of the face, skin, eyes, nose, and mouth, and which enables us to chew
 VI. Abducens nerve, which works with the oculomotor and trochlear nerves to control eye muscles
VII. Facial nerve, which processes facial expressions and sensations of taste
VIII. Acoustic nerve, which helps to process both hearing and balance
 IX. Glossopharyngeal nerve, which helps to process speech and taste
  X. Vagus nerve, which is involved with many vital organs of the body, helping to regulate breathing, heartrate, and the digestive processes
 XI. Accessory nerve, which enables us to turn our head and shoulders by sending signals to the appropriate muscles
XII. Hypoglossal nerve, which enables us to move our tongue by sending signals to the appropriate muscles

The Cerebrum

The cerebrum is made up of two halves, the cerebral hemispheres (Figure 3.2). Each hemisphere is covered with a ⅛-inch blanket of neural tissue called the cerebral cortex. It contains between 70 and 85 percent of all neurons in the adult brain, specifically the cell bodies that give it a gray appearance. The axons that branch out from these cell bodies make up the white matter underneath the cortex. The appearance of the cerebral cortex is usually compared to the shell of a walnut. In utero, the cortex usually grows too large for the rest of the brain, so it gets pushed into folds that appear as a series of convolutions, called "gyri," and grooves, which are referred to as "sulci" if shallow or "fissures" if deep. When viewing the brain from the outer layer, the most prominent fissure is the longitudinal fissure, which almost divides the two hemispheres into the right and the left sides.

The left hemisphere is more tightly packed with neurons than the right. The right hemisphere, conversely, contains more white matter than the left. This difference helps to further explain the asymmetric functioning of the hemispheres.

The cerebrum • processes our thoughts,
             • differentiates and discriminates,
             • arbitrates and makes judgments,
             • evaluates and solves problems,
             • controls conscious and deliberate acts, and
             • controls conscious and deliberate movements.

Each hemisphere is divided into four lobes, named after the skull bones that cover them (Figure 3.3). The functions of the four primary lobes are shown in the chart "The Lobes of the Cerebral Hemisphere."

The occipital lobe is of extreme importance because the visual process is so crucial to all other functions. Except for vision, perceptual inputs have their primary routes to the opposite hemisphere of the brain. Each eye splits its visual field, feeding half to each hemisphere. For example, close your left eye and place the extended first finger of

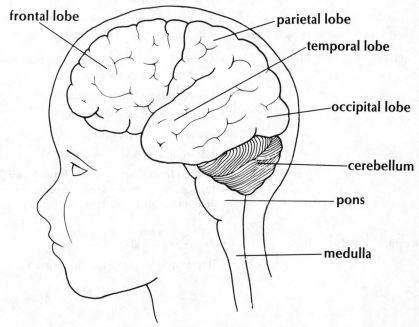

FIGURE 3.3. BRAIN, UNDISSECTED SIDE VIEW

THE LOBES OF THE CEREBRAL HEMISPHERE

Lobe	Location	Functions
Parietal	Top	• Responding to sensory input of pain, touch, temperature • Processing distance, size, shape, texture, intensity, and location • Proprioception, or the ability to determine the position of the body in space • Screening the above inputs for processing and handling, ignoring some and giving special attention to others
Temporal	Lower side	• Receiving sound • Processing what we hear • Processing auditory input in speech • Abstract thought • Short-term memory
Frontal	Front	• Controlling muscles of the speech center and those used in writing • Governing emotional expression • Producing empathy and altruism • Planning for future action • Controlling opposite sides of the body • The left frontal lobe contains Broca's area, the part of the motor speech area that enables people to produce language
Occipital	Back	• Processing visual impulses • Interpreting visual images that come from the eyes

your right hand vertically two inches in front of your right eye. Everything that you view to the left of your finger goes into the right hemisphere, and everything that you view to the right of your finger goes into the left hemisphere. The same split occurs for your right eye.

The occipital lobes must process a number of characteristics of light in order to produce the visual images called sight. The images that fall on the retina of the eyes stimulate the rods and cones there. (The cones deal with color and daylight vision; the rods deal with light intensity and night vision.) An area within the occipital lobes has a complete map of the surface of each retina. Each part of the image on the retina can therefore be interpreted by the brain. Various other cells in the occipital lobe account for color, movement, and interpretation of simple and complex shapes. Other cells coordinate the images from each side of each eye to produce three-dimensional vision. Visual discrimination, with all of its complexities, provides Andrea with the tools needed for the finest of visual tasks that might be required of her as she grows and develops.

The Corpus Callosum—A Bridge for Thought

The corpus callosum is the bridge between the two hemispheres that allows them to communicate with each other (Figure 3.4). They do so by means of commissural fibers (Figure 3.5). If you hold your two hands up next to each other in the form of fists, to represent the two hemispheres, and move them apart slightly, you can envision the space that is taken up by the corpus callosum. Its fibers cover a space of approximately 4 inches. Without them, there would be no communication between the hemispheres. These are the fibers that are severed in the split-brain operations referred to on pg. 18. These commissural fibers become myelinated with experience and maturity. Very little communication occurs between the two hemispheres prior to 2 years of age, but by the age of 4 there is constant communication. Thus, it is evident why the preschool years of 2 through 4 are so crucial in whole child development.

According to Colwyn Trevarthen (1987, pgs. 108–109), the corpus callosum has over a billion fibers at birth. During the three or four

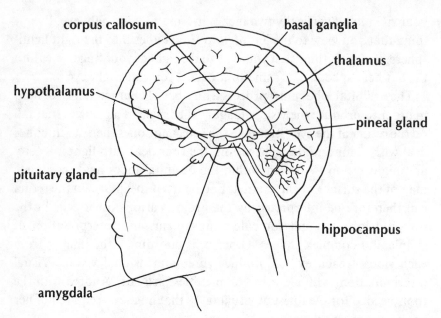

FIGURE 3.4. LIMBIC AREA AND BASAL GANGLIA

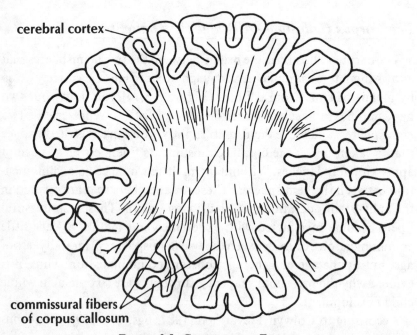

FIGURE 3.5. COMMISSURAL FIBERS

months following birth, however, large numbers of these fibers, called callosal axons, are redundant and are weeded out. The remaining ones sort themselves in an orderly fashion to form contacts between the two hemispheres that are limited to certain areas of the cortex. From four months on, this interhemispheric bridge grows, as the fibers become thicker and as they become myelinated. In a mature adult, the average corpus callosum is approximately 3½ inches long and ¼ inch thick (A. Smith, 1984, pg. 117).

Joseph Pearce, in *The Magical Child Matures* (1985), refers to correspondence he had with Roger Sperry in 1974 in which Sperry indicated that his findings showed that the corpus callosum begins to develop at the end of the first year and does not attain full development and function until age 4. We know now that the corpus callosum is, in fact, in place even before birth. Recent research has shown that relatively specific anatomical connections within each hemisphere develop at different rates and at different postnatal onset times (Thatcher et al., 1987).

Although overall development is continuous, there are many examples of growth spurts or sudden increases in rates of growth, indicating that there are certain sensitive periods for achieving new states of development and for specific new types of learning. Spurts of development occur between birth and 3 years of age, between 4 and 6, between 8 and 10, between 11 and 14, and between 15 and adulthood, culminating in bilateral connections between the frontal lobes. This developmental pattern could be a reason why very young children tend to function as though they have only a right hemisphere until they start developing language skills between 2 and 4 years of age. At 4, they may still be doing most of their processing with the right hemisphere, but they have also begun to use the two hemispheres in partnership.

Association and Projection Fibers

Two other types of fibers are actively involved in brain function: the association fibers (Figure 3.6) and the projection fibers (Figure 3.7). The association fibers connect the various parts of the same hemisphere. They crisscross back and forth over each hemisphere, connecting

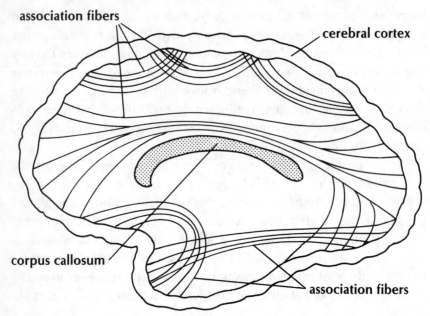

FIGURE 3.6. ASSOCIATION FIBERS

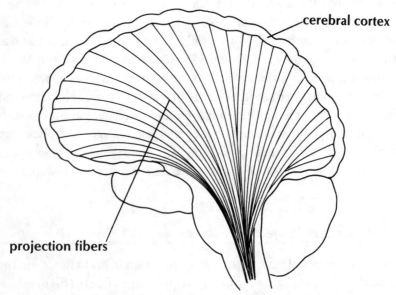

FIGURE 3.7. PROJECTION FIBERS

the motor and the sensory areas in those hemispheres and playing dominant roles in memory, reasoning, emotions, will, and intelligence. The projection fibers are the ascending and descending nerves that transmit the impulses between the cerebral cortex and other parts of the central nervous system. They go out from the brain stem in a fanlike pattern, reaching into all parts of the cerebral hemispheres.

The Basal Ganglia—A Governing System for Body Movement

Situated underneath each hemisphere are several clusters of nerves called the basal ganglia (see Figure 3.4). These are located in the white matter of the brain much like seeds in an apple and vary in size and shape from almonds to plums and even to sea horses. One of their primary functions is their involvement with movement, relaying commands from the cerebral cortex to such lower centers in the brain as the cerebellum and the brain stem, which we will discuss shortly.

With the help of the basal ganglia, the ears play an important role in achieving vestibular balance and learning to cope with gravity. Within the inner ears are a series of ducts which, because of their partially circular shape, are commonly called semicircular canals (Figure 3.8). Whenever the head is moved, fluid flows through one of the ducts, alerting tiny hairlike cells that it contacts at the base of the ducts. These hairs, in turn, activate nerve fibers that send messages to the rest of the body about what changes must be made by the muscles, ligaments, joints, eyes, and inner ear to cope with the changing forces of gravity due to the change in the position of the head. The actual messages are coordinated by the basal ganglia, which are responsible for helping the muscles to retain or, if necessary, regain, their equilibrium.

The Limbic System—A Site for Our Emotions

The limbic system (see Figure 3.4) is located at the junction of the mid-brain (at the top of the brain stem) and the front half of the brain, which is called the forebrain. It forms a concentric ring in each hemisphere,

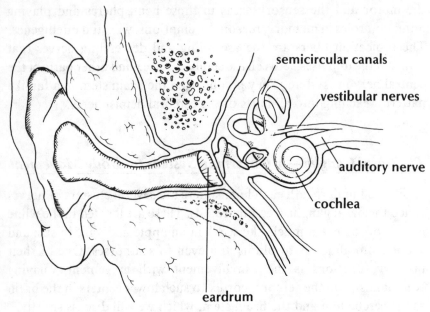

FIGURE 3.8. INNER AND MIDDLE EAR

folded in at a central core, at a connection that also serves the basal ganglia. It is the center of control for the manifestation of our emotions, much of our hormonal activity, and the functions of the autonomic nervous system previously described.

Tiny organs in the limbic system are involved in these processes, including the amygdala, the nearby septum pellucidum, and the hippocampus. The hippocampus, in addition, may be involved in providing a means for variability in learning (O'Keefe and Nadel, 1978) and thus is crucial to our willingness to develop programs that present learning in untraditional ways.

The Thalamus—The Relay Station of the Brain

The thalamus (see Figure 3.4), located deep in the forebrain at the top of the brain stem, serves as a relay center to send signals from the body and lower portions of the brain to the appropriate centers in the two hemispheres above it. It assists in alerting and activating higher centers of the brain by monitoring the travel of stimuli that are received from the body.

The Hypothalamus—The Body's Thermostat Center

Directly underneath the thalamus is a small but critical portion of the limbic system called the hypothalamus (see Figure 3.4). No larger than the end of your thumb, the hypothalamus, along with the pituitary gland attached to it, controls the following vital functions of the body:

- temperature,
- appetite (and thus food intake),
- water balance (and thus thirst),
- wakefulness and sleepiness,
- bladder contractions (and thus urination),
- cardiac muscle contractions,
- food movement through the digestive tract,
- metabolism of fats, proteins, and carbohydrates,
- hormonal activity related to the sex organs, and
- counteraction to feelings of aggression.

The Cerebellum—The Little Brain

At the base of the brain, in the back, is a special cluster of neurons called the cerebellum (see Figure 3.9). It bulges out from the back of the midbrain and is shaped like a butterfly, its wings spread out under the lower back of each hemisphere. It is sometimes called the "little brain." Containing some of the largest neurons in the brain, it controls co-ordination and proprioception, without which we would have no postural control or balance. It controls the amount of tension in our muscles and thus monitors our control of those muscles, frequently through reflex activity. It connects to the brain stem in three places: to the midbrain, to the pons, and to the medulla. Though it monitors

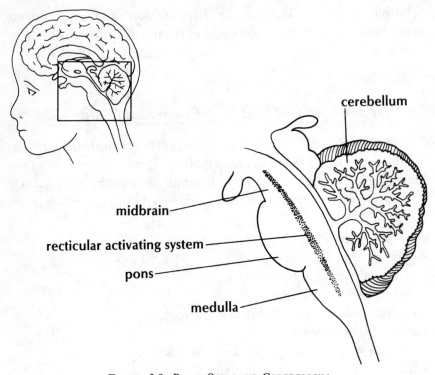

FIGURE 3.9. BRAIN STEM AND CEREBELLUM

many of our voluntary movements, when it is damaged, other motor areas can be reeducated to control those movements because the movements originate in other parts of the central nervous system.

The Brain Stem—The Site of Our Vital Signs

Beginning from the top of the spinal column extending up into the lower middle of the brain is a three-part system called the brain stem (see Figure 3.9). Less than 3 inches long, it is the pathway for over one million sensory and motor fibers that transmit messages between the spinal cord and the cerebral cortex.

The Medulla

This lowest part of the brain stem, the medulla (see Figure 3.9), is actually a continuation of the spinal cord. At its junction with the spinal cord, most of the motor fibers that come from the left side of the cerebral cortex cross over to the right side of the spinal cord. These fibers will synapse with the spinal nerves on the right side of the spine and cause movement in the skeletal muscles of the right side of the body. The fibers that come from the right hemisphere will synapse with nerves on the left side of the spine and thus control the skeletal muscles of the left side of the body. The medulla also registers some of the sensory impulses that travel from the spinal cord through sensory fibers up to the cerebral cortex in a right-to-left and left-to-right pattern similar to that of the downward-traveling motor fibers.

The medulla also is the center for reflexes that regulate heartbeats and adjust breathing and the diameter of blood vessels. Other reflex actions mediated by the medulla are coughing, vomiting, sneezing, hiccuping, eye-blinking, and swallowing. Because of these many vital functions necessary to the maintenance of life, a blow to the base of the skull where the medulla is located often proves fatal or, at the least, can cause serious bodily malfunctions.

The Pons

The middle section of the brain stem, the pons (see Figure 3.9), is a 1-inch bulge of white matter that serves as a bridge between the upper and lower parts of the brain stem and between the brain stem and the cerebellum.

The Midbrain

The top part of the brain stem is the midbrain (see Figure 3.9), a 1-inch long connecting link between the lower parts and the centers above it. It contains two bundles of motor fibers that convey impulses from the cerebral cortex through the brain stem and down into the spinal cord. Large bundles of sensory fibers are also partially contained within the midbrain; they convey impulses to the cerebral cortex from the spinal cord. Certain auditory and visual reflexes are involved with the midbrain, as well as the nerves that control the movements of the eyeball and changes in the sizes of the pupils.

Reticular Activating System

Traveling up the center of all three compartments much like a hot dog in a bun, but no larger than the tip of your finger, is a core of neurons called the Reticular Activating System, commonly referred to as RAS (see Figure 3.9). This critical system acts like a dimmer switch in a light fixture, influencing the levels of alertness of the centers above and controlling the speed at which signals are transmitted from the sensory messages received by the spinal cord.

The fine interplay between these many parts of the central nervous system is nurtured through multisensory experiences. Activities that involve the specialized functions of both hemispheres help to integrate the two hemispheres as well as to fine-tune coordination between all parts of the body.

Summary

The basic functioning units of the brain are neurons, or nerve cells, whose electrical and chemical impulses are the means through which the body functions. A neuron consists of a cell body from which extend a number of thick fibers called dendrites, which receive impulses from other cells. At the end of the dendrites are thousands of little sprouts through which impulses are transmitted to other cells by synaptic action, which is the biochemical release of chemicals from one cell to another. The nerve cell sends out its most important signals through fibers called axons, which control the various parts of the body. An axon can be very short, or it can be several feet long and extend from the motor portion of the brain to the part of the body that it controls.

Axons are covered with myelin, a fatty substance that serves as insulation much like that covering electrical wires. Myelination, which occurs through experience and maturity, allows impulses to travel faster.

The brain stem, at the top of the spine, is made up of the medulla, the pons, and the midbrain, all important centers of basic bodily functions. The cerebellum, which bulges from the back of the midbrain and under the back of each hemisphere, controls coordination and proprioception, without which we would have no postural control or balance. The limbic system, located over the midbrain, contains the thalamus, which relays sensory impulses to the rest of the brain, and the hypothalamus, which controls many important body functions, including body temperature, hunger, and thirst. Nearby are the basal ganglia, knotlike collections of nerves that help relay information regarding motor activity from the cerebral cortex to the brain stem. The upper part of the brain is composed of the cerebrum, which consists of two cerebral hemispheres. Commissural fibers of the corpus callosum transmit messages from one hemisphere to the other. The cerebral cortex, which is the outer layer of the cerebrum, is the major decision-making area of the central nervous system. The cortex is divided into four primary areas—the frontal, occipital, parietal, and temporal lobes—all of which play important roles in our body functions and perceptions.

For Further Study

1. Read a book from the library on the brain, written for the layperson. Describe five implications for educators about learning and development based on the information in the book.
2. Record your mood changes during one day. Attempt to identify physical reactions and conditions within your system that parallel these moods.
3. Observe a preschool classroom. Record incidents that require children to make emotional decisions as they interact with other children.
4. Observe an elementary grade classroom. Record incidents that require the use of fine eye-hand coordination.

References

O'Keefe, J., and L. Nadel. 1978. *The Hippocampus as a Cognitive Entity.* Oxford: Clarendon.

Pearce, Joseph C. 1985. *The Magical Child Matures.* New York: Dutton.

Pool, J. 1987. *Nature's Masterpiece: The Brain and How It Works.* New York: Walker.

Smith, Anthony. 1984. *The Mind.* New York: Viking.

Thatcher, R. W., et al. 1987. "Human Cerebral Hemispheres Develop at Different Rates and Ages." *Educational Digest* (October).

Trevarthen, Colwyn. 1987. "Brain Development." In *Oxford Companion to the Mind*, ed. Richard L. Gregory. New York: Oxford University Press.

CHAPTER 4

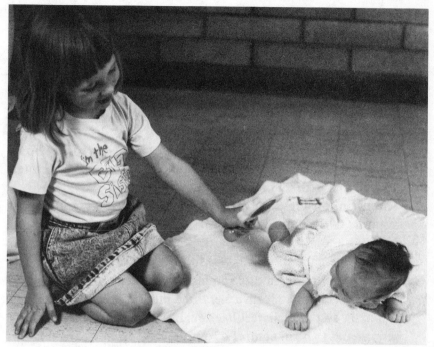

PHOTO 4.1

Processes of Child Development

*E*lizabeth, age 8 weeks, is lying on a blanket on the living room floor. Her sister, Laura, shakes a rattle nearby. She turns her head toward the rattle, a motor-perceptual act, thus adding visual input to the auditory input she already had received. She turns her head back to its original position. Laura shakes the rattle again. This time, Elizabeth purposely turns her head with anticipation. She will probably repeat this type of action several times. Eventually, it will become a perceptual-motor skill.

Toward Perceptual-Motor Skills

In the time that the central nervous system is developing, the corresponding motor system is also developing. As the motor system develops, so do our perceptual skills, in accordance with the following sequence:

1. Sensations are received, coded into impulses, and sent to the brain via the sensory nerves.
2. Based on the individual's previous experience, personal knowledge, and feelings at the time, the received impulses are interpreted, analyzed, and sorted.
3. The brain, through its two hemispheres, selects an appropriate response to the message.
4. Through the motor nerves, a responding impulse is sent to the appropriate parts of the body. Motor response then occurs.
5. Part of the outgoing motor impulse is utilized to give feedback to the brain, helping to form generalized motor patterns that remain within the system. This feedback enables us to supervise our motor actions and to be in control of our movement.
6. The above sequence of sensory and motor integration forms the basis for conceptualization, which is the result of cognitive activity.

Thus, perception is more than just taking in information. It involves an entire system of incoming and outgoing information and actions that are dependent on one another and that are closely linked to the motor-perceptual and the perceptual-motor processes. We are not born with these processes developed, even though the mechanisms are there. They develop along with the central nervous system and are closely related to motor activities and movement experiences. Without normal developmental experiences, perceptions may be distorted, just as the accompanying movements may be possibly distorted (clumsy, awkward, jerky, inaccurate, or misdirected).

So many structures of the brain are involved in the control of movement that this control appears to be one of the fundamental functions of the brain. Life itself begins with a song of movement, as the lively sperm seeks the ovum's point of penetration, and the multiplication of cells begins in a rhythmic pattern of replication. The growing fetus, continuing this replication in a specific order, is capable of responding to certain stimuli with a jerk of its embryonic limbs as early as the eighth week of gestation. At 16 weeks there is a stirring and stretching, with minute jerks and thrusts, growing ever stronger as the weeks in utero progress. Motoric activity continues, culminating in the amazing muscular contractions of birth itself, which demonstrate the tremendous power of the reflex system, from which the infant's future movement activities will spring and its entire system of perceptual-motor skills will develop.

Sequential and Simultaneous Motor Development

Development in young children is cephalocaudal (from the Latin words *cephalo*, which means head, and *cauda*, which means tail), that is, development begins at the head and moves downward, progressing toward the feet. Simultaneously, development occurs proximodistally (from the Latin words *proximo*, which means near or center, and *distans*, which means far or outer), that is, development begins near the center of the body and gradually moves outward to the peripheral areas. Thus, the ability to control movement of the neck develops before the ability to control movement of the shoulder; shoulder movement must be achieved before control of the muscles of the upper arm is attained. Then comes the elbow, followed by the lower part of the arm. By about 2½ years of age, the development of control has moved to the wrist. From there it continues its outward journey, moving through the areas of the palm and then through the fingers, section by section and joint by joint. Finally, at an average age of between 5 and 5½ years the control of movement reaches the fingertips.

Simultaneously, other parts of the body are developing outward and downward, step by step, with the upper and inner areas of the body always preceding the next area in which developmental control will occur.

Though this is the normal order of human development, there is great variation in the times and rates of growth among individuals. Too rapid a development may result in parts or stages being skipped entirely; too slow a development may result in or be the result of mild to severe neurological disorders. The exact rate and time of development, however, is less important than the attainment of each step. The norms developed by the Gesell Institute (Gesell, 1940) are recommended as general guidelines.

Sensory System

Even before birth, the body is continuously receiving sensory information from both the external (sensory) and internal (kinesthetic) environment, as has already been discussed. Therefore, we treat the functioning of the sensory system not as a separate stage of development but rather as a concurrent part of all development. The sensory system is an integral part of the sequence of perceptual-motor achievement:

1. *Sensorimotor development:* Through our senses and kinesthetic awareness, we learn to respond motorically.
2. *Motor-perceptual development:* We then develop a perception of what the motor act will bring about.
3. *Perceptual-motor development:* Then we deliberately repeat the motor-perceptual act through a process of trial and error to achieve an expected result.
4. *Conceptualization:* From our perceptual-motor activities, we begin to develop concepts.

Relaxation

In all of the following developmental stages, relaxation is one of the most important conditions through which infants and children learn to use their sensory and motor input and output systems. Moshe Feldenkrais (1970, pg. 54) states that muscles can do only two things according to the messages relayed by the brain: They can contract to a

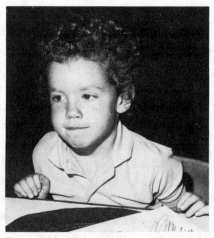

PHOTO 4.2. Four-year-old Zachary is staring out the window, momentarily oblivious to the world about him. He is daydreaming his own world and would go on sitting in this position for five or ten minutes if he were not interrupted by the teacher's reminder.

PHOTO 4.3. The teacher has said impatiently, "Zachary, we're waiting for you." He jerkily refocuses his vision but takes a few moments to grasp what is going on. A feeling of embarrassment overwhelms him when he realizes that everyone else is standing at the door waiting for him. He immediately becomes tense and self-conscious.

PHOTO 4.4. After clumsily pushing back his chair, he awkwardly joins the group, the teacher's reminder still echoing in his ears. His behavior during the next hour will probably be erratic, wavering from disruptiveness to slipping back into the comfort of his daydreams.

level above the level of tonus (muscle tension) at which they are habitually maintained, or they can reduce their contraction below that level. In other words, when these muscles receive impulses via the sensory and motor systems, they can either contract and become tense, or they can relax and be more receptive to new information.

When children are able to be appropriately relaxed, the incoming and outgoing information travels through the system more completely, more accurately, and more efficiently. Increased tension has the opposite effect and can significantly decrease incoming information. Even a slight increase makes it more difficult for children to process information and make appropriate decisions and responses. Imagine the difficulty when there is a great deal of tension and a corresponding decrease in the ability to absorb incoming information. Thus, we can substantially increase the amount of learning taking place by having children feel relaxed, secure, and physically comfortable within an appropriate and motivational environment.

Stages of Development

Reflex-Motor Development and Motor-Reflex Development

Human infants come into this world totally helpless and needing a longer period of care and nurture than do other mammals. To help them survive during their initial adjustment to the environment, they are born with certain automatic reflexes that bring about involuntary movements according to the specific stimuli (sensory input) received by the sensory neurons via the sensory receptors. The chart, "Reflexes Present in Newborn Infants," shows a number of these reflexes.

Some of these are called primitive postural reflexes. They initiate the development of movement skills during an infant's first three months, but they are meant to become inhibited by the end of the first year of life, unlike other reflexes—such as the reflex that makes our hands flail out to balance ourselves if we start to fall—that normally remain active throughout life. These primitive reflexes are normally inhibited by being appropriately used and thus weakened so they can be overridden

REFLEXES PRESENT IN NEWBORN INFANTS

Reflex	Purpose	Duration
Blink:		
Blinks at flash of light— sign of normal light perception	To protect eyes	Lifelong
Rooting:		
Turns head toward light touch on cheek, opens mouth, tries to suck	Preparation for nursing, high correlate with alertness	Birth to 3 or 4 mos.
Sucking:		
Sucks rhythmically when finger or nipple is in mouth	Nourishment	1–4 days to 3 mos.
Babinski:		
Big toe extends and other toes spread when the outer edge of the sole of the foot is stimulated	Signifies that lower spinal cord is receiving appropriate signals	Birth to 1½ yrs.
Knee jerk (patellar reflex):		
Jerks knee when tendon below knee is tapped	Unknown	Lifelong
Palmar grasp:		
Closes hand tightly when pressure is applied to palm; grips	Basis for learning voluntary grasp	Birth to 3 or 4 mos.
Moro (startle reflex):		
At loud noise or sudden drop of body, extends arms, fans out hands, throws head back, extends legs, and then clenches hands to chest	Basis for learning voluntary protection	Birth to 9 mos.
Swallowing:		
Swallows when food or fluid is in mouth	Self-preservation	Lifelong
Sneezing:		
Sneezes because of nasal irritation	Self-preservation	Lifelong
Sneezes because of bright lights	Self-preservation	Birth to 3 or 4 mos.

Reflexes Present in Newborn Infants—*Continued*

Reflex	Purpose	Duration
Primitive Postural Reflexes		
1. Labyrinthine responses:		
Prone flexion:		
When placed face down, flexes muscles that bend the joints: knees bend and are drawn up under abdomen; arms are tight at the side with elbows bent; head is turned slightly to one side and chin is tucked in	Assists in the development of awareness of gravity	Birth to 4 or 5 mos.
Supine extension:		
When face up with head to one side, extends arms and legs, bends knee on side that face is turned toward, and reaches upward with arm on other side, bending elbow	Assists in learning to deal with gravity	Birth to 4 mos.
2. Tonic neck responses:		
Asymmetric:		
When lying on back with head to one side, extends arm and leg on side that face is turned toward and flexes arm and leg on other side, bending knee and elbow	Introduction to idea of laterality, with each side of body having a different response	Birth to 4 to 6 mos.
Symmetric:		
When on stomach with head tilted backward, extends arms, including wrists and fingers; flexes hips and knees, bringing knees under abdomen, and subsequently puts self in creeping position	Introduction to the motoric activity that will lead to creeping, pulling to standing position, and walking	Birth to peak strength between 6 and 8 mos; totally suppressed by 3 yrs.

and replaced with newly learned motor patterns. Uninhibited, the primitive reflexes have first call on all actions of the body and interrupt the free flow of sensory and motor impulses. This interruption interferes with normal development of dynamic balance, manipulative skills, and successful entry into higher levels of learning.

The tonic neck reflexes (see Photos 4.5 and 4.6) merit special attention because they are crucial to helping the child initially get into appropriate positions to move through space, but many children do not successfully mature through them. Consequently, these reflexes have first call on these children's neural pathways throughout their lives, interfering with their fluidity of movement.

PHOTO 4.5. ASYMMETRIC TONIC NECK REFLEX. Sara, 8 weeks old, is lying on her back, looking to her right. Her right arm is extended directly out in front of her face, and her right leg is extended straight downward. Her left arm and leg are flexed. She will be in this position many times, but one day will be different: she will throw her flexed arm across her face and turn herself over. After she does this once, she may not do it again for another week or two, but when she does, she will probably repeat the movement as a learned motor behavior throughout the day. By 3 months of age, she will have learned the process well and will be able to turn herself over at will.

PHOTO 4.6. SYMMETRIC TONIC NECK REFLEX. Stafford has been wriggling on his stomach for several weeks. Now, at age 6 months, he lifts his head. The symmetric tonic neck reflex causes his arms to extend and his knees to bend so that he is in a creeping position. He seems surprised and looks around as if to say, "Look at me. I did a trick." He does get attention and responds even to the feeling of excitement. Being pleased, he continues the activity to get more attention. Soon he begins a to-and-fro rocking motion, trying to figure out where to go from there. He practices this new motion frequently. He still has not been able to get any place, but he has learned to use his arms and his legs separately from his torso. Meanwhile, motivated to move from where he is, he gets down flat on the floor and crawls forward, starting the process of learning to alternate his left arm and right leg with the right arm and left leg. In so doing, he will learn that he has two opposite sides of his body that can work in unison and balance each other.

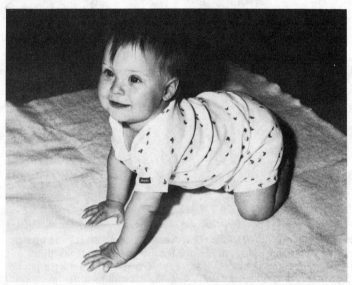

PHOTO 4.7. A few weeks after Photo 4.6 was taken, Stafford's mother put him on the floor on his stomach. He began his usual rocking motion, trying to get his mother's attention. Suddenly, one hand and knee moved forward. He seemed surprised and delighted, looked around, and tried again. Now the opposite hand and knee moved forward. And again. He had learned to creep.

Listed here are some of the causes of reflexes not being used appropriately by otherwise normally developing children:

1. moving too fast through early developmental stages,
2. not lying on stomach, especially not on the floor or other hard surface,
3. not learning to turn self over when lying on back,
4. not crawling,
5. not creeping,
6. walking earlier than average,
7. not moving freely until learning to walk, because of overuse of walkers, swings, and playpens, and
8. walking much later than 15 months of age.

In Chapter 10, you will find exercises to help inhibit primitive reflexes.

Figure-Ground Awareness

We are all aware of the figure-ground games given to children. They are shown a landscape and asked, "Can you see the animals hiding in the field?" Or they may be shown a tree and asked, "Can you find the bird in the tree?" The visual skills that it takes to differentiate the important foreground subject from the background begin to develop during the early weeks of life when the infant first learns to separate the active part of the body from the rest of the body. For example, Elizabeth, the infant in the scenario opening this chapter, was turned over on her back and reached out to hit the rattle her sister was holding. In that motion, Elizabeth's shoulder, arm, and hand were the "figures," and the rest of her body was the supporting "ground." She was experiencing kinesthetic figure-ground awareness; in other words, she was internally processing sensory messages in her brain about which part of her body was moving, giving herself feedback to problem-solve when she begins to make voluntary movements, so that she can put all her body parts together to move in a harmonious and productive manner.

Differentiation

All purposeful movement is differentiated movement, but it doesn't come about naturally. The brain has to learn to distinguish between the various muscles, tendons, and joints of the body and the movements they can perform. This knowledge develops cephalocaudally (from the top down) and proximodistally (from the center of the body to the periphery, or in to out). The awareness develops sequentially. For example, at 2 months of age, Sara has learned to control her neck muscles and is in the process of learning to control her shoulder muscles and tendons and those of the central part of her upper chest. From her shoulder she will progress to her upper arm, from upper arm to elbow, from elbow to lower arm, and from lower arm to wrist. She should acquire knowledge of the muscles, tendons, and joints of her wrist at about 2½ years of age. It will take another 2½ years to extend that knowledge through the palms of her hands down through the separate joints of her fingers and finally to the fingertips. Simultaneously, she is developing comparable awareness about her torso, hips, buttocks, thighs, knees, calves, and, at about age 2 or 2½, her ankles. From there her awareness will move down through the various sections of her feet until it reaches her toe tips. All of this information is stored in the brain. The information concerning the right side of the body is generally stored in the left hemisphere. The information concerning the left side of the body is generally stored in the memory of the right hemisphere. Though there are sometimes exceptions to this rule (see pgs. 111 and 113), it is readily seen why brain integration to enable the whole body to function in a wholesome manner is so important.

As Sara gathers the above information, she first learns to move parts of her body one at a time. Later she will begin to use both arms or both legs in a bilateral manner, that is, both at the same time in the same way. As she develops an awareness that she has two separate sides of the body, she may demonstrate homolateral movements—meaning that she will move only the arm and leg on one side of the body at a time. Finally, sometime between 6 and 10 months of age, she will learn to move in cross-lateral patterns, that is, moving an opposite arm and leg simultaneously while the other arm and leg do not move.

Differentiation

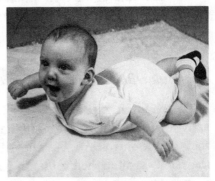

PHOTO 4.8. At 8 weeks, Sara has learned to control her neck muscles and is in the process of learning to control the muscles and tendons in her shoulders and the central part of her upper chest.

PHOTO 4.9. At 5 months, Sara has learned that, when placed on her stomach, she can arch her back, extend her arms, and balance herself briefly with a near-rocking motion. She is developing control over the movement in her upper torso. Within the next three months, she will extend this knowledge to more complex motor acts, including creeping and pulling herself up to a standing position while holding on to the side of the crib.

PHOTO 4.10. At 3½ years, Charles is demonstrating differentiation as he moves his hand and fingers while trying to manipulate a pair of scissors.

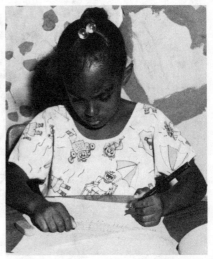

PHOTO 4.11. At age 5, Missy demonstrates differentiation as she learns to write her name.

Another kind of differentiation is that control of the large muscles (gross motor) is learned before control of the small muscles (fine motor) is developed.

Vestibular Balance and Opposition to Gravity

The children in Photo 4.12 are able to perform gravity-defying activities as a result of the vestibular balance they have learned during their developing years. They have learned to differentiate the parts of their body around their center of gravity at any given moment in order to maintain posture. They have learned to organize the parts of their body in order to maintain their balance in opposition to the force of gravity, in whatever position they may happen to find themselves. Two primary structures are involved:

1. **Semicircular canals** (See Figure 3.8). As the head turns, bends, twists, or otherwise changes position, fluid in the semicircular

PHOTO 4.12. VESTIBULAR BALANCE

canal of the inner ear brushes against the tiny hairlike bodies lining the canal to indicate to the self "which way is up."

2. **Proprioceptive sense organs.** The nerve endings in the muscles, tendons, and ligaments are constantly sending messages to the various integrative centers of the brain about the amount of muscular tension that is present, the strength of the pull on a muscle, or the amount of stretching of a ligament. These, integrated with the information from the semicircular canals, assist the body in maintaining its vestibular balance.

Movement and Motor Control

This next stage of development is evidenced when children learn to initiate a movement, monitor its duration, and know when to terminate the movement. In other words, movement control has three components: initiation, monitoring, and termination. As children continue their development, they learn to judge the space around them

PHOTO 4.13. MOTOR CONTROL

and where they are in relation to that space. They learn to function rhythmically, and develop an awareness of temporal cues, which leads to an understanding of duration and termination. An important factor in the development of spatial and temporal awareness is ocular control.

Ocular Control

Ocular control requires three types of skills:

1. fixating—that is, focusing on an object and being able to hold and maintain it within the visual field;
2. tracking—that is, following an object with the eyes in vertical, horizontal, and diagonal patterns; and
3. converging—that is, bringing both eyes together when looking at an object at close range (see pg. 70 and pg. 220).

Colwyn Trevarthen, professor of child psychology and psychobiology at the University of Edinburgh in Scotland, reports that a newborn, just minutes old, may watch the mother's mouth intently if she protrudes her tongue or opens her mouth wide and will imitate the mother by opening his or her mouth wide or sticking out his or her tongue (1987). A baby born without trauma or sedation is visually alert at birth and may be observed fixating bright places, tracking an object in different directions around the body, and otherwise displaying the ability to visually orient to a stimuli. As infants increasingly interact with their environment during the ensuing weeks, their visual skills increase accordingly. As they learn to deal with the midline of their body, they simultaneously learn to use both eyes in unison, developing the ability for binocular vision at approximately 9 months of age.

Coordination

Hand-eye coordination is the ability for the hands and eyes to work in unison to perform a task, with the hands leading the eyes through the activity. *Eye-hand coordination* develops soon afterward, with the eyes leading the hands through the activity (Photo 4.14). *Foot-eye*

PHOTO 4.14. EYE-HAND COORDINATION

PHOTO 4.15.
EYE-FOOT
COORDINATION

coordination is the ability for the feet and the eyes to work in unison, with the feet leading the eyes through the activity. *Eye-foot coordination* follows, with the eyes leading the feet through the activity (Photo 4.15). For example, the eye spots a hopscotch square to jump into. The feet, directed by the coordinated brain, jump into the correct space. These steps in the development of coordination help children learn how to perform the various movements necessary to go on to more mature developmental stages. From learning to move specific parts of the body to integrating the whole self in a graceful, balanced, and fluid way, appropriate movements will occur according to their purpose.

Perceptual Motor Match

This section could also be called "Visual-Auditory-Kinesthetic-Tactile-Olfactory-Gustatory-Vestibular Motor Match." Motor match is the ability to use one or more of the senses in a perceptual task that requires matching the particular perception to a particular body movement. For example, playing patty-cake is a visual motor match— "visual" being the mode of perception of what is to be done, and the "motor match" being the motor activity that carries out the perception. When a child hears a noise and turns in its direction, the hearing of the noise is the auditory perception and the turning of the head toward the noise is the motor match.

A 9-month-old infant feeding herself is a good example of several perceptions working in unison (Photo 4.16). Looking at the food and directing her hand first to the spoon and then to the food matches visual perceptions with the movement activity of obtaining the food. Olfactory perception may also be involved, because the odor of the food may make the mouth water and may increase the intensity of the visual perception. As Kathryn puts the spoon into the food and struggles to get the food to balance and stay on the spoon, the effort to "match" is taking place. As the spoon is brought toward her face—first up above her nose, then over to her ear, then back to her nose, and finally onto her lips (but maybe not yet into her mouth)—the very struggle to achieve sends impulse after impulse to her brain. When the food finally makes it into her mouth, the match is achieved, and

PHOTO 4.16. PERCEPTUAL MOTOR MATCH

Kathryn feels the satisfaction of accomplishment. The entire process is enhanced by yet another sense: the gustatory sense (taste), which helps to intensify the integrative effect of the entire process. This satisfaction leads to the motivation to try again—and again. Finally, the appropriate movements are established because a generalized motor pattern of "spoon to mouth" has been embedded in the brain. This generalized motor pattern results in perceptual-motor action. Whenever Kathryn wants to accomplish "spoon to mouth" in the future, the generalized motor pattern will go into effect through the various neurons that have memorized the action.

Locomotion

Locomotion is the ability to purposefully move our bodies from one point in space to another, according to an internal goal or to external directions that require a response. Locomotor patterns may involve crawling, creeping (on hands and knees), walking, jumping, or other methods of propelling one's body through space. For example, when a child drops a ball and is asked to pick it up, the acts of going to the ball, of remembering the purpose of going to the ball once there, and of picking up the ball constitute the total locomotor skill. The skill is a combination of already learned generalized motor patterns.

Crossing the Midline

Newborn infants see the world as though half of it were on one side of the body and half on the other side. In whatever way one hand moves, the other moves with it. For example, if the infant moves the right arm toward the right, the left arm will simultaneously move toward the right. One arm is moving away from the midline of the body, however, while the other is moving toward the midline. When very young infants reach for an object overhead with one arm, the arms reverse their actions as soon as the midline is reached, and the arm on the side of the body over which the object is moving does the reaching. The infant can grab the object only on the side where the object is.

To recognize that one has two sides to one's body, a prerequisite for using both sides of the brain productively, one must recognize the midline of the body—that is, the point at which the two vertical sides of the body meet—and to be able to work at that point. This may mean bringing the hands together at the midline of the body, whether at the feet (as in tying shoes) or at the eyes or at the waist. For example,

PHOTO 4.17. MIDLINE AWARENESS

playing patty-cake is a midline skill (Photo 4.17). Holding your hands together as in prayer is a midline skill. Focusing on a word is a midline skill. The children in Photos 4.10, 4.11, and 4.14 are practicing midline skills.

Laterality

As infants develop the ability to cross the midline of the body, they develop the basis for laterality—knowing that they have two functioning sides of the body that can work independently of one another or in unison. As they develop this awareness, they begin to be able to control their movements upward and outward. As the need to contend with gravity increases, they reorganize their awareness into higher developmental levels of laterality, which is the basis for developing a dominant brain hemisphere and left–right-hemisphere thinking processes.

Laterality could be described as horizontal brain activity. It is another way of saying, in a psychological sense, that each hemisphere handles thought and contributes to behavior in its own way. In a physical sense, it means being aware of the two sides of one's body and knowing the difference between them. To recognize that one has two sides to one's body, there must be a recognition of the midline of the body.

In developing laterality, children are also in the process of laying the foundation of directionality. But not until about 7 years of age does the concept of laterality progress into directionality, with awareness not only of right and left but also of up and down, front and back, and close and far. Simultaneously, the thought processes of the two hemispheres are strengthening the force of their own laterality.

Handedness

As laterality develops and the awareness of the two separate sides of the body grows, one side becomes the leading side and is considered to be the dominant side. Preference for one side or the other appears to begin to develop at about the age of 2 years, eventually resulting in a child being right-handed or left-handed. Those who are right-handed have a clear-cut division of labor between the two hemispheres, with the right hand being controlled by the left hemisphere and the left hand being controlled by the right hemisphere. There is some evidence, however, that if a person is left-handed and left dominant, the neurons controlling their movements may come from both right and left hemispheres (Flowers, 1987, pg. 301).

Through experimentation during the developmental stages, infants and toddlers learn to sort out what is on one side and what is on the other. They try first one hand, then the other, frequently alternating until they find which they prefer for a particular task. Anatomically, the two sides are separate (pgs. 35, 36, 47). The neurological functions of the left side are governed by the right hemisphere, and those of the right are governed by the left. These differences are distinct and must be learned, primarily through movement and self-exploration. (Laterality, by the way, does not mean knowing left from right. It means knowing within oneself that there are two sides to the body no matter what they are called.)

Balance and posture are directly dependent on laterality, because when the body moves, the two sides of the body must cope with balance around a center of gravity.

Directionality

When laterality has been achieved and an internal awareness of the midline of the body and its two sides has been developed, there is usually an accompanying awareness of the separateness of the top half and the bottom half of the body, and of the front half and the back half. This knowledge of the various directions of the body leads to the next stage of development: the concept of directionality. Thus, once a child is aware of what direction an approaching object is coming from, the child must then understand that when the object reaches and starts going beyond the midline of the body, the direction is at that point changing away from the body. From this understanding, the child is able to perceive an object or another person as moving in a particular direction, facing a certain way, or otherwise positioned against a background.

Receipt and Propulsion

Once directionality is established, the child can then develop the ability to determine the speed and direction of moving objects in relation to self. Thus, children learn to perceive whether something (such as a ball) is coming toward them, or whether an object is moving away from them (which occurs when they throw the ball).

PHOTO 4.18. RECEIPT AND PROPULSION

Rhythm

Gradually, the child begins to develop a sense of rhythm. This is the ability to perform a movement or a series of movements with a consistent time interval. Rhythm allows us to put together a series of movements in a coordinated manner and to perform them with smoothness and freedom.

Visual Monitoring

These stages culminate in visual monitoring—the ability children have of using their eyes to check the environment to determine where they are and where they are going. Without appropriate development, there is a tendency to "eye-guide," or to watch the body or body parts while performing a task in order to reassure oneself that the task is being performed properly. With developmental maturity, children can perform the same tasks without having to watch themselves to see if they are moving correctly. They can judge their movements by observing the space around them and by mentally evaluating the results of their movements.

A Milestone in Integration

When children can visually monitor their environment, usually by age 11, it can be assumed that the brain hemispheres have been appropriately developed. Integration of the sensory and perceptual-motor systems of both sides of the body indicates integration of the sensory and perceptual-motor systems of both sides of the brain. The mechanisms for conceptualization are therefore in place, through the ongoing processes of sensorimotor and perceptual-motor integration. The accompanying sense of body image, which has been internalized, leads to a wholesome self-esteem.

Thus, we can see that whole child development is the result of the dynamic interaction of genetics with the environment. The achievement of laterality at age 7 (pgs. 71–72) correlates with the beginning of Piaget's stage of concrete operations (complex mental processes and the use of logic; Piaget and Inhelder, 1969). The development of a good sense of body image and self-awareness at age 11, the last of Kephart's primary stages of sensorimotor and perceptual-motor development, correlates with the beginning of Piaget's stage of formal operations (the highest level of cognitive functioning). This process of whole child development will now go on toward further learning, achieving, and maturing.

Summary

The process of child development begins with sensory information coded into impulses that are sent to the brain through the sensory nerves. The impulses are interpreted by the brain through its two hemispheres and a response occurs with the transmission of impulses through the motor nerves. Perception is the result of a continual stream of incoming and outgoing information, with ongoing feedback to the brain. Movement is an important part of the developmental process, because so many parts of the central nervous system are involved with it and because it is the basis for the formation of perceptual-motor skills. Development occurs proximodistally and cephalocaudally in a sequential manner, with various areas developing simultaneously. The sequence is universal for all humans, but the times for achieving various stages of development vary. Too-rapid growth may mean that some stages are passed through too quickly; too-slow growth may indicate a mild to severe neurological disorder. Relaxation is crucial for infants and children to appropriately learn to use their sensory input and motor output systems. When the muscles of the body are relaxed, they are more receptive to new information. Tension has a deterrent effect and can dramatically decrease incoming information.

Infants are born with certain automatic reflexes that help them survive during their early months. These reflexes are called the primitive reflexes, because they are meant to become inhibited by the end of the first year of life. The tonic neck reflexes are especially important because they help infants into positions from which they can learn various motor skills, such as turning, creeping, and standing. When these reflexes are not inhibited appropriately, they have first call on all sensorimotor impulses throughout life and may interfere with fluidity of function. The stages of development that normal children go through start with the primitive reflexes. Through their sensorimotor system, they develop figure-ground awareness, differentiation, vestibular balance, movement control, coordination, perceptual motor match, locomotion, midline awareness, dominance, laterality, directionality, awareness of receipt and propulsion, rhythm, and finally the ability for visual monitoring. Cognition is ongoing, and when all of these stages have been accomplished, the mechanisms for conceptualization are in place.

For Further Study

1. Visit a library and look up the work of Newell Kephart, whose research forms the basis for the developmental processes described here.
2. Visit a special education class and document how many children appear to have problems in motor function.
3. Visit an infant center and document reflex activity.
4. Interview 30 persons about their left- or right-handedness. Ask if they ever use their other, nondominant hand for certain tasks. Find people who are ambidextrous and observe their activity, noting whether they change hands mid-task.

References

Feldenkrais, Moshe. 1970. *Body and Mature Behavior*. New York: International Universities Press.

Fiorentino, Mary R. 1973. *Reflex Testing Methods for Evaluating Central Nervous System Development*. Springfield, IL.: Chas. C. Thomas.

Flowers, K. A. 1987. "Handedness." In *Oxford Companion to the Mind*, ed. Richard L. Gregory. New York: Oxford University Press.

Gesell, Arnold. 1940. *The First Five Years of Life*. New York: Harper & Row.

Piaget, Jean, and Barbel Inhelder. 1969. *The Psychology of the Child*. New York: Basic Books.

Trevarthen, Colwyn. "Brain Development." In *Oxford Companion to the Mind*, ed. Richard L. Gregory. New York: Oxford University Press.

CHAPTER 5

From Skill to Purpose

THE DEVELOPMENTAL PROCESSES described in Chapter 4 provide children with the tools for further learning and development. Each new skill requires time and experimentation to acquire, and young children persist in the repetition needed to master it. From the first step away from the sofa to the resulting plop on diapered bottom, the child experiments over and over with the processes involved in walking, and similar experimentation will take place for all the other skills that will develop in the ensuing weeks, months, and years.

Motivation to Explore

Once children have mastered a skill, it becomes a means to new ends and they will use it to expand their world. The motivation to explore increases with the development of each new skill. Hunt (1966) recognizes this pattern as intrinsic motivation and identifies three stages through which it develops.

Stage 1. Newborn infants respond to sensory stimulation as a result of inborn reflexes. What evokes listening for the newborn soon evokes looking toward the stimulus. The resultant visual stimuli may result in reaching and, later, in grasping. Once grasped, the object elicits sucking as the infant brings it to its mouth. Thus, the drive to explore and discover begins. Piaget ([1936] 1952) considered these types of behaviors to be largely independent sensorimotor systems at birth.

Stage 2. The second stage of intrinsic motivation involves recognition of the pattern of the stimuli and a drive to have it continue. Piaget calls this the "reversal transformation," which is the beginning of intentionality. An example is the game of peek-a-boo. The adult, soon tiring of the game, wants to quit. But the infant will crawl to the weary adult in order to keep the game going. The pattern involved in the game becomes predictable for the infant, who delights in each new surprise "peek." The resultant emotional satisfaction serves as reinforcement. The more the infant hears and sees, the greater the drive becomes to hear and see more.

Stage 3. The third stage relates to novelty. D. O. Hebb (1964) realized years ago that children desire to discover something new within the context of the familiar. Novelty introduces variety and contradictions in the experience of children. The new must be made to fit what has already been learned. Such novelty becomes the chief motivation for further cognitive learning and for improvement of perceptual-motor skills.

Symbolism

Simultaneous to the developmental stages that lead to sensorimotor and perceptual-motor integration, children begin learning to organize their world through symbolism as well as to experience it concretely. Because each brain hemisphere processes symbols differently, an awareness of these differences can help us understand why individual children respond so differently to the stimuli that comes their way. In order to understand these differences, we need to explore the nature of symbolism.

A symbol in its simplest form is something that stands for something else. For example, a leaf from a tree is the real thing. A picture of a leaf, the spoken word "leaf," or the letters that spell that word, *l-e-a-f*, when in that order, are all symbols that stand for the actual leaf.

The ability of human beings to develop a world of symbolism allows us to understand things beyond their physical attributes. For example, you may be holding a windup alarm clock. It is something tangible that can be explored and manipulated. It can be wound, the hands can be turned, the alarm can be set, and the clock can be taken apart with a screwdriver and the gears can be observed. To share your understanding of the clock, however, you need to apply symbolism. The clock can be given a name, it can be photographed, or a picture can be drawn of it. It can be described in words, and its separate parts can be diagrammed and labelled. This material can be organized into an essay. The result is that the clock can be understood by others symbolically without even seeing the real thing.

Symbol Systems

Symbolism allows us to experience higher cognitive activity. Whenever several symbols that relate to each other by a given set of rules are used in combination, they form a symbol system. Some symbol systems are informal, and others are very formal and highly structured. Examples of items from which informal symbol systems can be developed are

- clothing,
- jewelry,
- homes,
- money,
- hairstyles,
- recreational activities, and
- automobiles.

Individuals, groups, and cultures assign symbolic values to items such as those listed. These values form symbol systems with rules that are often implied and seldom consciously recognized. For example, we may buy a new car for a number of reasons besides mere transportation; a new car symbolically means status, position, success, or possibly power. These values develop informally within the culture or subculture and are seldom articulated.

Formal symbol systems are much more elaborate and follow a complex set of rules. Examples of formal symbol systems are

- spoken language,
- written language,
- mathematics, and
- music.

The rules for these systems are developed formally by the culture and are precisely articulated.

Development of Symbolism in Children

The collective symbolic experience of the culture into which a child is born sets the stage for the development of symbolic understanding by that child.

1. **Manipulation.** Piaget's work helps us understand the processes by which symbolism is developed in children (Piaget and Inhelder, 1969). During their first two years of life, children spend much of their time in sensory and motor experiences. As they experiment with objects through shaking, feeling, sucking, smelling, visually examining, and hearing, the repetition of their actions in a variety of ways develops schematic patterns of response within the nervous system. These patterns, which are the direct result of individual multisensory experiences, become the basis for symbolic activity.
2. **Representation.** The process of discovering that something stands for something else can be called symbolic acquisition (Godwin, 1987). Using Piagetian theory, D. P. Weikart (Weikart et al., 1976) uses the term *representation*. As children continue experiencing their environment, they begin to develop symbols to represent their experiences and the things and persons involved in those experiences. Through repetition and imitation, as children learn that certain actions can represent others that are similar but not exactly alike, the basis for informal symbolism begins to take form. At the same time, as they begin to acquire language, their initial words—even "Ma-ma" and "bye-bye"—form the basis of formal symbol systems they will use.

3. **Imagery.** Although both hemispheres "know" words, putting those words into meaningful language is primarily a function of the left hemisphere in most people. By the same token, although both hemispheres "know" imagery, the production of imagery is primarily a function of the right hemisphere. Children acquire the ability to control their wrist movements at approximately 2½ years of age. At that age, if they have a crayon and paper, the scribbles they produce will gradually take the shape of circles, which are frequently given names such as "dog," "house," or "baby." Even though the circles are indistinguishable to the casual observer, to young children they are symbolic expressions of the imagery their brain is producing.

As the development of muscular control moves down into the hands and fingers, by 3½ years of age the scribbles become much more complex, and the explanation of what they symbolize also becomes more complex. Instead of "dog," it might now be "dog eating," or "doggy sleeping." This type of symbolic activity might also take place at the piano. Laura, age 3½, may say, "Daddy, I'll play 'Jingle Bells' for you." She then proceeds to hit a series of piano keys while she sings notes at random, symbolically producing a song that she is mentally imagining.

4. **Spoken Language.** As indicated above, the early babbling of children leads to the first spoken words, which become the basis for the first formal symbol system to be learned—that of spoken language. The process is a natural part of nurturing. Mom and Dad respond to those babbles that sound like "Mama" or "Dada." Shortly, children learn that certain sounds receive attention, so they start repeating them. Soon, through modelling and adult reinforcement, they discover that certain sounds stand for things around them. At this point the child is beginning to understand the basics of symbolism and to expand symbolic acquisition. The child plays with words a great deal, showing delight with the process although not yet knowing the rules involved. For example, Bobby might point to a picture of a cow and say, "See Grandpa. Moo-ooo." Gradually, however, he will develop a functional understanding of the words he knows as he internalizes the rules of formal language.

5. **Functional Understanding.** As children develop a functional understanding of the rules of language, they learn to apply these rules but have no conscious understanding of them. They learn the rules simply by copying the language styles of models. Much of their language develops from trial and error and from coaching by the people in their environment. If a parent, for example, doesn't use the correct sentence structure as a basis for her language, the child will also learn the incorrect structure. Although the symbol system of spoken language is very complex, modelling is the most powerful tool of early language acquisition.

Implications for Educators: The Symbolic Sequence

As these beginnings of symbolism develop, a corresponding and harmonious development of perceptual, conceptual, and motivational processes also develops. As the growing and learning process becomes formalized, what we call "education" plays an ever-increasing role in these developmental processes. Effective education is therefore based on understanding the interaction of children with the environment, which in turn stimulates the cognitive processes and the use of symbols to increase their understanding.

1. **Referent Manipulation**

   As previously stated, early multisensory experiences associated with manipulation of objects in the environment initiate the memory systems through which symbolic interpretation will be applied. These objects are called referents. The memory systems associated with each modality become integrated with new percepts gained from new experiences. How an item smells is associated with previously experienced odors. As the child plays with or manipulates the item, he or she relates to and modifies previous imagery according to new and changing experiences with that item. Past auditory, tactile, and kinesthetic values also come into play with the present experience resulting in changing concepts. Although both brain hemispheres come into play, right-hemisphere functions predominate at this early level of learning, which can be said to occur from inside to outside.

2. **Descriptive Symbolism**

As manipulation progresses, children move into the next level of understanding by applying the formal symbol systems through which the formal educational process begins. The first level is descriptive, since these symbols help to label, identify, describe, classify, and visualize aspects of the referents being explored. Rich descriptive language is spoken and written form is used. We name referents, discuss them and their functions, and classify them. We use these referents in asking questions to stimulate thinking. We place written labels and names on items and locations that apply to the referents. We show pictures, photographs, look at models, read stories, see filmstrips and videotapes, and sing songs about the referents. We build rebus charts combining words with pictures to enhance children's understanding. We discuss their feelings and perceptions about their investigations. Thus we apply many aspects of symbol systems to broaden understanding. This is an outside-to-inside learning process, and it is especially relevant to the understanding and growth in learning of children who show strong preferences for right hemisphere functions.

3. **Symbolic Manipulation**

Learning reverts to an inside-to-outside process in the third level of experience. It provides children with the opportunity to manipulate symbols—along with their referents—directly, in order to enhance their understanding. Although this is the third level of learning, many aspects of descriptive symbolism and symbolic manipulation occur concurrently.

Symbolic manipulation assumes a number of dimensions. Rather than simply exploring referents, at this level children manipulate or produce symbols that look like, represent, measure, explain, describe, or define the referents or concepts related to them. By drawing a picture, they apply a visual set of symbols that brings about understanding of what is being represented and helps to crystallize related feelings and ideas. For example, a child's drawing of an elephant after a trip to the zoo may bring about an increased understanding of the experience and its accompanying feelings, which the child will internalize for later adaptation.

The classroom therefore becomes an environment rich with opportunities for children to symbolically represent and therefore better understand reality. From exploring things in space with blocks, Legos, and clay to symbolically playing out roles of the people in their lives, they incorporate symbolism in their daily activities. From charting the growth of plants to creating stories and decorating bulletin boards that report on the experience, children acquire through symbolism the vast background of information they need to pursue more complex cognitive tasks and to better understand the world in which they live.

Summary

The aspects of cognitive development that occur through direct interaction with the environment include perceptualization, motivation, conceptualization, and symbolism, which develop in harmony with each other. Child-environment interaction begins with the primitive reflexes, which are genetically built into the nervous system to provide the basic tools for development. As infants move through these reflexes, cognitive processes begin to modify basic movements, which in turn integrate their sensorimotor systems as the senses become increasingly involved in the process. Such activity creates organized patterns of behavior that develop into informal symbolic activity. Soon the formal symbol system of language emerges as children learn to differentiate sounds. Motivation drives them to use their newly acquired skills to investigate an ever-broadening world. Finally, as they acquire and master movement skills, socialization becomes formalized and many children enter preschool, day-care, kindergarten, or elementary schools. As the growing and learning process becomes formalized, what we call "education" plays an ever-increasing role in these developmental processes. Effective education is therefore based on the understanding that children's right-hemisphere interaction with the environment stimulates left-hemisphere cognitive processes and that the combination will maximize the learning potential of every child.

For Further Study

1. Outline the differences between games played by rules and games played by symbolism, as described by Piaget (1962).
2. Make a list of all of the symbols you use on a particular day.
3. Observe children in a dramatic play activity in a housekeeping area of a preschool class. List the symbolic representations you hear and see.
4. Observe an elementary school class writing poetry. Read some of the poetry and describe the symbolism the children use.

References

Godwin, Douglas C. 1987. "Development of Symbolism in Young Children." Paper presented at the East Texas Methodist Day-School Conference, at Tyler, Texas.

Hebb, D. O. 1964. *Organization of Behavior.* New York: Wiley.

Hunt, J. McV. 1966. "The Epigenesis of Intrinsic Motivation and Early Cognitive Learning." In *Current Research in Motivation,* ed. R. N. Haber. New York: Holt, Rinehart & Winston.

Piaget, Jean. [1936] 1952. *The Origins of Intelligence in Children.* Trans. Margaret Cook. New York: International Universities Press.

———. 1962. *Play, Dreams, and Imitation in Childhood.* New York: Norton.

Piaget, Jean, and Barbel Inhelder. *The Psychology of the Child.* New York: Basic Books, 1969.

Weikart, D. P., et al. 1976. "The Development of Representation." Paper presented at a workshop sponsored by the High Scope Foundation, Ypsilanti, Michigan.

SECTION II

Assessments of Hemisphericity

CHAPTER 6

The Psychological Diagnosis of Hemispheric Dominance

THE PHRASES "right-brained" and "left-brained" are tossed about in many circles today. When someone exhibits a trait commonly ascribed to one of the brain hemispheres, that person receives one of these labels. From that point on, the individual is pigeonholed, and future behavior is viewed according to that label. Labels have this effect on us. Once we categorize an individual, we stop observing. We create a set of expectations that clouds our views of that person. Although in social circles this labelling may generally seem harmless, in classrooms, where learning, growth, and development are the focus, it is clearly harmful.

For this reason we have taken a conservative position in this book regarding the careless use of asymmetric labels. Children do exhibit these traits in various degrees and combinations, however, and the asymmetric model of brain function can provide us with new perspectives about their behavior. Using labels such as scatterbrained, uptight, lazy, unorganized, and rigid to describe what we have seen in children has resulted only in their feeling guilty rather than in changing their behavior. Society seems to attribute behavior thus labelled to character weaknesses and seems to believe that if children are reprimanded strongly for displaying it, they will change their character and behave differently.

Such pressures have been extended into our educational systems, where labelling of children is frequently based on how slow or fast they can function. Individual patterns of rhythmicity or a possible lag in overall motor development and its accompanying perceptual and conceptual skills are disregarded. Children who lag in overall development are apt to be using right-hemisphere functions more frequently than the average child because developmental integration has not been achieved.

New discoveries in hemisphericity are revealing that a number of personality traits come from cognitive organizational schemes through which children approach their world. By "organizational schemes" we mean those cognitive strategies that a child uses in perceiving, understanding, and interacting with the world. As indicated before, the degree that a given behavior comes from one hemisphere rather than the other is not the critical point. How we help children to utilize the functions of their preferred hemisphere and how we help them to acquire skills that will enable them to encompass the functions of both hemispheres with greater ease is what matters.

We must be continuously aware that these unique organizational schemes are real and produce unique approaches to the world. What we are calling a right-brain strategy is clearly different from a left-brain strategy. A child who exhibits a predominance of strategies from one hemisphere has a very different approach to and perception of the world than a child who exhibits a predominance of strategies from the other hemisphere.

Within this context, then, we approach the task of asymmetrical diagnosis and suggested guidance. Characteristics of hemispheric traits as they manifest themselves in young children are outlined below, along with diagnostic strategies. Observation of and discussion with young children become perhaps the most valuable tools for determining what is going on inside them. Other strategies may be employed on occasion. As traits are identified, activities can be selected from Sections III and IV to enrich, balance, or integrate them.

Few children will display all of the characteristics of one hemisphere or the other that are outlined below. Most likely, each child in an average classroom will have a combination of traits, although with more coming from one hemisphere than the other, because of the laterality he or she has established. We have observed that much preschool and kindergarten behavior favors right-hemisphere organization schemes. These tend to diminish over time in many children as the regimen of educational instruction in the primary grades begins to train the left hemisphere. Many children who favor right-brain strategies and do not or cannot make the transition to left-brain modes of thought do not do well in school unless provided with enough meaningful experiences to keep the flames of intrigue with the world around them burning. The risks of failure for these children increase every year. We have yet to discover how many of these children drop out—inside or out of the system. But we do have enough evidence to be concerned. The more we discover about the dynamics of right- and left-brain dominance, the more specific can be our intervention. In the meantime, an awareness of those traits that have been found to be unique to each hemisphere can provide new insights into children's behavior. Activities planned for the development of these traits can enhance their productive use.

Psychological Dominance: Assessment Guide

In Chapter 1, 14 specific asymmetrical traits for processing information by each brain hemisphere were identified (pg. 13). These traits work in harmony to produce behaviors that tend to be right- or left-hemisphere oriented. We have combined these traits into nine categories of behavior. A child's preferred mode of processing thought can be assessed by observation of these behaviors. The nine categories are Reasoning, Motivation, Perception, Organization, Language Expression, Temporal Awareness, Emotional Expression, Graphic Expression, and Musical Expression. There is much overlap of categories in the following assessment guide, just as there is much overlap of brain function. Use as many of the assessment activities as possible for each child being assessed. At the conclusion of the assessment, a subjective summary can be written based on your observations.

Reasoning

Observe children in one or more of the following kinds of activities:

A. Acting out a role in a role-play center with props and clothing (for example, a firefighter in a fire station)
B. Discussing events that took place on a particular weekend or holiday
C. Cleaning up the room as a class
D. Constructing something—a building made from empty food containers or a bird feeder, for example (watch for different approaches to the problems involved, such as design, gathering materials, and construction)

Patterns of Reasoning

LEFT HEMISPHERE	RIGHT HEMISPHERE
___ 1. Interested in facts	___ 1. Interested in possibilities
___ 2. Repetitive	___ 2. Inventive
___ 3. Puts things in order	___ 3. Uses haphazard arrangements
___ 4. Verbally explains thoughts	___ 4. Explains by demonstration
___ 5. Uses factual examples	___ 5. Uses metaphorical examples

Examples of Behavior

LEFT HEMISPHERE	RIGHT HEMISPHERE
___ 1. Duplicates roles being played out, exactly and unimaginatively	___ 1. Expands on role playing with original ideas
___ 2. Uses much language in playing roles	___ 2. Uses much acting and movement in playing roles
___ 3. Uses materials traditionally	___ 3. Uses materials innovatively

___ 4. Repeats events as they occurred

___ 4. Elaborates on events

___ 5. Explains thoughts with appropriate choice of words

___ 5. Uses gestures and body language in explanations

___ 6. Explains thoughts and events by comparison with previous experiences of the same types of thoughts and events

___ 6. Explains thoughts and events by comparison with previous experiences of different thoughts or events, with a metaphorical relationship that may seem far-fetched to a listener but logical to the child

___ 7. Organizes activity methodically

___ 7. Pursues activity randomly

___ 8. Arranges materials in orderly manner

___ 8. Arranges materials randomly

___ 9. Makes plans

___ 9. Responds to tasks spontaneously

___ 10. Interested in doing things "the right way"

___ 10. Suggests alternatives to traditional methods

___ 11. Some actions are repetitive

___ 11. Keeps trying new approaches

Motivation

Observe children in one or more of the following kinds of activities:

A. Building a seasonal bulletin board over several days (observe for patterns of self-containment versus constant seeking of approval)
B. Create playdough with child (watch for patterns of exactness versus trial and error)
C. Exploring how a piece of mechanical equipment works—such as an old windup alarm clock (already partially dismantled), a record player, or a radio

Patterns of Motivation

LEFT HEMISPHERE	RIGHT HEMISPHERE
___ 1. Teacher's expectations are of utmost importance	___ 1. Driven by natural curiosity
___ 2. Pursues "proper" activities	___ 2. Pursues alternatives

Examples of Behavior

LEFT HEMISPHERE	RIGHT HEMISPHERE
___ 1. Listens for directions and guidance	___ 1. Dives into task without waiting for adult guidance
___ 2. Does exactly what told to do	___ 2. Experiments with task to explore possibilities, or how it works
___ 3. Checks for feedback and approval	___ 3. Suggests to you or others how to proceed
___ 4. Seeks approval when task is done	___ 4. Eager to show others what is going on
___ 5. Relies on feedback to determine feelings of success or satisfaction	___ 5. Enjoys tactile and creative values of projects

Perception

Observe children in one or more of the following activities:

A. Creating several faces from construction paper ovals plus a choice of several kinds of ears, eyes, noses, hair, mouths, and free forms
B. Working a jigsaw puzzle from which one key piece is missing (note at what point the child detects that piece is missing, and ask what can be done to compensate for it)
C. Drawing a picture of their choice, which you interrupt by reading a short story or showing a short filmstrip and then asking questions

about it while they continue drawing (note if the drawing drastically changes)

Patterns of Perception

LEFT HEMISPHERE

___ 1. Responds to auditory directions

___ 2. Responds on the basis of known expectations and previous knowledge

___ 3. Needs correct parts to complete task

___ 4. Accepts sensory input at face value

RIGHT HEMISPHERE

___ 1. Responds to tactile input

___ 2. Responds to shapes and forms

___ 3. Improvises to complete a task

___ 4. Converts sensory input into imagery

Examples of Behavior

LEFT HEMISPHERE

___ 1. Matches pieces of face to form "proper" images

___ 2. Detects missing piece late in the process

___ 3. Cannot complete puzzle without all the pieces

___ 4. Focuses either on drawing or listening

___ 5. Responds to questions according to focus

RIGHT HEMISPHERE

___ 1. Less concerned with finished face than with joy of making it

___ 2. Quickly detects that a piece is missing

___ 3. Is satisfied without the piece or wants to make a new piece

___ 4. Can attend to both drawing and listening, flitting from one to the other

___ 5. Continues drawing while answering questions

Organization

Observe children in one or more of the following activities:

A. Working one or more of several available puzzles
B. Making mosaic picture of something they like at home
C. Role playing in a medical role-play center
D. Cleaning and straightening materials in toy cupboard or (for elementary school children) cubbies or desks

Patterns of Organization

LEFT HEMISPHERE	RIGHT HEMISPHERE
____ 1. Mimics real-life roles in dramatic play	____ 1. Expands on roles in dramatic play
____ 2. Systematic	____ 2. Spontaneous
____ 3. Precise	____ 3. Disjointed
____ 4. Has a place for everything	____ 4. Items located haphazardly
____ 5. Works with items one at a time	____ 5. Gathers materials in bunches

Examples of Behavior

LEFT HEMISPHERE	RIGHT HEMISPHERE
____ 1. Tends to build puzzle in one direction, carefully examining one piece at a time	____ 1. Experiments with different pieces and various locations within boundaries of the puzzle
____ 2. Meticulous in organizing mosaic, placing glue on background very carefully as needed	____ 2. Approaches mosaic in broad, holistic way, spreading glue according to feeling and impression
____ 3. Uses mosaic pieces one at a time	____ 3. May pour mosaics onto glue

_____ 4. Systematically plans and executes cleaning

_____ 4. In cleaning, is concerned with getting everything "back in" rather than in its "proper" place

_____ 5. Materials rearranged, sometimes in a more orderly manner than before cleaning

_____ 5. Tendency to stuff things in when putting them back where they came from

_____ 6. Takes pride in organized appearance of newly arranged areas

_____ 6. May avoid cleaning for fear of not being able to organize well

_____ 7. Role-playing materials arranged true to life experience with doctors

_____ 7. Arranges materials for role play according to their value in exploring the various roles

_____ 8. Uses materials systematically

_____ 8. Uses materials inspirationally

Language Expression

Observe children in one or more of the following activities:

A. Discussing and writing or dictating a story about what was seen and heard on a class nature walk (on the way, have them look for things they like, and on the return, have them listen for sounds)
B. Role playing in a home role-play center filled with items, such as dolls, teddy bears, and cooking utensils, that will stimulate familiar roles
C. During a conversation period, telling about something that happened to them or something they enjoyed doing that week; afterward, dictating or writing a story about the same subject
D. Free play or lunch (listen to them as they converse)
E. Creating a four- or eight-line poem about one of a list of topics

Patterns of Language Expression

LEFT HEMISPHERE	RIGHT HEMISPHERE
___ 1. Uses oral language to express interests	___ 1. Uses oral language to express imagination
___ 2. Uses oral language to meet needs	___ 2. Enjoys producing sounds, even if not meaningful
___ 3. Uses language purposefully	___ 3. Uses free-flowing facial and body language
___ 4. Seldom touches people or things	___ 4. Frequently touches people and things
___ 5. Uses written language correctly	___ 5. Is more adept at presenting ideas in an original, interesting way than in using correct grammar or spelling
___ 6. Stories have a beginning, a middle, and a logical conclusion	___ 6. Stories are sometimes related in an illogical order, lack a conclusion, or jump to an ending, leaving big gaps
___ 7. Poetry is precise and usually factual	___ 7. Poetry is emotionally expressive and imaginative
___ 8. Poetry usually rhymes	___ 8. Poetry may not necessarily rhyme; may be off-beat in tempo

Examples of Behavior

LEFT HEMISPHERE	RIGHT HEMISPHERE
___ 1. Logically expresses what was seen and heard on a field trip	___ 1. Excitedly recalls what was experienced on a field trip

___ 2. Relates events exactly as they happened

___ 3. Relates what sounds were heard

___ 4. Relates facts about events and experiences

___ 5. Retells stories and relates experiences in a poised manner

___ 6. Mimics language patterns in role-play experiences

___ 7. May use language rather than actions in playing roles

___ 8. Inflexible

___ 9. Retells stories factually

___ 10. When interrupted, will go back to the beginning and start over

___ 11. Writes poetry about abstract ideas

___ 2. Embellishes events with little stories

___ 3. Imitates sounds that were heard

___ 4. Makes up stories about events and experiences metaphorically related to other aspects of life

___ 5. Retells stories and relates experiences emotionally

___ 6. Uses language imaginatively in order to expand on role play

___ 7. May use actions rather than language in playing roles

___ 8. Flexible; willing to try new ideas of others

___ 9. Fantasizes in retelling stories, frequently getting off subject

___ 10. Ignores interruptions, even though train of thought may be lost

___ 11. Writes poetry that creates visual pictures

Temporal Awareness

Observe children in one or more of the following activities:

A. When you announce "five minutes before clean-up" and then "clean-up time" during a free play period

B. Estimating time an errand will take by setting a timer (with a buzzer) before they leave

C. Awareness of class routine, ability to stay within appropriate time limits for class activities, ability to finish activities, and ability to be ready on time for the next activity

Patterns of Temporal Awareness

LEFT HEMISPHERE	RIGHT HEMISPHERE
____ 1. Responds to time constraints	____ 1. Slow response to time constraints
____ 2. Accurately estimates spans of time	____ 2. Inaccurately estimates spans of time
____ 3. Displays awareness of time sequence	____ 3. Displays lack of awareness of time sequence
____ 4. Very conscious of passage of time	____ 4. Oblivious to passage of time

Examples of Behavior

LEFT HEMISPHERE	RIGHT HEMISPHERE
____ 1. Begins to finish current activity when five-minute warning is given	____ 1. Little or no change in behavior after five-minute warning
____ 2. Begins to clean up immediately when "clean-up time" announced	____ 2. Slow to respond to "clean-up time" announcement; may need reminders
____ 3. Usually brings activities to a closure at end of a given period	____ 3. Projects are often not completed within an allotted period
____ 4. Fairly accurate in estimating time	____ 4. Unable to project time even approximately
____ 5. Apologizes when late	____ 5. Unaware of being late; may lie to cover up unawareness of time

___	6. Gets to new activities and events as expected, or even early	___	6. Frequently arrives late or is unaware of what is next on agenda

Emotional Expression

Observe children in one or more of the following activities:

A. Discussing humorous, sad, and frightening films, filmstrips, or videotapes, shown on separate occasions (What parts were funny, sad, scary? What would have made it funnier, sadder, or scarier?)

B. Discussing short stories or incidents that are humorous, sad, or frightening (ask the same questions suggested in A)

C. During a conversation period, recounting something funny that happened to them

Patterns of Emotional Expression

	LEFT HEMISPHERE		RIGHT HEMISPHERE
___	1. Reserved in emotional responses	___	1. Openly responsive emotionally
___	2. Maintains steady facial expressions	___	2. Facial expressions display much emotional content
___	3. Tends toward greater display of negative emotions	___	3. Tends toward greater display of positive emotions
___	4. Enjoys humor	___	4. Produces humor
___	5. Sees serious side of situations	___	5. Sees humorous side of situations

Examples of Behavior

	LEFT HEMISPHERE		RIGHT HEMISPHERE
___	1. Responds to humor, sadness, fear, and other emotional states in a controlled manner	___	1. Expresses appropriate emotions freely, spontaneously, and with body language

Examples of Behavior

LEFT HEMISPHERE	RIGHT HEMISPHERE
___ 2. Is analytical and realistic in solving sad or fearful situations	___ 2. Creates optimistic solutions to sad and fearful situations
___ 3. Accepts stories, films, tapes at face value	___ 3. Embellishes stories with own versions, especially humorous ones
___ 4. Displays slow transition between emotions	___ 4. Emotions change rapidly
___ 5. Emotions are slow to surface because there is much control over them	___ 5. Often controlled by emotions, which are quickly ignited
___ 6. Difficulty in recalling humorous experiences; relates only essential facts	___ 6. Easily recalls humorous experiences; relates them in a humorous style
___ 7. Laughs infrequently	___ 7. Laughs openly
___ 8. Laughs when others laugh	___ 8. Enjoys making others laugh, being silly, clowning

Graphic Expression

Observe children in one or more of the following activities:

A. Drawing a picture of something important to them and talking about it afterward
B. Drawing or painting and then talking or creating a story about some aspect of a field trip
C. Creating a holiday display to take home, using clay and other three-dimensional materials

Patterns of Graphic Expression

LEFT HEMISPHERE	RIGHT HEMISPHERE
____ 1. Draws exactly what is expected	____ 1. Expands drawings from what is expected to include own ideas
____ 2. Draws exact representations; gives factual explanations	____ 2. Adds own expressive imagination to what is expected
____ 3. Uses media according to rules	____ 3. Experiments with media
____ 4. May enjoy copying other people's creative art	____ 4. Enjoys originating artistic creations

Examples of Behavior

LEFT HEMISPHERE	RIGHT HEMISPHERE
____ 1. Uses drawings to illustrate events	____ 1. Uses drawings to illustrate a scenario or to solve a problem
____ 2. Repeats techniques or styles in drawings or paintings	____ 2. Constantly seeking new ways of expression through drawings or paintings
____ 3. Needs frequent coaching in describing art work	____ 3. Enjoys giving elaborate explanations of what is in art work
____ 4. Needs frequent reassurance that art project is progressing appropriately	____ 4. May wish to do another art project when assignment is completed
____ 5. May need prodding to develop ideas for display	____ 5. Attacks display project with confidence; often gives others help or ideas

Musical Expression

Observe children during one or more of the following activities:

A. Group singing (observe children for spontaneity, facility, and enthusiasm)
B. In small group of three or four in music center equipped with musical instruments and records
C. Creating a song as a class, with each child contributing a word, idea, or phrase

Patterns of Musical Expression

LEFT HEMISPHERE	RIGHT HEMISPHERE
____ 1. Expresses music mechanically well	____ 1. Expresses music spontaneously
____ 2. Follows directions and does what leader does	____ 2. May deviate from given directions, adding original musical sounds
____ 3. Enjoys reading notes and words to song	____ 3. Innovates according to mood of the moment
____ 4. In creating a new song, is primarily interested in tempo, rhyme, and accuracy	____ 4. In creating a new song, is most interested in original ideas and emotional content
____ 5. Use of musical instruments is prosaic	____ 5. Use of musical instruments is experimental
____ 6. Seldom initiates musical activities	____ 6. Frequently hums, chants, raps

Examples of Behavior

LEFT HEMISPHERE	RIGHT HEMISPHERE
____ 1. Follows teacher's direction in singing in group	____ 1. Sings songs in own way without monitoring group or teacher

—— 2. Sings songs in group watching teacher's lips

—— 3. Uses rhythm instruments in a mechanical way

—— 4. Plays records in the music center to listen to

—— 5. May contribute a single idea or word to a new song

—— 2. Face reveals that the music is felt while it is sung

—— 3. Uses body movements along with the rhythm instruments

—— 4. Uses music center to generate own music

—— 5. Offers many suggestions in creating a new song

PSYCHOLOGICAL PROFILE OF HEMISPHERIC DOMINANCE

_____
(name of child)

After you record the highlights of your observations using the example below, you might add a summary statement.

Left Hemisphere   **Right Hemisphere**

Reasoning

Patterns: _____   _____
Behavior: _____   _____

Motivation

Patterns: _____   _____
Behavior: _____   _____

Perception

Patterns: _____   _____
Behavior: _____   _____

Organization

Patterns: _____   _____
Behavior: _____   _____

Language Expression

Patterns: _____   _____
Behavior: _____   _____

Temporal Awareness

Patterns: _____   _____
Behavior: _____   _____

Emotional Expression

Patterns: _____   _____
Behavior: _____   _____

Graphic Expression

Patterns: _____   _____
Behavior: _____   _____

Musical Expression

Patterns: _____   _____
Behavior: _____   _____

CHAPTER 7

The Physiological Diagnosis of Hemispheric Dominance

THE PHYSIOLOGICAL DIAGNOSIS of hemispheric dominance is based on the physical and physiological development of the child, which was discussed in Chapter 4. Whereas the diagnosis of psychological dominance discussed in Chapter 6 is somewhat subjective, the following assessments are based on objective observations.

Handedness and Laterality

Is the child right- or left-handed? To determine this, check each of the following, because different hands may be preferred for different tasks.

1. Which hand does the child use for

	Left	Right	Either
• writing or crayoning?	___	___	___
• cutting?	___	___	___
• eating?	___	___	___
• ball throwing?	___	___	___
• hammering?	___	___	___
• threading a cord through a bead?	___	___	___
• combing hair while looking in a mirror?	___	___	___
• brushing teeth while looking in a mirror?	___	___	___

2. Which hand does the child use to pick up objects from a table?

   Have the child seated at a table, with hands on lap. Distribute eight crayons of different colors randomly on the table top. (Using crayons will lead the child to think that you are testing for color awareness—thus avoiding self-consciousness about hand choice.) Repeat this exercise as many times as necessary to establish a definite pattern. Sometimes the child will pick up with the hand that is most convenient at the moment: for example, the child may use the hand last in motion, thus utilizing the momentum of the previous motion to perform the new motion.

   Number of times using right hand _____
   Number of times using left hand _____
   Preference shown (circle one):
   　　　left　　right　　no preference indicated
   Number of times crossed midline _____
   Number of times avoided crossing midline _____

3. Which hand does the child use to pick up objects from a table when visual perception is absent?

   Tell the child to close eyes (or blindfold child). Place eight crayons randomly on the table top. Ask the child, "Can you find one crayon to give me?" Repeat this exercise four times.

   Number of times using right hand _____
   Number of times using left hand _____
   Preference shown (circle one):
   　　　left　　right　　no preference indicated
   Number of times crossed midline _____
   Number of times avoided crossing midline _____

4. Which hand does the child use to pick up objects from the floor?

   Have the child stand in one spot, with feet 4 inches apart. Place crayons randomly in front of child's feet, and ask child to pick them up. Repeat this exercise as many times as necessary to establish a definite pattern.

Number of times using right hand   ____
Number of times using left hand   ____
Preference shown (circle one):
        left   *right*   *no preference indicated*
Number of times crossed midline   ____
Number of times avoided crossing midline   ____

Foot Preference and Laterality

Testing for foot dominance can be undertaken with preschool children. We have observed that children sometimes use the dominant foot for an action and sometimes they use it for support. For example, when hopping, a child may hold up the dominant foot because that is a harder task than the actual hopping.

1. Have the child gently kick a ball placed directly in front of the midline of the body. Repeat activity three times.

   Number of times using right foot   ____
   Number of times using left foot   ____

2. Have the child kick a quarter placed on the floor directly in front of the midline of the body. Repeat activity three times.

   Number of times using right foot   ____
   Number of times using left foot   ____

3. Have the child run toward a ball and kick it hard. Repeat activity three times.

   Number of times using right foot   ____
   Number of times using left foot   ____

Enter the total for all three activities below.

Total number of times using right foot   ____
Total number of times using left foot   ____
Preference shown (circle one):
        left   *right*   *no preference indicated*
Number of times crossed midline   ____
Number of times avoided crossing midline   ____

Eye Preference

1. Make a tube of a piece of 9″ × 12″ paper by rolling it and fastening it with tape. Place the tube on a table directly in front of the child's midline. Ask the child to pick up the tube and sight for a distant object with one eye closed. Repeat three times, sighting three different objects.

   Number of times using right hand and right eye _____
   Number of times using left hand and left eye _____
   Number of times using left hand and right eye _____
   (cross-dominance)
   Number of times using right hand and left eye _____
   (cross-dominance)

2. Repeat the first exercise with a 4-inch-long tube, and have the child sight for objects at close range, such as on the table top or on a book cover.

   Number of times using right hand and right eye _____
   Number of times using left hand and left eye _____
   Number of times using left hand and right eye _____
   (cross-dominance)
   Number of times using right hand and left eye _____
   (cross-dominance)

When the dominant eye is not on the same side as the dominant hand or foot, this is called cross-dominance. This crossing may be due to one or more of the following causes:

1. Laterality is not developed, so neither side is dominant.
2. Laterality is delayed, with the possibility that dominance is not yet fully established.
3. Laterality has been established on the side of the dominant hand, but illness or injury weakened the formerly dominant eye, so the other eye became dominant while hand dominance remained the same.
4. A left-handed person has been forced to write with the right hand, so dominance eventually moved to the right hand for most activities although the left eye remains dominant for vision.

5. There is a highly developed ambidexterity, with the individual being capable of using either eye, hand, or foot at will.

All of the above reasons, except ambidexterity, may cause confusion in hand-eye coordination tasks such as writing or doing arithmetic and also may cause confusion and uncertainty in reading. Ambidexterity may be an indication of a highly skilled person; it causes difficulty in eye-hand coordination only if dominance has not been developed.

Hemispheric Preference

By averaging the number of right and left uses in the hand, foot, and eye preference exercises above, you may be able to determine hemispheric preference. Most people who show a preference for the left in tasks such as these are right-hemisphere dominant. In 70 percent of left-preference people, the right-hemisphere functions are similar to those listed in Chapter 1 (pg. 13) and in the description of psychological dominance in Chapter 6. But in the remaining 30 percent of left-preference persons, half (15 percent) show speech control in the right hemisphere, and the other half (15 percent) show speech control coming from both the right and left hemispheres.

Although most right-handed people are left-hemisphere dominant, some are right-hemisphere dominant, and some, like the 15 percent of the left-handers referred to above, show speech coming from both hemispheres. Right-handed people have the greater ability to respond with both hemispheres, even though one hemisphere is dominant. It is therefore practically impossible to determine hemispheric dominance on the basis of hand, foot, or eye preference alone.

Hand Positions for Writing

Most people, when writing, slant their paper slightly to their left and hold their writing hand below the line of writing, reaching up to the line with the pen or pencil or other implement to make the desired markings. Their writing instrument is at an angle away from the body (see Photos 7.1 and 7.2). People who write in this manner, whether left- or right-handed, are believed to be left-hemisphere dominant for language.

Hand Positions for Writing

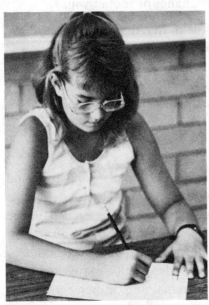

PHOTO 7.1. WRITING WITH RIGHT HAND BELOW LINE OF WRITING

PHOTO 7.2. WRITING WITH LEFT HAND BELOW LINE OF WRITING

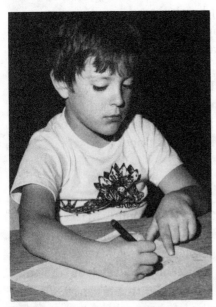

PHOTO 7.3. WRITING WITH RIGHT HAND ABOVE LINE OF WRITING

PHOTO 7.4. WRITING WITH LEFT HAND ABOVE LINE OF WRITING

About 60 percent of left-handed people hold their writing instrument above the line of writing and bend the wrist downward in order to get the desired marks on the line (see Photos 7.3 and 7.4). Those who write in this somewhat inverted position, whether right- or left-handed, are believed to be right-hemisphere dominant for language.

A certain percentage of people develop equal skills in the functions of both sides of the body. They may show either the right- or left-handed writing position and can use either their left side or right side for most tasks. Such people have possibly developed the ability to use the processing skills of either hemisphere equally well, and they often may display superior cognitive skills. Ambidexterity, or the ability to use each hemisphere to its fullest, is not to be confused with lack of dominance. A lack of hemispheric dominance, or the inability to use the functions of either hemisphere in a productive manner, may be the cause of a deficiency in learned skills, personality disorders, or other abnormal conditions.

Eye Directionality

There is yet another method of determining whether one is right- or left-hemisphere dominant. Studies have indicated that when the right hemisphere is actively processing information, the eyes momentarily shift toward the left, and when the left hemisphere is actively processing information, the eyes momentarily shift to the right. In other words, there is an automatic reflexive eye movement toward the side of the body that is opposite to the hemisphere dominating the thought process at that moment. It has been found that this reflexive movement is most evident during times of stress, a fact that might be kept in mind when trying to assess a particular child's dominance. Such an assessment is obtained by asking a series of questions (samples follow) while observing the resultant eye movements. These movements fall into four patterns that correspond to four categories of learners:

- *Auditory learners.* The auditory center of the brain is in the left hemisphere. In accordance with the theory of reversal, people whose eyes shift primarily to the right when processing thought may possibly learn best through auditory stimuli (see Photo 7.5). Adults who show a predominance of right-directed eye movements are often involved in the sciences because they are very analytical in their thinking.

- *Visual learners.* People whose eyes shift primarily to the left when processing thought may learn best through visual stimuli (see Photo 7.6). Adults who show a predominance in left-directed eye movements may have a tendency to be involved in the humanities and in the social sciences.

- *Tactual learners.* Some people seem to be always looking straight up rather than to one side or the other (see Photo 7.7). These are very special people who may not show either a right- or a left-hemisphere dominance. Their primary method of taking in information is through their tactual processes, including touch, awareness of body movements, and possibly, kinesthetic awareness. Barbara Vitale (1982) and others label this type of learner the "haptic learner." Such people learn best by doing.

- *Indeterminate learners.* Thomas Blakeslee (1980) introduces a fourth type of eye movement: bidirectional. People who exhibit this type of eye movement fall somewhere in between the visual and the auditory learner. These people's eyes shift in both directions, regardless of the type of questions they are asked or of the amount of stress that is introduced.

Sample Questions

1. If I have seven cookies and you give me three more, how many will I have? (Adjust numbers of cookies according to age of child.)

   Direction of eyes   _____

2. What is your address?

   Direction of eyes   _____

3. What is the name of the hospital where you were born? If you don't know the name, what town is it in?

   Direction of eyes   _____

Eye Directionality

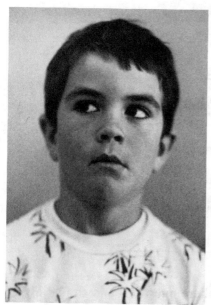

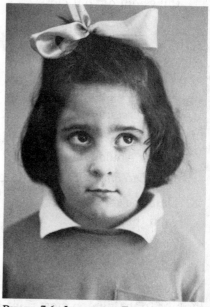

PHOTO 7.5. RIGHTWARD EYE
MOVEMENT: AUDITORY LEARNER

PHOTO 7.6. LEFTWARD EYE
MOVEMENT: VISUAL LEARNER

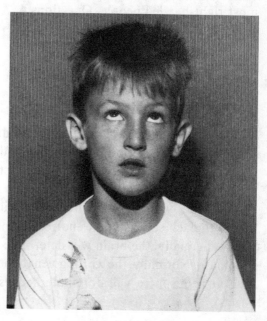

PHOTO 7.7. UPWARD EYE
MOVEMENT: TACTUAL LEARNER

4. What would you say if you woke up and saw someone stealing things out of your closet?

   Direction of eyes   _____

5. Describe your bedroom.

   Direction of eyes   _____

6. When you go outdoors, what are some of the things you see?

   Direction of eyes   _____

7. If your house were on fire, what things would you try to save? Where would you take them?

   Direction of eyes   _____

8. Describe some of the things you would save in the fire. Tell what they look like.

   Direction of eyes   _____

Questions 1 to 4 are left-hemisphere questions and should evoke looking to the right in most right-handed people. Questions 5 to 8 are right-hemisphere questions and should evoke looking to the left in most right-handed people. Questions 4, 7, and 8 have an element of stress added.

Dichotic Listening

Thomas Blakeslee (1980) describes the dichotic listening test as one of the easiest for determining hemispheric dominance, providing there is access to the necessary equipment: a stereo tape recorder with a stereo headset, so that different sounds can be given to each ear simultaneously, and a stereo tape that will present a different set of words to each ear. Though auditory signals from both ears will be received equally, the brain will determine which set of words will be dominant. Normally, the words given to the right ear and processed by the left hemisphere will dominate because of the left hemisphere's dominance in interpreting speech. If the words given to the left ear are dominant, then that person is likely to have right-hemisphere dominance for what is normally considered to be a left-hemisphere function.

The test can be carried further by using nonverbal sounds, such as humming or whistling, in the tape, with different tunes going to each ear. For most people, the nonverbal sounds heard by the left ear will dominate because of the right hemisphere's dominance over nonverbal sounds. Dominance can then be determined for the person being tested by combining the results of the verbal input and the nonverbal input.

Which ear processed the greater number of messages?

1. **Verbal:** *Right* ____ *Left* ____
2. **Nonverbal:** *Right* ____ *Left* ____

Do not jump to the wrong conclusion, however, if a child appears to show language dominance in the right hemisphere in this test. Such a finding should be cause for a hearing test by a medical doctor, to ensure that there is no natural hearing loss in the left ear. Only if the medical test is negative can a reversed dominance then be assumed.

Physical Asymmetry

If a child has developed a strong dominance, one side of the body will be larger, fuller, and stronger than the other side. Comparisons can be made of the hands, feet, ears, nostrils, eyes, and even width of the mouth. Comparisons can be made as to which side is preferred for carrying a heavy object (for example, a pail of water) from one place to another, which foot can kick a ball the farthest, and which hand can grip your hand the tightest.

Strongest side _____

Fullest side _____

PHYSIOLOGICAL PROFILE OF HEMISPHERIC DOMINANCE

_____
(name of child)

Hand Preference   Left ___   Right ___   No preference ___
  Crosses midline   Yes ___   No ___

Foot Preference   Left ___   Right ___   No preference ___
  Crosses midline   Yes ___   No ___

Eye Preference
  Close range   Left ___   Right ___   Cross-dominance ___
  Distance   Left ___   Right ___   Cross-dominance ___

Eye Directionality   Left ___   Right ___
                  Up ___   Bidirectional ___

Dichotic Listening
  Verbal input   Left ___   Right ___   Mixed ___
  Nonverbal input   Left ___   Right ___   Mixed ___

Physical Attributes
  Fuller side   Left ___   Right ___   Neither ___
  Stronger side   Left ___   Right ___   Neither ___

       Full Figure   Photo of
       Photo of   Child's Face
       Child

Summary: _____

_____

_____

_____

_____

Summary

A final determination of a person's hemispheric preference must take into account as many variables as possible. Once the physiological attributes have been determined, they need to be evaluated as a whole with the psychological attributes. Just as there are wide variances in character, personality, health, and appearance among individuals, so wide variances are also to be expected among people's patterns of brain functioning.

References

Blakeslee, Thomas. 1980. *The Right Brain.* Garden City, NY: Doubleday/Anchor.
Vitale, Barbara M. 1982. *Unicorns Are Real.* Rolling Hills Estates, CA: Jalmar Press.

Developmental Activities

CHAPTER 8

Activities for Whole Child Development

THE ACTIVITIES in the following chapters are geared toward maximizing the development of hemispheric functioning of children between 2 and 8 years of age, with emphasis on the preschool child. Within each chapter the activities become progressively more difficult. Because the neurological system continues developing through age 11, variations are sometimes suggested to expand or to modify the activities for children ages 9 through 11. All of the activities are open-ended, so the reader can modify and add to them in whatever ways are most appropriate in a particular setting or with a particular age group.

The activities are generally arranged according to the type of developmental skill being exercised, but there is much overlap between the various types of experiences. Because there is such a vast network of interconnections among all parts of the body and the central nervous system, the activities are intended to maximize both motor and cognitive skills. Many right-hemisphere functions and those that integrate both left-hemisphere and right-hemisphere processes are utilized, including perceptual-motor skills, spatial awareness and sensorimotor integration, symbolism and metaphoric language, imaging, feelings and emotions, and creativity.

Perceptual-Motor Skills

The development of perceptual-motor skills is based on the physiological growth of the child (as described in Chapter 4). The stages of development are exercised through sequential movement activities geared toward solidifying the natural development that is taking place or that has already taken place. These activities also help us recognize possible lags in development, as evidenced by poor coordination, inability to perform basic motor skills in a way that is comparable to other children of a similar age, poor balancing skills, clumsiness, and frequently, emotional tension or aggressiveness. When emotional tension or aggressiveness is predominant, it is important to trace it to the possible causes. These may be the social environment in the home or some physical disorder, including poor vision or a hearing problem. But sometimes the cause is immature or uncoordinated physiological development due to too slow a movement through the various stages as a result of a lack of movement opportunities or sensory stimulation. Or the cause may be too fast a movement through the various stages as a result of artificially prodding the child into activities rather than letting the child discover them naturally. The result of moving too quickly or too slowly through the stages of development can be unresolved steps in the process of coordinating all the body parts with the central nervous system.

Spatial Awareness and Sensorimotor Integration

Since right-hemisphere–dominant people have acute spatial awareness, exercises related to space and shapes are scattered throughout the various activities; in addition, Chapter 12 is devoted primarily to space. Once right-hemisphere–dominant children realize how well they can handle problems that have to do with space, their self-esteem is boosted, because they have often already experienced difficulty with certain left-hemisphere activities.

Spatial perception is a very important skill, since all of our actions are related to the location of ourselves and of objects in space. Spatial awareness involves several senses: sight, sound, touch, and kinesthesia. Kinesthesia is the internal awareness of the location of any part of our body—or what position it is in—at any given moment. This awareness, combined with the balancing powers of the vestibular system (see pgs.

64–65), helps us to know how we relate to the space around us. This knowledge is further strengthened by what we see with our eyes, which is dependent on what position our heads are in. Thus, the importance of sensory integration is obvious, and the interrelation of all the senses and their functions is taken into account throughout the activities that follow.

Everything we look at is located in space by our ability to integrate more than one sense at a time. We are guided not only visually but by sound as well. If a scent is involved, then we are also integrating smell into the series of senses. If we are looking at or reaching for food, the gustatory sense, or taste, comes into play even before the food is in our mouth. Once we have located the object in space, if we want to touch it, we must involve the motor system of the body. Thus, from sensory integration we move to sensorimotor integration, or coordination. In other words, the sensory information that our mind has processed must be coordinated with the information the motor system has received from the cerebral cortex as to what type of movements must be performed. We take all of these skills for granted, but they are not easily achieved by young children. They call for much practice, much exercise of all of the senses, and much opportunity to use the sensory and motor input in both hemispheres in order to achieve spatially coordinated behavior.

Symbolism and Metaphoric Language

Although both hemispheres recognize words per se, the left hemisphere (Broca's area—see pgs. 37 and 38) processes words so that they become meaningful language, putting them in the appropriate sequence and syntax. The right hemisphere has its own means of communication, such as the use of symbolism (see Chapter 5) and metaphors or analogies. Drawing on these right-hemisphere strengths, many of the activities we present make strong use of both symbolism and metaphoric thinking—which is a symbol system of its own. (See especially Chapters 19 and 20.) Metaphoric language jumps over the barriers of syntax and logic, ignores sequential connections, disregards classifications and orders of things, and makes its own clarifications and relationships to help us understand an event, an idea, or a fact.

Imaging

Imaging, or the ability to see pictures in the mind, is a powerful symbol system. It is a right-hemisphere function that can be capitalized on to help right-dominant children in their learning. Even right-hemisphere dominant children need training in this skill. Many exercises throughout the following chapters incorporate the ability to see pictures in the mind. These activities fall into three categories, although the categories may overlap one another in any given activity. The categories are visualization, guided imagery, and fantasy.

Visualization

Imaging is the biological ability of the brain to form a picture. When that picture is initiated from the environment, it is called visualization—or, by some, visual thinking. It is practiced when there is a real situation with real objects that are pictured in a real scenario. By picturing what is going on, problems may often be solved. By picturing various aspects of a situation in the mind, sometimes what had seemed muddled and confused is suddenly viewed with new clarity or new understanding. By picturing the components of a problem, the problem may seem much simpler, and the solution may now seem obvious. By picturing formulas, words, shapes, forms—anything that is important to a learning situation—the learning is made easier. The mind pictures become equivalent to audio-visual aids that we are so accustomed to in our daily lives.

Visualization is imagery that is created from the environment. People use visualization for different reasons—to help orient themselves to the space around them or to help recall past incidents, for instance. The most frequent use, however, is to make a kind of a mental notebook to help sort out the components of difficult problems. This kind of visual thinking is sometimes transferred to pencil and paper—with diagrams, maps, and doodles outlining the thoughts that are being internally brainstormed. When put together, these elements help show a composite picture of all the aspects of a particular problem, event, situation, or condition.

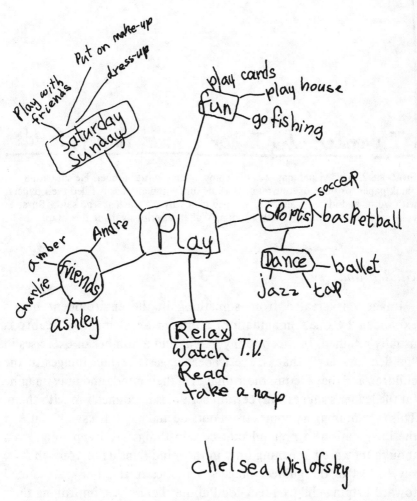

FIGURE 8.1. This visual map was drawn by Chelsea, a third grader. Her teacher gave the class the topic of play to visualize and told them to allow their streams of consciousness to dictate the words that they wrote down. The activity took place in a darkened room with soft music.

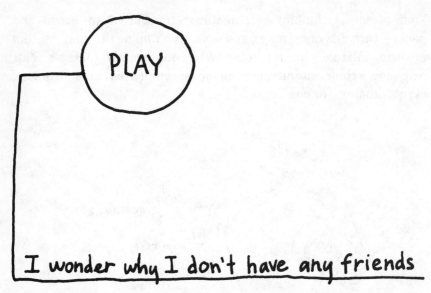

FIGURE 8.2. This visual map was drawn by Walter, a fifth grader. He sat with a blank paper for three or four minutes while other students busily filled their papers with words and ideas. Walter was nudged gently by the teacher, who said, "Surely, you can write something." With a groan, Walter laboriously made this map.

Guided Imagery

Imagery is created from something in the environment but is expanded by one's imagination, although an element of reality is usually retained. In this book, you will find a number of exercises in "guided imagery"; that is, the leader suggests certain images to the children and they picture these images in their minds and may imagine (at the leader's suggestion) certain activities in connection with them. This type of imagery comes from outside and capitalizes on the use of the imagination to pretend that certain things are happening, even though they are happening only in the mind ("inside of yourself," we say). Most of the guided imagery activities in this book are aimed toward helping children feel good about themselves, improving their self-image, and boosting their self-esteem.

Imaging is intensified when the senses of vision, hearing, touch, smell, or taste are evoked. There are great differences, however, in the way people respond to these various sensory inputs. For example, as explained in Chapter 7 (pgs. 113–14), some people respond best to auditory cues, some respond best to visual cues, and still others respond best to tactual input. Research has shown, however, that preference for the type of sensory input may not always be a matter of constitutional differences; it may be a choice of what seems most appropriate for a given occasion (Kolers and Smythe, 1979). It is important when doing imaging exercises with a group that all three forms of sensory cues be used in order for the greatest number of children to have a successful experience.

The practice and use of imaging, through guided imagery experiences such as those in this book, can greatly enrich the inner lives of children and can vastly enhance their ability to plan, organize, create, invent, and solve problems.

Fantasy

The magical world of fantasy expands imagery and helps children soar into new worlds on the wings of their imaginations. Whereas imagery and visualization come from the environment, fantasy comes purely from the inner self. It is the ability of the brain to form ideas, no matter how farfetched they may seem. Just as nighttime dreaming is a means by which the events, desires, and stresses of our daily lives are sorted out, so daydreams and fantasies enable children to sort out their innermost thoughts, wishes, and perplexities. They may not necessarily find the answers in dreams and fantasies, but children do find a way of mentally "talking" about them that may help relieve their confusion and their lack of understanding of the real world. Encouraging children to tell their fantasies to you, to draw pictures of both their dreams and their fantasies, or to dictate or to write them down in story form can often lead to insights about them that might otherwise never come to light.

Not only are fantasy experiences valuable as an escape or a "balance" mechanism, but when children are encouraged to open up the right hemisphere of the brain to fantasy, they are being encouraged to listen to their dreams, to exercise their imaginations, and to set their sights on what may seem to us to be unrealistic and unachievable goals. But when they are given approval, the steps they may take toward achieving these goals can lead them to achievements that they might not otherwise have experienced. They may even discover unexplored territories that will lead them to solve some of our worldwide problems. Thus, fantasies, when not so overwhelming that they overshadow all other activities, need to be encouraged, talked about, and even written down. When children are inspired to write down their fantasy stories (without adult pressure for correct spelling and grammar), their thoughts flow freely, beautifully, and with great originality.

Fantasies are child-initiated. We can only inspire; we can't create another person's fantasy.

A Comparison of the Three Imaging Processes

Here is an example of the difference between the three imaging processes. The situation is your returning to school following a brief vacation and deciding that the room arrangement has to be changed to give a fresh approach for the following weeks.

1. **Visualization.** You visualize the actual furnishings and imagine how they will look when rearranged. You may decide to draw a "map" (Figure 8.3) of some of the ideas you are beginning to develop about the new room arrangement and your goals in connection with it.
2. **Imagery.** Inspired by some of the ideas of the visual map, you mentally replace the visualization of the actual furnishings with new but realistic furnishings. You may even imagine yourself going shopping for the new furniture and equipment. Your imagination becomes active; you may even start imagining great new learning environments and may mentally explore their dimensions. With color, action, and perhaps even music, you get caught up in the excitement and challenge of the newly imaged environment and suddenly find yourself deeply immersed in fantasy.
3. **Fantasy.** The environment you envision may have colorful animal-shaped furnishings made out of some type of luscious material that

is soothing to the touch. The furniture is lightweight, flexible, yet sturdy, and when you sit in a chair, your body sinks into the comforting shape it creates around you. Other chairs look like giant bubbles, and the desk, in the shape of a large yellow banana, is

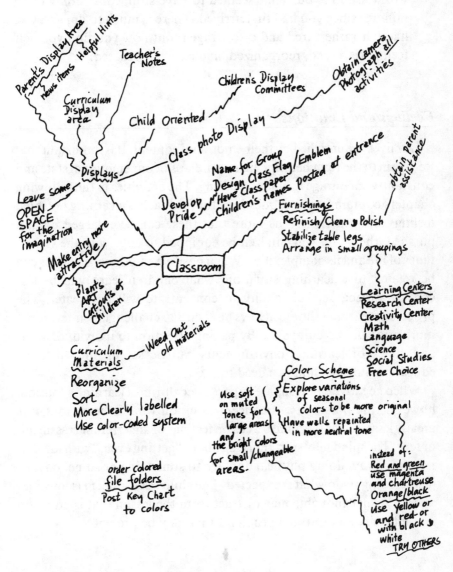

FIGURE 8.3. VISUAL-THINKING MAP FOR NEW ROOM ARRANGEMENT

spotted with a colorful array of gadgets. As you look closer, you find that they will do everything from sharpening pencils to creating games and grading papers. They will even . . .

Suddenly you come out of your reverie and see the reality of the world around you. Time seemed to have stopped. It's only three minutes since you had first arrived. There is much to do, and you had felt rather tired and discouraged, but now you find yourself feeling refreshed, reorganized, and eager to proceed.

Feelings and Emotions

Our lives are enriched by their emotional content. It is important that we give in to the right hemisphere's awareness of our emotional state and constantly encourage its understanding. The activities in the following chapters contain frequent questions for feedback concerning personal feelings and reactions. The more that these can be enlarged on and pursued, the better will children be equipped to cope with the vicissitudes of life and its complexities. When positive emotional elements can be related to a learning situation, what children learn will be less confusing because their ability to concentrate will be greater. The process of learning should always be exciting, challenging, interesting, motivational, and enjoyable. By paying attention to individual needs and styles of learning, environments can be set up in which the educational curriculum is indeed fun.

When negative emotions are experienced during a learning situation, however, the possibility of concentrating on what is being taught is greatly lessened, as the mind dwells on feelings of anger, embarrassment, or fear. The mind may start thinking about "getting even," with ideas of running away, doing physical damage to something or somebody, or just refusing to do what is expected. The child's self-esteem is lowered, and his or her thoughts may distract from the lesson that is going on and intensify any learning problems that may be present.

Creativity

Creativity isn't actually an approach to learning, but rather the result of an approach or approaches. Creativity, the authors believe, is the direct result of a wholesome blending of imaginative, intuitive, artistic skills of the right hemisphere with the organizational and arrangement skills of the left. The fantasies and original ideas created by the right hemisphere are dependent on strong input from the left in order to present them in such a way that others can understand, appreciate, benefit from, and enjoy them. Often, what we look upon as creativity is actually innovation, invention, and self-discovery as materials and ideas are explored. When this exploration results in a change in an idea, attitude, object, or event, creativity may be said to have occurred. Creative actions celebrate the individual, even when the actions are part of a group effort. The combined creative actions of the individuals can result in the celebration of the group, but the group is ineffective without the unique contributions of its individual members. This concept of contributions by all members of a group or class is one of the primary thrusts of the activities in this book.

Reference

Kolers, Paul A., and W. E. Smythe. 1979. "Images, Symbols, and Skills." *Canadian Journal of Psychology* 33: pgs. 158–84.

CHAPTER 9

Relaxation

INFANTS BEGIN to learn how to use their sensory and motor systems through relaxation. When children are appropriately relaxed, the incoming and outgoing information travels through the system more completely, more accurately, and more efficiently than when the body is tense and inflexible. When tension increases, the incoming information can be significantly decreased, which makes it difficult for children to process information and make appropriate decisions and responses. It is possible to double, and even triple, the amount of learning taking place when children are relaxed, secure, and physically comfortable, provided that the environment is appropriate and motivating.

Because so many children today have undue tensions in their lives as a result of societal stresses, we will introduce numerous methods of helping them to achieve relaxation. We suggest that one or more of these methods be employed at the start of as many activities and academic lessons as possible.

Relaxation activities can help children learn to recognize their own body tension and learn that certain activities over which they have control will relieve that tension. They will eventually learn that they have control over the stillness or lack of stillness of their bodies and, subsequently, that they have similar control over the stillness or lack of stillness of their minds. Relaxation activities can be introduced before imagery and visualization experiences and after intense intellectual activity, long periods of quiet activity, and vigorous physical activity.

The basic principle in muscular relaxation is to start with the head and neck and move downward, and with the top of the spine and move outward, simulating the cephalocaudal and proximodistal principles of development of muscular control (pg. 53). Another activity we often use to promote relaxation is imaging. This important right-hemisphere activity is interwoven throughout the remainder of this book.

The Relaxation Boat

Preparation: As shown in Photo 9.1, children sit opposite a partner, legs stretched out in front of them and straddling their partner's legs. Partners should move close enough so that they can comfortably hold each other's hands. (Children should take their shoes off for this activity.)

PHOTO 9.1. THE RELAXATION BOAT

Leader: I want you to pretend you are all little boats sitting in the water. You are light and bouncy, because the water is holding you up. You are funny little boats. You can do all kinds of tricks.

Close your eyes gently and see what kind of boat you are. What color are you? Imagine that you are that color all over. Do you see a flag flying from your mast? Does the water feel warm or cool against your body? Don't tell me about it. Just think about it inside of your head. Do you feel bouncy? Do you feel light because you are floating in the water? Think quietly about other things that you feel because you are a boat.

(At this point you can go from child to child and gently massage the back of the neck and the shoulders of each one for approximately ten seconds to help them begin relaxing. If you have someone to assist you, perhaps you can spend fifteen seconds in neck and shoulder massage for each child. This can be done, in fact, prior to any of the exercises in the book.)

Leader: Now let's play the relaxation boat. Everyone can hold hands and rock very gently to and fro. This is to the tune of "Row, Row, Row Your Boat."

ROCK, ROCK, ROCK MY BOAT
(Tune: "Row, Row, Row Your Boat")

Rock, rock, rock my boat gently to and fro.
Rock and rock and rock and rock—rock it as we go.

(Children rock gently to and fro, holding hands.)

Leader: Now everyone can stop rocking and just pull against each other.

Now pull, pull, pull my boat—pull it hard and tight.
Pull it, pull it, pull it, pull it—until it feels just right.

(Children gently pull against each other, pulling their arms taut, but not hard enough to rock.)

Leader: Now let go of each other's hands.

Roll, roll, roll my boat, roll it 'round and 'round.
Roll it, roll it, roll it, roll it—do not make a sound.

(Children move their arms around and around, rotating their shoulders.)

Now shake, shake, shake my boat, gently shake it slow.
Shake and shake and shake and shake, shake it to and fro.

(Children shake arms very gently with short, quick, staccato movements.)

Now wiggle, wiggle, wiggle the boat, wiggle soft but fast.
Wiggle, wiggle, wiggle—and now you stop at last.

(Children continue shaking, slowing down gently.)

Leader: Now change position so that the soles of your feet are against each other. Support your body with your arms stretched to the floor.

Push, push, push my boat, push it all the way.
Push, and push, and push, and push, and that is all today.

(Children push against the soles of their partner's feet.)

Shake, shake, shake my boat, shake it hard and fast.
Shake and shake and shake and shake—and now you stop at last.

(With soles no longer touching, children shake their legs.)

Loosening the Tight

Another, more traditional, relaxation exercise can be used with any of the activities throughout the book.

Leader: Everyone make your head feel real tight. Hold. Now let it go loose.

Now make your shoulders feel real tight. Hold. Now let them go loose.

Now make your arms feel real tight. Hold. Now let them go loose.

Now make just your hands feel real tight. Make a fist. Hold. Now relax.

Now make your hips feel real tight. Hold. Now relax.

Now make your legs very tight and tense. Hold. Now relax.

Now make just your feet very tense. Hold. Now relax.

Now make your body—all the parts of your body—very tight and tense.

Now just hold it. Take a deep breath. And relax. Relax your whole self.

Now lie down on the floor, close your eyes, and let your entire body be relaxed.

(Play soft music on record or cassette player.)

VARIATIONS:

1. All parts of the head can be relaxed, for example, jaw or chin, mouth, forehead, neck, eyes, and eyebrows. Children sometimes suggest the ears, which are interesting to try but not possible for most people.
2. Other small parts of the body may be added to the exercise, depending on how long you want the activity to last.

Hanging Loose

This relaxation exercise helps children learn the "hanging-loose" stance, a postural activity that brings about immediate relaxation once the skill is achieved. This is a centering activity; it helps children become aware of their center of gravity and allows the body to move into a natural state of balance. Before starting this exercise, you should help children relax their minds with a quiet period, perhaps by playing some soothing music or having them participate in a guided-imagery fantasy.

The effect you are seeking is similar to that when children play at being a rag doll. The shoulders droop, the chin drops down toward the chest, the chest goes down into the hips, the stomach protrudes somewhat, the spine is curved, and the legs appear about to collapse (see Photo 9.2). When the stance is achieved, which may take quite a bit of practice, you should be able to push gently on one shoulder so that it goes back and the other shoulder comes forward as the upper torso twists at the waist. As you move your hand away, the torso should twist slightly the other way, then back again, perhaps two or three times, until it returns to its original position. An easier test for relaxation is to tap gently against one of the dangling arms to see if it moves to and fro reflexively, a movement similar to one you try to get by tapping the shoulder. It may be wise for you to learn this stance yourself before trying to get children to do it, although it may be easier for them because they may have less natural tension than you do.

PHOTO 9.2.
HANGING LOOSE

Leader: Let your arms fall to your sides and just let them hang loose.

Now let your head hang loose, with your chin down toward your chest.

To do this, you'll have to let your shoulders hang loose also.

Feel your chest going into your stomach.
Feel your stomach going into your legs.
Feel your legs going into your feet.
Feel your feet going into the floor (ground).

OH DO YOU SEE ME HANGING LOOSE?
(*Tune*: "Here We Go 'Round the Mulberry Bush")

Oh do you see me hanging loose,
    hanging loose, hanging loose,
Oh do you see me hanging loose,
    so early in the morning?

My arms are loose down by my side,
    by my side, by my side,
My arms are loose down by my side,
    so early in the morning.

My shoulders droop, my body droops,
    my body droops, my body droops,
Oh see now how my body droops,
    so early in the morning.

My body digs into the floor,
    into the floor, into the floor,
My body digs into the floor,
    so early in the morning.

Although this activity takes much practice to learn well, it is worth the time. It can be used to relax a tense classroom by telling everyone to stand up and then saying, "Hang loose." Children can also learn to use the technique on their own for momentary relief of tension.

Rag Doll

Hanging Loose may be varied by playing Rag Doll and rag doll games. In the song that follows, the left-hemisphere process of language gradually moves into the right-hemisphere process of humming.

RAG DOLL
(Tune: "The Farmer in the Dell")

The rag doll hangs her arms.
The rag doll hangs her chin.
Her whole self is hanging loose.
Now let's all sing it again.

The rag doll hangs her arms.
The rag doll hangs her chin.
Her whole self is hanging loose.
Hmm hmmm hmm hmmm hm hm-hmm.

The rag doll hangs her arms.
The rag doll hangs her chin.
Hmm hmmmm hmmm hm hm-hmmmm hmmmmm.
Hmm hmmm hmm hmmm hm hm-hmm.

The rag doll hangs her arms.
Hmm hmm hmmm hmmmm hmm hmmm.
Hmm hmmmm hmmm hm hm-hmmmm hmmmmm.
Hmm hmmm hmm hmmm hm hm-hmm.

Hmm hmm hmmm hmmmm hmm hmmm.
Hmm hmm hmmm hmmmm hmm hmmm.
Hmm hmmmm hmmm hm hm-hmmmm hmmmmm.
Hmm hmmm hmm hmmm hm hm-hmm.

Leader: Oh, the poor rag doll is so tired now that she just sinks down onto the floor and rests.

(Recorded music can be played while the "rag dolls" are resting.)

Roots

The following fantasy can be used to enhance the feeling of grounding that children will get from "hanging loose." Play Hanging Loose and then continue as follows.

Leader: Now I want you all to close your eyes. Feel yourself hanging loosely all over. Feel your feet go deeper into the floor . . . and deeper yet . . . and all of a sudden, it's not you at all. It's part of a tree that's standing there, and its roots are going way down into the ground for food and water. They dig deeper and deeper and stretch themselves in all directions. They have such a tight grip inside the ground that even though you are hanging loose, you are very strongly planted in the one spot.

Gradually you notice that the sky is getting darker, even though it's the middle of the day. Clouds are coming from all directions, and the sun disappears from view. A cold wind begins to blow, and you just dig your roots deeper into the ground. You sit down and cuddle up to protect yourself from the wind. You sway to and fro because you are still very loose and very relaxed. Suddenly the wind blows so hard that you tighten yourself all over to brace yourself against it. You feel your whole self get very, very tense. And just as suddenly the wind begins to slow down, and you let yourself begin to get loose all over again. The clouds move away and the sun shines down. And you relax and smile at the sun. Slowly, you stand up, tall, your roots still deep in the ground. You spread your branches out to the sun, straighten yourself to the sky, and become yourself again. You open your eyes and look at your friends and say, "Hello."

Other Relaxation Activities

Throughout the following pages, many activities are preceded by similar relaxation exercises. These exercises can be used with the given activities, or they can be used with any other activity. They can also be used alone for relaxation at any time. Many other relaxation games are included in Clare Cherry's book, *Think of Something Quiet—A Guide for Achieving Serenity in Early Childhood Classrooms* (1981).

CHAPTER 10

Inhibition of Primitive Reflexes

IN ORDER TO DEVELOP a true integration between the left and right hemispheres, all the developmental stages must be achieved. One that classroom teachers frequently overlook is inhibition of the primitive reflexes. Until they become inhibited, primitive reflexes will have priority over all brain activities and may interfere with thought processes, causing hesitation and interfering with the natural flow of impulses. Children who have only partially inhibited their primitive reflexes (see pgs. 56–59, 61) will benefit from crawling and creeping activities. They will also benefit from some of the following postural reflex exercises.

Postural Reflex Exercises

🐾 Little Puppy Dogs 🦴

The children stand in a row in front of the leader. Then they get down on their hands and knees, with arms perpendicular to their shoulders and about 6–10 inches in front of their knees. Elbows must not bend during this exercise. The leader should demonstrate this exercise the first two or three times so the children will have the proper reflex-inhibiting movement (see Photo 10.1).

Leader: All right, puppy dogs. Get ready. Now turn your head to the side so your chin is touching your shoulder. Now do the same thing with your chin touching your other shoulder.

(Repeat three times.)

PHOTO 10.1. LITTLE PUPPY DOGS

Now you can do the same thing, but this time your head is bent down so that your chin is right above your elbow. Keep your elbows very straight while you do the same thing with your chin near your other elbow.

(Repeat three times.)

Little Kitty Cats

Leader: Now I'm going to say "alley-go-zoop," and all the little puppy dogs are changed into kitty cats.

All right, kitty cats. Keep your arms very straight while you hunch your back way up like this.

(Demonstrate.)

Still keeping your arms straight, bring your chest way down as low as you can without bending your elbows.

(Repeat three times.)

◟ The Ankle Game ◞

Still on hands and knees, the children cross one ankle over the other, as shown in Photo 10.2.

Leader: Hold your ankle over your other foot, while your foot is spread as flat as you can make it go. Now change feet and hold them the same way.

(Repeat three times.)

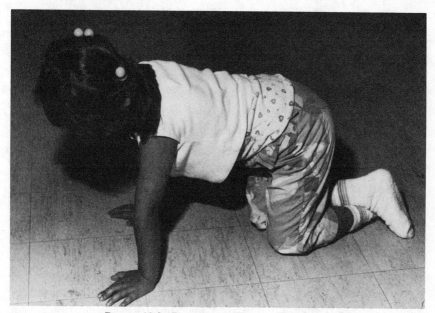

PHOTO 10.2. POSITION OF FEET IN THE ANKLE GAME

◟ Cats and Dogs Song-Game ◞

Once the above exercises are mastered, they can be practiced with the following song-game.

SEE THE LITTLE CATS AND DOGS
(*Tune:* "Down by the Station")

See the little cats and dogs standing in a row-row,
Waiting for the leader to say it's time to go-o.

See them look to one side, all so very qui-et.
Then they look the other way, doing it just right.

(Repeat three times.)

See them bending down their heads and looking to the side,
And now they turn the other way, eyes open wide.
They did it all again, they did it for a week.
Then they said, it's time to pee-eek.

They looked to one side, holding very still now.
They looked the other way. This is how it's done.
They did it over again, head high and over shoulder.
Turn around and have some fun.

They put their heads down, and turned to the side now.
They looked the other way, keeping heads down.
They looked the first way, and held so very still.
And they said, let's do it again!

Crawling and Creeping

The following activities are geared toward helping children relive their earliest crawling and creeping experiences in order to fill in possible gaps in their motor development. As for other activities, it is advisable to first help the children to relax their minds and bodies. The first exercise in the crawl-creep series reviews the homolateral movements an infant makes when first learning to move its body in a horizontal motion. This exercise helps to establish the fact of two separate sides of the body.

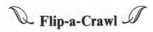 Flip-a-Crawl

Children lie down on carpet, face down, turned to one side, as shown in Photo 10.3.

Leader: I want you to pretend you're a little baby lying in a crib. It feels so soft and safe. It feels so good you decide to

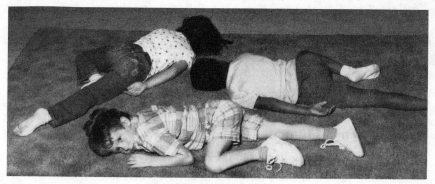

PHOTO 10.3. FLIP-A-CRAWL

suck your thumb. You don't really suck it, but you put your thumb opposite your mouth so that it will be nearby when you're ready to suck it.

Now, because you're just a little baby, you'll stretch one hand and one leg down straight on one side of your body. That's right. Now you can bend your knee on the other side of your body so that it is a little ways under your elbow on that side.

Oh, you're such quiet little babies, lying there so softly. Close your eyes for a few moments and see if you can feel how soft the bed is and how comfortable and cozy you are. If you try real hard, you can even see a picture of the baby in your head. See the little baby lying in its crib.

(If children seem to be very relaxed at this point, hum a little tune for two or three minutes to continue the relaxation.)

Everyone open your eyes and look at that thumb opposite your mouth. Now, when I say "flip," I want you to put your bent arm and bent leg straight, turn your head so it is looking the other way, and bend the arm and leg on the side that your head is turned to.

(As heads are turned, they should stay touching the floor.)

Flip!

(Children reverse their position.)

Flop!

(Children go back to original position.)

Flip!

(Reverse.)

Flop!

(Back to original again.)

(Continue for three minutes at a slow, steady rhythm. As children become skilled at the changes in position, each session can be concluded with one minute of very quick changes.)

From wiggling and squirming during the early weeks of life, from homolateral patterns such as those practiced above, infants move into cross-lateral (cross-pattern) crawling. This movement, which requires the arms to pull the body forward and the legs and feet to push, sensitizes the eyes and hands to the principle of coordinated cross-lateral movement, an important step in the later development of eye-hand coordination and visual motor perception. While the child is moving forward on the floor in a rhythmic pattern, the brain registers the sensation of the body against the floor surface. This sensation of full body movement on a flat surface will be later reflected in the child's ability to write on a flat surface with a fluidity of movement.

The Crawl Box

This is a marvelous piece of equipment to help children learn to perform a rhythmic cross-lateral crawling pattern (see Photo 10.4).

MATERIALS:

2   8-foot-long pieces of ¾″ × 8″ plywood shelving for sides
1   8-foot-long piece of ¾″ × 30″ heavy-duty plywood for bottom
2   8-foot-long pieces of ¾″ × ½″ rounded-top molding for top edges
1   10-foot-long piece of carpeting, 30 inches wide
1   30-foot length of lightweight clothesline rope
24 screw eyes through which to crisscross rope
6   angle bracket and screws

DIRECTIONS:

Fasten shelving along plywood base to form a tunnel without a roof (see Photo 10.4). To steady the box, screw a pair of angle brackets near each end and toward the middle. Cover the floor of the crawl box with the carpeting, turning it under 1 foot at each end. Cover the top edge with molding, and place the screw eyes along the outside of each top edge. Thread the rope side to side through the screw eyes, forming a crisscross pattern over the box.

PHOTO 10.4. THE CRAWL BOX

CRAWL BOX CHANTS

As children crawl flat on their stomachs through the box, the leader chants:

        _____ is going through the crawl box,
        _____ is going through the crawl box,
        _____ is going through the crawl box,
        Crawling all the way-ay-ay-ay-ay.

Here is another chant for crawl box activities. You can also alternate the direction for hand and knee every other line, or substitute arm for hand, leg for knee, and so on.

        First one hand and then the other,
        First one hand and then the other,
        First one hand and then the other,
        Crawling all the way-ay-ay-ay-ay.

        And one knee bent, then the other,
        One knee bent and then the other,
        One knee bent and then the other,
        Crawling all the way-ay-ay-ay-ay.

VARIATIONS:

1. Crawl through a tunnel made by placing chairs in a row and tipping them so that the backs form a V-shaped opening.
2. Crawl in and out under tables throughout the room.
3. Crawl on a 2-foot-wide strip of carpeting that forms a pathway through the room.
4. Crawl the length of a hallway.
5. Play "Alligators" chasing fish around the room and trying to snap them up for dinner.
6. Crawl along zigzag pathways on the floor made with tape or chalk.
7. Crawl in various shapes made on the floor with tape or chalk.
8. Crawl to various tempos of dance music.

➷ The Animal House Creep ✍

The cross-lateral creep is an important accomplishment for children. It should be achieved, with a rhythmic even movement, by the time the child is between 10 and 12 months of age. Creeping comes about as a natural follow-up to crawling. When creeping, children are learning not only to function in the important bilateral manner, but they are also learning to use both eyes in concert. As the hands move forward rhythmically, the eyes pick up that movement and visual-motor integration increases.

Children creep as the following rhyme is chanted.

THE ANIMAL HOUSE

The cats are creeping through the house.
They creep as quiet as a mouse.
The cats are creeping one by one.
They know that soon they'll have some fun.
But now they are so very quiet,
'Cause it's the middle of the night.

Across the house in another room,
The dogs are creeping in the light of the moon.
They are also as quiet as can be,
Because they're trying to hide from me.
So slowly creeping along they go,
So soft, so quiet, and ever so slow.

And since this is an animal house,
Here comes creeping a tiny mouse.
It says to the cats, "You can't catch me."
It says to the dogs, "You can't even see."
It says to its friends, "We better run,
Because I'm afraid they really might come."

So run, run, run went their little feet,
Running so fast, then out to the street.
Run, run, run, they went back inside,
Then found a little hole in which to hide.

The mice cuddled up in their hole so tight,
The cats and the dogs all said, "Good night."
There wasn't a whisper, not even a peep,
The cats and the dogs all went to sleep.

VARIATIONS:

1. Creep to various tempos of dance music.
2. Creep to a slow march.
3. Creep while pushing a small cardboard box, such as a shoe box, with forehead.
4. Creep while pushing a styrofoam cup with forehead. (Cup will go in various directions, causing the child to change directions.)
5. Push small cars back and forth across the room, following after them by creeping.
6. Have a creeping parade.
7. Creep while blowing a feather across the room.
8. Creep backward.
9. Creep on all fours, forward and backward. This is an excellent exercise for postural development and for strengthening muscles.
10. Creep on a grassy outdoor area. The tactile sensation of the grass intensifies the internalization of the activity.

CHAPTER 11

Postural Skills and Opposition to Gravity

CHILDREN FIRST LEARN as infants to cope with the pull of gravity. As they progress through the various developmental stages, this first learning expands to an awareness of the ever-shifting center of gravity and how to maintain appropriate posture. When these skills are well developed, the result is a wholesome body image, the foundation for a strong self-esteem. The activities in this chapter are geared toward strengthening the ability to integrate the left and right sides of the body and the upper and lower halves of the body against the pull of gravity. Activities such as hopping, jumping, and leaping develop postural control and a healthy understanding of how to coordinate the entire body in movement.

Jumping

Jumping calls for equal use of both sides of the body as well as differentiated use between the upper and lower halves of the body. Children who have missed certain developmental stages will have difficulty getting the body off the ground. Such children should play a great number of games on the walking board or balance beam, because they need to be able to "feel" balance in order to lift themselves off the ground. Walking board activities (see pgs. 188–93) can help them improve postural control. They can also practice jumping by holding the back of a chair while lifting themselves off the ground. The following instructions can help give them the appropriate lift:

Bend your knees a little. Bend your waist as you lean forward just a little ways. Bend your elbows so they are at your waist and your arms are out in front. Now feel where your center is. Take a deep breath. Jump!

Jack Be Nimble

Provide objects of progressively greater heights for the children to jump over.

> I jump so fast, I jump so high,
> I jump right over this pumpkin pie.
> *(A plate or pie tin to represent a pie)*
>
> I jump so fast, as quick as a fox,
> I jump right over this little box.
> *(A small box)*
>
> Jack be nimble, Jack be quick,
> Jack jump over the candlestick.
> *(A candlestick)*
>
> See how I jump, just take a look
> While I jump over this great big book.
> *(A large book)*
>
> I jump so fast, as quick as a fox,
> I jump right onto this little box.
> *(A small box)*
>
> I'm up on top, I can touch the sky.
> When I jump off, I go so high.
> *(A large box)*

VARIATIONS:

1. For older children, use progressively more difficult obstacles to jump over, onto, and off of.
2. Turn body around while jumping.

3. Jump along a path around the classroom.
4. Jump with feet wide apart.
5. Jump with one foot far in back.
6. Take many little fast jumps.
7. Take slow high jumps.
8. Jump in a square pattern.

ᘐ Jumping Jacks ♫

Stand with feet together and arms at side. On the count of 1, jump so that feet land apart and arms go up with hands touching directly overhead. On the count of 2, jump and bring feet together and arms to side. Repeat ten times at normal speed. Vary speed: slow, average, fast.

ᘐ Jumping Around ♫

I'M JUMPING, I'M JUMPING
(*Tune:* "A-tisket A-tasket")

I'm jumping, I'm jumping, straight ahead I'm jumping,
And then I jump the other way, back to where I came from.
Now sideways I'm jumping, right to the side I'm jumping,
And now I'm squatting near the ground,
 and still jump, jump, jump, jump.

Now backward, and backward, right straight back I'm jumping,
And then I jumped up to the sky, and jumped so very high now.
So high now, so high now, I jumped so very high now.
And then I jumped while bending low,
 and still jump, jump, jump, jump.

VARIATIONS:

1. Jump around while holding a friend's hand.
2. Jump around while holding two friends' hands, one on either side.

3. Jump around while facing a partner (not holding hands).
4. Jump around while blindfolded.
5. Jump around very, very slowly.
6. Jump around very, very quickly.

✷ The Tree Jump ✷

The children are seated on ground for this imaging exercise.

Leader: Everyone close your eyes and take a deep breath. Now let it all out. Take another deep breath. Let it out. Now take one more deep breath and fill all the corners of your body with oxygen. Now push it all out and slowly take little, tiny, short breaths while I count to 20. *(Slowly count 1 to 20— breathing too quickly could cause hyperventilation.)* Now take one more deep breath. Let it all out. Keep your eyes closed and just take short little breaths while I count to 20 again. *(Slowly count 1 to 20.)*

Now just listen to your heart breathe and imagine that you are in the woods. There are tall trees all around you. See that tall one over there? It looks like it would be easy to climb to the top. You go over to it, grab hold of a low branch, and start pulling yourself up. You grab hold of another branch and pull yourself up some more. Then you come to a lot of little branches that are almost like steps. You climb up on one after the other. You are going higher . . . and higher . . . and higher . . . until finally you reach the very top of the tree. You hold on tight as you look all around you. You can see the tops of all the other trees. And far away you can see the town and all the houses. They look so tiny from where you are.

Then you look in back of you. There is a tree next to you that has a little platform on it that someone has built. It is a wooden platform, and it looks very strong. You know you are very strong, too. So you stand up on a branch, you bend your knees a little, you bend your waist a little, you bend

your elbows at each side, and then you count: 1 . . . 2 . . . 3
. . . and you jump! You jump from the tall tree to the
platform on the other tree. As you look around, you feel
very proud that you jumped so far. But now it's getting dark.
So you quickly climb down the new tree, your feet touch
ground, and you run home.

Now you can stretch your arms way up high, open your
eyes, and come back into the class.

FOLLOW-UP QUESTIONS

- When you were way up high at the top of the tree, how did it feel?
- Was it warm or cold up there?
- What were some of the things you could see when you were up at the top?
- If you were a bird, what would you think if you saw a child at the top of your tree?
- What are some other places that go very high up into the air like tall trees?
- If you were dreaming, what are some of the other kinds of high places that you could jump from? Where would you land after the jump?
- What would you have done if you saw a horse sitting on top of the other tree?
- What would happen if a rabbit jumped up on a rainbow?
- Would you rather be a bird or a piece of cake?
- Would you rather be a tree or a tall building? Why?

ART ACTIVITY

Cut out many pieces of construction paper of various shades of brown
and tan, to be used for tree trunks and limbs. Supply sheets of white or
light yellow construction paper.

Have the children make a picture of a wooded area where there are
many trees, using the brown scraps of paper for the tree trunks and the
branches and coloring in the leaves and anything else needed with
crayons.

Frog Jumps

FROGGIE CHASED THE WEASEL
(Tune: "Pop Goes the Weasel")

All around the little pond,
The froggie jumped some quick jumps.
The froggie said, "It's lots of fun,"
Until he came to a tree stump.

He stopped and looked and figured out
How to make a big jump.
He took a breath and gave a leap,
And fell and got a big bump.

The frog got up and jumped again,
And then he chased the weasel,
All around the little pond,
Pop! Goes the weasel.

The Jump Line

On large sheets of paper, use crayons while listening to recorded music. Draw a line down the middle of the paper, so the line is vertical as you face it. As the music plays, make marks on the paper, while keeping your hand jumping back and forth across the line to the rhythm of the music.

VARIATIONS:

1. Use chalk.
2. Use wide-tip markers.

The Jump Drip

PREPARATION:

Spread a large paper in an area that can be easily washed of paint—perhaps outdoors on the grass. Prepare tempera paint of a fairly creamy consistency. Use extra-thick brushes. Half-inch trim paintbrushes can be used. To help keep the paint under control, demonstrate to children how they can tap the wrist of their brush-holding hand up and down against the wrist of their other hand to get the paint to drop off.

ACTIVITY:

Hold a can of paint with the brush in it. As the music plays, dip your brush in the paint and shake it onto the paper by "jumping" your hand up and down very gently. Every time the music stops momentarily, change colors.

VARIATION:

Dip your brush in the paint (without holding the container). Let the paint drip onto the paper from the force of your body jumping up and down. Every time the music stops momentarily, change colors.

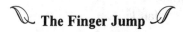
The Finger Jump

PREPARATION:

Use large sheets of paper suitable for fingerpainting. Set out fingerpaints. Each child should have available two colors that blend well, such as yellow and blue, yellow and green, green and blue, yellow and red, red and orange, yellow and orange.

ACTIVITY:

Tell the children that this is going to be a jumping fingerpainting. They may use the paints in any way they like as long as their hands keep jumping up and down.

SEE MY HANDS GO UP AND DOWN
(*Tune:* "London Bridge")

See my hands go up and down,
    up and down, up and down,
See my hands go up and down, my fair lady.

Take the paint and put it down,
    put it down, put it down,
Take the paint and put it down, my fair lady.

Jump around and over and out,
    over and out, over and out,
Jump around and over and out, my fair lady.

Cross your hands and jump them now,
    jump them now, jump them now,
Cross your hands and jump them now, my fair lady.

Jump my palm with front and back,
    front and back, front and back,
Jump my palm with front and back, my fair lady.

Now my hands are full of paint,
    full of paint, full of paint,
Now my hands are full of paint, my fair lady.

Stop it now and wash my hands,
    Wash my hands, wash my hands,
Stop it now and wash my hands, my fair lady.

Because this is really a "jumping" experience, help the children to calm down by giving them a bucket of soapsuds to wash their hands in. Follow the activity with a period of relaxation.

Hopping

Hopping is a more sophisticated form of getting the body off the ground by gaining postural control over the shift of gravity.

𝒬 Chair Hop 𝒮

To teach toddlers to hop, have them hold onto the back of a chair while they jump on one foot five times and then on the other five times. Three-year-olds should be able to hop a minimum of three hops on one foot for a distance of one to two feet. Four-year-olds should be able to do six hops for a distance of two to four feet. And five-year-olds should be able to do eight to ten hops for a distance of four to six feet. Children who cannot achieve these minimum goals should practice by holding onto a chair back. They should also be involved in many walking board activities (see pgs. 188–93) to help improve their postural control.

WAYS TO PRACTICE HOPPING

1. Hold onto the back of a chair on which someone is sitting (for weight). Hop five times on one foot, then five on the other. Continue until tired.
2. Practice hopping while holding onto someone's hand.
3. Play "broken leg." Some nonhoppers will suddenly acquire the skill as they get caught up in the dramatic play activity and unconsciously gain control over their center of gravity.
4. Play being an automobile that gets a flat tire and has to "hop" home.

Hopscotch Games

Hopscotch games are excellent integrative activities that use both sides of the body, alternating between bilateral (both sides doing the same thing), homolateral (only one side in action at a time), and cross-lateral (opposite arm and leg working together) movements. In addition to the traditional hopscotch games, those that follow are excellent developmental activities that require use of both sides of the body:

1. Start out with games that require one hop, then both feet down (see Figure 11.1).
2. Use two hops and both feet down (see Figure 11.2).
3. Use three hops and both feet down (see Figure 11.3).
4. Continue to make games increasingly more difficult in above manner (see Figures 11.4, 11.5, and 11.6).

The Hopping Circle

With chalk, mark numbers from 1 to 50 in a large circular or snail pattern.

Hopscotch Patterns

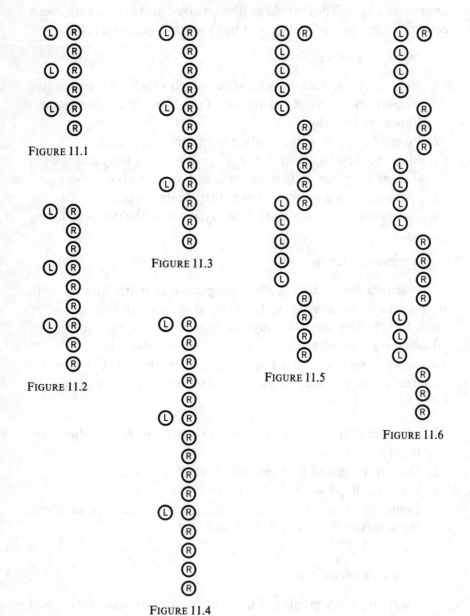

FIGURE 11.1

FIGURE 11.2

FIGURE 11.3

FIGURE 11.4

FIGURE 11.5

FIGURE 11.6

1. Enclose numbers in the shape of a foot.
2. Enclose numbers in alternating geometric shapes, such as a circle and triangle, then a square and a rectangle, which can be taken into consideration in any of the following activities.
3. Enclose numbers in series of geometric shapes, such as four circles, four triangles, and so on. Children can alternate feet with each new shape.

ACTIVITIES:

1. Children hop on as many numbers as they can. As soon as they need to put one foot down, they change feet until the next stop. They continue to change the hopping foot each time they need to stop.
2. Children make a given number of hops on one foot, then change to the other foot, continuing to alternate until circle is completed. They might start out with three hops on each foot and keep increasing the number until they are doing eight hops on each foot. The goal is to change feet according to a given pattern rather than to increase endurance on one foot.
3. To recorded music, the children can hop on the circle. The leader stops the music every five to ten seconds, at which time the children change feet.
4. Same as above, using both feet to hop. One foot goes on the number, the other foot to the side of it.
5. Same as above, except that numbers are placed in a random pattern around the area being used, so that children have to be aware of the changing directions.

VARIATIONS FOR OLDER STUDENTS:

1. Same as any of the above, except moving backward.
2. Same as any of the above while holding a half-filled glass of water. The goal is not to spill the water.
3. Same as above, holding the glass of water, but changing the holding hand each time the hopping foot is changed so that the holding and the hopping are performed by the same side of the body.

4. Same as above, holding the glass of water, but changing the holding hand each time the hopping foot is changed so that the holding and the hopping are performed by opposite sides of the body.

ART ACTIVITIES:

1. Create designs for various hopscotch games.
2. Create a hopscotch design, using color codes to tell whether you put down one foot or two. Show code on side of paper.

⤞ The Hopping Maze ⤝

Using different colors of chalk or different shapes, draw hopping patterns that crisscross in many directions around the room. Have the various patterns in different colors or different shapes overlap one another (see Figure 11.7). Have children divide into teams, each selecting a different color or shape.

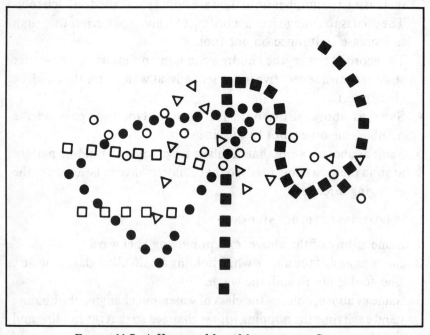

FIGURE 11.7. A HOPPING MAZE MARKED WITH SHAPES

Each team follows its color while hopping on one foot or the other until the end of the pattern is reached. Each child may change the hopping foot as needed.

VARIATIONS:

1. Hop to recorded music.
2. Hop to recorded music, but change the hopping foot every time the music is stopped.
3. Teams change colors in order to experience a different pattern.
4. Hop on right foot only, with left eye occluded (use patch).
5. Hop on left foot only, with right eye occluded (use patch).

The Hopping Rope

Lay a rope on the floor or ground.

The children hop back and forth across the rope, changing feet whenever both feet touch the ground. Once the children are comfortable with this exercise, play recorded music while they hop back and forth across the rope.

Jump Rope

Hopping and jumping activities can be expanded with jump rope activities. These integrated activities are excellent for learning to use all parts of the body in unison (and thus, all parts of the brain in partnership). Successful jump rope experiences lead to a wholesome body image as well. And, as stated previously, a good body image is the basis for self-esteem.

The Long Rope

One person holds the rope (15–20 feet recommended) at each end. A third child then practices jumping over the rope in the following activities.

1. Jump over rope as it is held 6 inches above the ground, then 8 inches, and finally 10 inches. Older children may go much higher.
2. Jump over rope as it is held slightly above the ground and swung gently to and fro.
   a. Jump using both feet in unison.
   b. Run and leap.
   c. Jump, using right foot only.
   d. Jump, using left foot only.
   e. Jump back and forth over the moving rope, alternating feet with each jump.

The Turning Long Rope

Two children hold the rope and turn it at an even speed for the jumping child.

1. While the rope is up, run through to other side and back again.
2. Jump over the turning rope one time, jump out, and back one time.
3. Jump over turning rope six times with both feet.
4. Jump over turning rope two times with one foot and then two times with the other. Gradually increase the number of times for each foot if child is capable of doing so.
5. Jump over turning rope six times, touching knees with both hands during each jump.
6. Jump over turning rope six times, touching ankles during each jump.
7. Jump over turning rope six times, touching floor during each jump.
8. Jump over turning rope, touching knees, then ankles, then floor during successive jumps. Repeat twice.
9. Same as 6, 7, or 8, doing each touch twice during each jump.
10. Jump over turning rope six times while bouncing a ball.
11. Jump over turning rope six times with a partner, while throwing ball back and forth to each other.
12. Jump over turning rope six times, turning around in a circle as the jumps occur.

13. Jump over turning rope six times, holding a partner's hand who is also jumping.
14. Jump over turning rope while playing patty-cake with a partner.
15. Jump over turning rope, making up a trick, and having others copy.

🍃 The Short Rope 🍃

This is the standard jump rope, usually approximately 7–8 feet long. Beginners should first learn to turn the rope as they jump over it with two feet at the same time at normal speed. Then they can quicken the speed of the turns and, after that, make two jumps in between each turn. When they are adept at the two-feet jump, they can practice jumping with one foot in the following increasingly challenging exercises.

1. Jump with right foot only.
2. Jump with left foot only.
3. Jump, alternating right and left feet.
4. Jump two times on right foot, two times on left. Continue pattern four times making a total of eight jumps. Increase to ten, twelve, and fourteen jumps.
5. Move forward while jumping on alternate feet.
6. Move backward while jumping on alternate feet.
7. Move sideways while jumping on alternate feet.
8. Jump rope with skipping movement.
9. Jump rope with skipping movement to music.
10. Jump rope with two feet while turning around and around.
11. Jump rope with two feet with eyes closed.
12. Jump on right foot with left eye closed.
13. Jump on left foot with right eye closed.

VARIATIONS:

1. Jump rope with two feet or alternating feet while bringing rope around twice between jumps.
2. Jump a rope that another person is holding by one end and swinging in a circle on the ground (see Photo 11.1).

PHOTO 11.1. TWO-PERSON VARIATION OF SHORT-ROPE JUMPING

3. Jump rope like a silly clown.
4. Jump rope like you are on a tightrope high up in the air.
5. Jump rope like a very, very old person.
6. Jump rope like a very, very tall person.
7. Jump rope like a very, very short person.
8. Jump rope like a very, very crooked person.
9. Jump rope like a very, very wiggly person.
10. Jump rope like a very high-stepping person.
11. Jump rope like a person who takes very tiny steps.
12. While jumping rope make up your own trick for others to copy.

◟ Difficult Jump Rope Activities ◞

1. Jump rope on a walking beam.
2. Jump rope on a large board raised 2 inches off the floor.
3. Jump rope on a sturdy table. (Leader must check to make sure table is sturdy enough to withstand jumping.)

Leaping

All jumping activities should be supplemented with leaping activities. Leaping is like running, except the body is off the ground longer—in other words, leaping combines running and jumping. Each leap should be preceded by running to help build up the momentum of the movement.

1. Leap over a 1-foot-wide space.
2. Leap over a 2-foot-wide space.
3. Leap over a 3-foot-wide space.
4. Leap over a 6-inch-high box or platform, not more than 2 feet wide.
5. Leap over a 12-inch-high box or platform, not more than 1 foot wide.

Continue as above, increasing the difficulty of the task in keeping with the children's increasing skills.

◟ Leaping Games ◞

1. *Leap the River.* Draw a "river" (2 feet wide) winding across the room. Then say, "Here is a river. How many times can you leap back and forth across it?"
2. *Leap the Puddles.* Draw 2-foot-diameter circles six feet apart scattered around a large area. Then say, "Here are some puddles on the ground. How many puddles can you leap over?"
3. *High Leaps.* Stretch a rope 2 inches above the ground across a grassy area. Have the children practice leaping over the rope, raising it as their skill increases.

CHAPTER 12

Spatial Relationships and Directionality

THE DEVELOPMENT of spatial awareness and directionality are closely akin to the development of postural control and laterality, which will eventually lead to the development of body image. Each of these types of development occurs in its own way, not concurrently, but certainly in synchronicity with one another.

Awareness of spatial relationships is a strong right-hemisphere skill, somewhat indicative of the wider spacing of neurons in the right hemisphere. During infancy, children are generally aware only of the space within their own visual field at any given moment. At first, objects out of view are totally nonexistent for them, but gradually they develop the concept of object permanency. As children develop into the locomotor stage and as they become able to move from object to object, they begin to develop an understanding of the shape and size of the room that they are in and of the location of the various items they are interested in. Finally, as their perceptual skills increase, children start perceiving the space beyond their immediate location and develop a memory for spaces that they have been in on previous occasions.

People with strong right-hemisphere preferences may have an excellent awareness of spatial relationships, shapes, forms, size comparisons, and arrangements, and yet have much difficulty with directionality in relation to their own selves. These are the people who always have difficulty with knowing which way is right or left, but they may do well with north, south, east, and west, because these directions are stable and do not relate to one's own body. Directionality comes later in the sequence of natural development (pg. 73) than spatial

170

awareness, but activities related to the two skills are so closely related that we have intermingled the two in this chapter—just as many other developmental skills will overlap throughout this book.

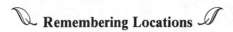 Remembering Locations

First, have children walk to and touch various items in the classroom. Then, have them stay in one place and point to the same items. Next, have them close their eyes and point in the direction of the same items. Finally, have them close their eyes and turn their bodies in the direction of the same items instead of pointing.

Arrange the classroom so children can position themselves in places that are over, under, above, below, on top of, underneath, between, in front of, in back of, to the side of, and on the other side.

VARIATIONS:

1. Same as above, but have children place objects in the places you ask them to.
2. Same as above, but have children point to the locations listed above.

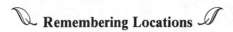 Big Steps, Little Steps

1. Have children walk around the periphery of the room, using giant steps. Repeat activity using baby steps.
2. Have the children walk diagonally across the room, using long steps. Repeat activity, using short steps.
3. Mark a space in the middle of the classroom, and have them walk to it, using toe-to-heel steps. Walk away from the middle using backward steps.

 Friends

Divide class into two teams, with each team standing on opposite sides of the classroom. Then sing this song. On the second verse, children from one side go to bring children from the other side back to their side.

MY FRIENDS ARE OVER THE OCEAN
(*Tune:* "My Bonnie Lies Over the Ocean")

My friends are over the ocean.
My friends are over the sea.
My friends are over the big room.
Oh bring back my friends to me, to me.

Oh bring back, bring back,
Oh bring back my friends to me, to me.
Oh bring back, bring back,
Oh bring back my friends to me-e-e-e.

Sing the first verse again while the children go back to their side of the room. Sing the second verse again, and have the second group go across the room to bring the children of the first group to their side this time. Repeat, alternating the group that goes to get the other.

Shape Spaces

Create a large circle with a rope or with tape on the floor. Ask the children to find the answers to the following questions.

1. How many steps does it take to go across the circle?
2. How many steps does it take to go across the whole room?
3. How many giant steps does it take?
4. How many toe-to-heel steps does it take?
5. How many steps does it take to go from the edge of the circle to the wall of the room?

VARIATIONS:

1. Use a triangular shape.
2. Use a square shape.
3. Use a rectangular shape.

Art Activity: Shape Design

With crayons, draw a circle, triangle, square, and rectangle on a 9" × 12" piece of construction paper. Place drawing over another sheet of paper and staple together.Cut out shapes; you will have two of each shape. Arrange shapes on a third piece of paper (at least 18″ × 24″) in an original design.

VARIATIONS:

1. Repeat with three pieces of each shape, using the same size of background paper.
2. Repeat with four pieces of each shape, using the same size of background paper.

 **Your Own Round Place**

PREPARATION:

With chalk, tape, or rope, make a circle on the floor or the ground that is large enough for all the children to sit inside comfortably.

Leader: Everyone find a place to sit in the circle. Draw an imaginary circle around that space.

(Part I) The space you're in is your own space. No one else can be in it. Close your eyes and take a deep breath. Now let it all out. Think about your own little round space. Take another deep breath and let it all out. Now while I count, I want you to take 20 little short breaths. (Slowly count to 20.) Now feel yourself in the circle. Feel how smooth and round the edges are. Think of how that is your very own space . . . no one else can get into it.

All of a sudden you feel your space blowing up like a big soft cushion, and you sink down right in the middle of it. Way, way down.

Now, still keeping your eyes closed, I want you to imagine that the space is getting tinier. It's getting so tiny that you have to make yourself get tiny, too. Make yourself just as tiny as you can.

Now start pushing on the sides of the circle with your elbows and feet and the rest of your body. Stretch it. Stretch it. That's the way. Now it's getting bigger and bigger and even bigger yet. Now it is a giant circle and you have all that space to stretch out in. But it's still your space. And if you open your eyes, you can see that your space is still yours.

Now I want everyone to stand up. Pull the wall up around you.

(Part II) Take one more look at your own round space. Now it's time for you to move. Look around and find someone else's space that you would like. Ask that person to change spaces with you. . . . Oh, you don't like your new space. Well, find someone else to change with you. *(Repeat two more times.)*

Oh-oh! Here comes a big wind. It's blowing all our circles away. Everyone can come back over here and sit on the floor.

PHOTO 12.1. IMAGING A ROUND PLACE. The children respond as the teacher says, "Now pull up a wall around you."

FOLLOW-UP QUESTIONS

- What did you think about when you knew you had your own little space, but it was getting tinier?
- Did you like the space best when it was tiny, very large, or just its regular size?
- How did your body feel when your space turned into a big soft cushion?

- What could have happened if your space turned into a rocket?
- What other kinds of spaces belong to us while we are using them? What about a chair when you are sitting in it? What about your bed when you are lying in it? What other places do you have?
- If you could paint your space any color you like, what color would you paint yours? Why?
- How would you have felt if a porcupine tried to get into your space?
- Make up a story about a porcupine who got into bed with you.

Design in the Round

MATERIALS:

Drawing paper cut into circles 12″ to 24″ in diameter
Drawing media

Leader: What kind of design could you make in your space? Here are some round pieces of paper. You can make a design on the paper to show me what kind of design you would like for your own space. Here are some crayons, some marking pens, and some chalk. You may use any of these you wish. When you're finished, we'll put all of your spaces up on the bulletin board and on the walls. You can look at your own space whenever you want to.

Repeat the imagery of circle spaces substituting triangles, squares, or long, narrow rectangles.

The House Place

Before children arrive, arrange the entire classroom as though it were one big playhouse or a greatly enlarged housekeeping area. Pile cushions in one area for the living room. Have the kitchen equipment set up for cooking and serving. Use a mattress or several exercise mats put together for the bedroom. Use shelves or tables tilted on their sides for walls.

When children arrive, take them on a tour of the "house." Provide them with the needed accessories to spend at least a two-hour session in free play. Add accessories as you take cues from the children's creative activities. Allow this set-up to remain for several days.

VARIATION:

Expand the house arrangement by setting up a market in an adjacent hallway, using empty food boxes and cans that children have been bringing from home at your request. You might even enlist the cooperation of co-workers and ask them to set up various shops in their classrooms.

With chalk, tape, or rope, mark a pathway to the various shops. Draw diagrams to show where to go to the various shops. Expand the diagrams into maps. Have the children create signs marking the various shops.

The Open Place

On completion of the "House Place" activity, have the children move all furniture and other objects from the classroom into an adjacent hallway or patio. If such an area is not available, move everything into one corner of the room or along the wall on one side. Function for one day with no furniture in the room.

Then allow each child to bring one item from the stored items into the classroom. Function for two days with these few items in the room. Ask the children why each item was selected. Give the children who want to do so an opportunity to trade one item for another.

If you wish, you can expand this activity by having each child add one more item and then work in the room this way for another two days. At the end of the activity, restore the classroom to its normal arrangement.

FOLLOW-UP QUESTIONS

- Which arrangement was the most comfortable? Which was the most fun? Which would you like to repeat if you could?
- How would the classroom have to be arranged if there were a giraffe in class?

- How would the classroom have to be arranged if there were only infants in the class?
- What accommodation would have to be made if a dinosaur came to visit for a day?
- What would happen if one of the students happened to be a real monkey?
- What would have to be done if the walls were made of thin paper?
- What would happen if there were no walls at all?
- What changes would have to be made if there were a tiger on the ceiling?

My Own Real Space

This activity is appropriate for first to third graders.

Leader: I have a surprise for you. Today we are all going to have our own real space. I've gathered together all the blocks I could find from all the other classrooms. I have some boards and some pieces of rope. You can each find a place in the room to mark for yourself. Here is a yardstick. This is 3 feet long. Your own space can be only 5 feet long, or 6 feet, which is twice as long as this stick. It can be only 5 feet wide. If you need help in fixing your space, please ask me. If you need to move furniture out of the way, that is all right. We're not going to use the furniture today, only our own spaces. When your space is finished, you may get your lunch pail and jacket, and whatever else you want, and put it in your space. You can make your space under some tables if you like. Or next to the desk or wall. Or even right in the center of the room.

When all of the spaces have been created, conduct the entire day with the children in those spaces, except during recess times. They can eat their lunches, read, sing, listen, and even write in their spaces. (See photo 12.2.)

PHOTO 12.2. MY OWN REAL SPACE. The children have rearranged the classroom to make their own spaces in it.

VARIATIONS:

1. This exercise can be done on a simpler scale for younger children by asking them to fix up a space for themselves in the classroom, without specifying a size. Unit blocks and other markers can be used for enclosures; exercise mats can be used for a space; furniture can be arranged to make a "walled-in" space; and any other ideas that the children originate can be capitalized on and utilized.
2. Take mats outdoors to a grassy area and create personal spaces.

Obstacle Courses

In playgrounds, use existing equipment, ladders, tires, and other objects to create an environmental obstacle course that will present challenges to children to go into, out of, under, over, around, squeeze in between, on top of, through, behind, to the side, up high, down low, and so forth.

VARIATIONS:

1. Lay out a rope to show the direction of the course.
2. Use large numbers to show sequence of items.

3. Have a large map showing sequence of items.
4. Go through obstacle course backward.
5. Go through obstacle course in reverse order.

⚘ The Space Puzzle ✐

Draw a diagram on paper showing the path that the children take from the classroom to the playground. Take the diagram with you as you follow the path with the class.

VARIATIONS:

1. Draw similar diagrams to familiar places that the children can go to with ease, such as another classroom, the restroom, the office, and other school locations.
2. Once the children have become familiar with diagramming paths, make the diagrams more complex, with lots of zigzag lines, turns, and doubling back.

⚘ Space Model ✐

Using unit blocks and other materials, have the children create a replica of the classroom, the entire school building, and the entire building plus the outdoor playground areas.

VARIATION:

Use toothpicks laid out flat on a cardboard surface as the construction material.

⚘ Mapping ✐

Have the children make simple maps of their "space model" areas.

VARIATION:

After the children have had some experience with mapping, have them create a map to scale, using tape measures and yardsticks. This map should be very simple so that the areas to be measured are limited. The map should indicate north, east, south, and west.

◟ Hoops ◞

Provide each child with a plastic hoop, which can be made from ¾-inch plastic tubing purchased at a hardware store. Tape the tubing together where the two ends meet.

Leader: Listen carefully and use your hoop according to the directions I give you.
Step through.
Hold the hoop high over your head.
Now hold it so that part is on top of your head.
Put it on the ground so you are in the center.
Step out and then step in again.
Stand to one side of the hoop.
Hold it in your left hand on the left side of your body.
Reach over and touch it with your right hand.
Hold it with your right hand on the right side of your body.
Hold it so it is in back of you.
Hold it so it is exactly in the middle in front of your chest.
Twirl it around while it's hanging from your right arm.
Twirl it around while it's hanging from your left arm.
Twirl it around while it's hanging from your waist.

CHAPTER 13

Midline Activities

MANY OF THE ACTIVITIES presented already have strong implications for midline development. Jumping and hopping, for example, require children to know they have two separate sides to their bodies. Because so many children have problems in establishing a strong midline awareness, the following activities are specifically presented to help develop this awareness. Midline development problems may be indicated by difficulties in knowing right from left, sequencing or following directions, eye-hand coordination, or reading, evidenced by reversals, losing the place, and skipping words.

Cross-legged Jump

Place a strip of tape on the floor.

Have the children stand on the left side of the tape. Tell them that when you clap your hands, they will place their left feet in front of their right feet and over the tape, leaving their right feet where they are. They are to do this by jumping. Part of the game is not to touch the tape. Say "Ready," and then clap. The children should all be cross-legged, with their feet straddling the line.

Tell them that when you clap again, they are to change feet across the line. Do this twice more, pausing to allow them to make adjustments.

Then tell them that you are going to clap a rhythm and they are to change on each beat. Clap in a slow, steady beat to allow adequate time for adjustments. Remind them not to touch the line.

When they are comfortable with the cross-legged jump, sing "We Are Cross-legged Kangaroos" and clap to the beat while the children jump.

WE ARE CROSS-LEGGED KANGAROOS
(*Tune:* "Old MacDonald," sung at appropriate tempo)

> We are cross-legged kangaroos,
> Jumping across the line.
> If our feet get tangled up,
> We'll fall on our behinds.
> With a cross-legged jump,
> And back over a hump,
> Our legs we then unwind.

VARIATIONS:

1. Jump cross-legged to records with different tempos.
2. Mark spaces with chalk or hoops to jump cross-legged into and out of.
3. Jump cross-legged while holding a partner's hand.
4. Jump cross-legged forward and backward.
5. Walk forward to beat, crossing line with each step.
6. Walk backward to beat, crossing line with each step.
7. Place footprints on each side of line. Children jump cross-legged over line, stepping on footprints to music.
8. Children high-step across line to snappy march records.
9. Watch a videotape of the film *The Music Man*. Let children make batons out of wrapping paper cores and hats out of construction paper. Let them be drum majors doing high steps across line to band music.

Arm Dancing

These arm-dancing exercises are extremely important developmentally for all children. They grew out of the need for midline activities, and they have proven to be valuable as an overall integrative activity and to give definition to growing skills in eye-hand, auditory-motor, and tactile-motor coordination. Arm dancing is a valuable remedial, as well as developmental, exercise.

PREPARATION:

Begin by giving each child two to four crayons of dark but contrasting colors and some paper that is sturdy enough for heavy rhythmic use (newsprint is not suitable). Individual 18″ × 24″ sheets of drawing paper or butcher paper may be used, but we recommend lengths of butcher paper—24 inches wide for 3-year-olds and 36 inches wide for 6-year-olds and up. Spread the butcher paper across the floor, so several children can participate alongside one another, or even across from one another. Afterward, the paper can be cut into sections to paint on—either on the crayoned or the reverse side.

Have the children lie on their stomachs, resting on their elbows until ready to begin.

Draw an *X* on the paper directly in front of each child.

ACTIVITY:

1. As the children listen to music, they draw large circular patterns around the *X* to the rhythm.
   - Have them use their dominant hand if they have established dominance.
   - Help them make the circles counterclockwise, the direction in which letters are formed in writing.

PHOTO 13.1. ARM DANCING. The children circle the *X* while listening to music.

- Tell them to move only their shoulders and arms and not to use their wrists or fingers as in drawing. Ask, "Do you feel your shoulder moving?"

2. When the music changes from one selection to the next, have the children change to another color of crayon. If you're having a successful, cooperative session, allow children to exchange colors.

3. Change the rhythm of the music occasionally.

4. For one-minute segments, have the children keep their eyes on the *X*; this will allow their peripheral vision to pick up the rhythmic movement of their hands.

5. Occasionally, for one-minute segments, have the children follow their hand movements. This is better done to slower portions of the music.

6. Next, remake the *X* and lightly outline a circle on each side of it. Have the children make a counterclockwise circle with each hand, keeping their eyes on the *X* at all times.

7. *Children who are 5 years of age and older* can use the two circles to form a sideways figure 8, or "lazy 8," with their dominant hand,

PHOTO 13.2. ARM DANCING WITH "LAZY EIGHTS"

keeping their eyes on the *X*. They can also elongate the figure 8 as the arm dancing continues.

1. Give each child a set of eight colors of crayons. Play one-minute segments of nursery songs, having the children change colors with each change of rhyme. When they are through, have the children point to the color they used for each rhyme. (This provides recall practice.) Two- and three-year-olds especially like this activity.

2. Tell a story:
   You're a 3-month-old baby. Your mother has placed you on the floor on your tummy. She gives you a crayon to hold in your hand. You hear music and start moving the crayon in a big circle, around and around, reaching your arm way, way out. Because you are only an infant, you can't move your wrists. So only your shoulders move to make the arms go around.

3. Using two circles on either side of the *X*, tell another story:
   I'm going to play some slow music while you close your eyes. I want you to feel your whole body as it feels the movement of the music. I want you to feel how your body is touching the floor. Feel where it is touching your chest, your hips, your tummy. Feel where your legs are touching and the way your toes are touching, too. Does it feel cold or warm? Hard or soft? Comfortable or uncomfortable? No fun or fun? Happy or sad? Listen to the music and think how it feels. Let it get into all the corners of your body while you slowly become part of the circles and part of the music. How does it feel to be a circle? How does it feel to be music? Now, just think about you!

   (Continue silently for two or three more minutes.)

4. Slower first- to third-graders can do five minutes of "lazy 8s" before the start of each day. You can also give them an opportunity before the start of each academic activity to silently draw circles around an *X* on a 12″ × 15″ sheet of drawing paper. (Notebook paper can be used, but a slightly larger size is less restricting.)

Music to Use with Arm Dancing

- Nursery songs. Change colors with each new song.
- "Around and Around We Go" on Millang and Scelsa's *We All Live Together*, Vol. 1 (Youngheart Records).
- Selections of dance music, especially folk dances.
- Other collections of familiar tunes.
- For older children, folk songs or more difficult selections.
- Music in 4/4 time. Ostrander and Schroeder (1980) have demonstrated that thinking seems to be more accelerated and deeper when accompanied by music in 4/4 time. This tempo allows for a stirring of thoughts and an awakening of ideas without the conflict of changing patterns. Baroque music by composers such as Bach, Handel, and Purcell has a steady beat that children can easily respond to.

References

Millang, Steve, and Greg Scelsa. *We All Live Together*, Vol. 1. Youngheart Records (Los Angeles).
Ostrander, Sheila, and Lynn Schroeder. 1980. *Superlearning*. New York: Dell/Delta.

CHAPTER 14

Strengthening Laterality

LATERALITY MEANS being internally aware of the two sides of one's body and knowing the difference between them (see pgs. 71–72). In order to achieve such awareness, children need to learn that they have a midline to their bodies (see pgs. 70–71), and they need to learn to get both sides to cooperate with each other. They also need to be able to cross their arms or legs over the midline of their bodies.

Experiences on the balance beam (also called a walking board) and on the balance board, such as those that follow, require balancing one side of the body against the other in order to cope with the force of gravity by maintaining equilibrium. The vestibular system (see pgs. 64–65) is developed in relation to gravity in order to eventually be able to dynamically achieve spontaneous balance in any position.

From practicing on the balance beam and on the balance board, the body gains the knowledge that there is a left side and a right side and that each can work independently. Balancing requires the use of both the right and the left sides of the body, playing one against the other. As children achieve skill in balancing, one side will take the lead and will usually become dominant, thus making the opposite hemisphere the dominant one. If the right side of the body takes the lead in achieving and maintaining balance, the left hemisphere will dominate that activity and will most likely be the dominant hemisphere for most other activities. If the left side of the body takes the lead, the right hemisphere will most likely be the dominant hemisphere for most other activities.

While children are strengthening their laterality by balancing activities, they are also laying the foundation for learning about directionality. This foundation is important because, as in other areas of motor development, skills build on previous skills. Although children do not achieve full awareness of directionality until approximately 8 to 9 years of age, it is important to introduce the concept earlier by familiarizing them with its many possibilities.

Laterality is strengthened by continually practicing increasingly more difficult balancing tasks, not simply by learning how to balance. Therefore, after they achieve each skill level, the children should go on to a progressively more difficult task, so that no matter how skilled, they will keep searching out new body patterns and new ways to achieve balance. The exercises that follow are in a progressively more difficult sequence. Allow the beginner who is not yet able or who does not yet have the self-confidence to balance to hold your hand for assistance. You can gradually let go, at first for a second or two, until your assistance appears unnecessary.

Walking Boards

Also called a balance beam, a walking board is a two-by-four board that is 8–12 feet long (see Photo 14.1). The wood should be smooth and have several coats of varnish to keep it from splintering. Be sure the wood is not warped and that, when placed on a flat surface, it does not wobble. The board is placed on end pieces, which raise it from the ground 2–4 inches.

Beginning Walking Board Activities

The following activities are for children who are 4 years and older. If they have trouble with an activity, they should hold the leader's hand. Their arms should dangle at their sides but can be used to achieve balance when necessary.

These activities can be adapted for 2- to 3-year-olds by using a board that is two-by-six rather than two-by-four; the board can be flat on the floor until they are fully at ease on it. At this age, children are more ready for bilateral movement (both sides moving the same) than for full development of the midline, which leads to cross-lateral movements. (The full development of the midline will not be completed until about age 7, in conjunction with the achievement of laterality—see pgs. 71–72).

1. To introduce walking on a walking board, have the children walk with one side leading the way. Thus, one foot is always in front of the other.
   Variation: Walk backward, with one foot always in back of the other.
2. Walk forward from one end to the other in a natural walk.
   Variation: Turn around and walk back to the beginning.

PHOTO 14.1. WALKING BOARD

3. Walk forward, placing heel and toe against each other.
   Variation: Walk backward.
4. Walk sideways from one end of the board to the other. (The body must be kept sideways, and you will need to help the children learn not to turn their chests toward the direction they are walking.)
5. Slide sideways from one end of the board to the other.
6. Walk forward with hands on hips.
   Variation: Walk backward.
7. Walk forward with arms crossed over chest.
   Variation: Walk backward.
8. Any of the above activities may be done with the board raised 2–4 inches at one end.

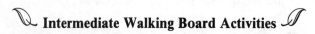
Intermediate Walking Board Activities

1. Walk the length of the board with a weighted lunch pail in each hand.
   Variations:
   a. Have a different weight in each lunch pail.
   b. Have a weighted pail in only one hand, with the other hand free.
   c. Have the weighted pail in the other hand.
2. Walk the length of the board while holding a 5- to 8-foot pole. (A broom or mop handle can be used.) Say, "Be a tightrope walker in the circus."
3. Walk the length of the board, stepping over pieces of wood that have been placed 8 inches apart.
   Variation: Place the blocks at unequal intervals.
4. Walk on a strip of tape that has been placed along the middle of the board.
5. Walk the length of the board, stepping on spots that have been marked 8 inches apart.
   Variations:
   a. Mark the spots at unequal intervals.
   b. Walk between the spots.
   c. Walk on alternate spots.

6. Walk the length of the board barefoot, stepping on dishwashing sponges that have been taped 8 inches apart.
   Variation: Place the sponges at unequal intervals.
7. Creep the length of the walking board.
   Variations:
   a. Creep backward.
   b. Creep forward with one leg and arm on the board and the other leg and arm on the floor.
   c. Creep forward with the opposite leg and arm on the board.
8. Gallop the length of the board and return.
9. Skip the length of the board and return.
10. Walk the length of the board with one foot on the board and the other on the ground.
11. Crisscross the length of the board. With feet on the floor, cross to the opposite side of the board with each step; in other words, when beginning with both feet on the right side of the board, the left foot crosses over, and then the right foot crosses over for the next step.
    Variation: Crisscross backward.
12. Any of the above activities may be done with the board raised 2 inches at one end and 4–8 inches at the other.
13. Creep the length of the board on hands and knees.
14. Creep the length of the board with one knee on the board and one on the floor.

Advanced Walking Board Activities

These activities require a great deal of individual motor planning. Allow the children to figure out how to handle the task, using their bodies and the walking board in whatever way serves their purpose. The only restriction is that they remain on the walking board, even if they have to stoop, place the tray down momentarily, or vary the activity in some other way.

1. Walk the length of the board holding a tray in both hands. The tray should be approximately the width of the shoulders.

Variations:
a. Walk backward.
b. Walk sideways.
c. Walk heel-to-toe.
d. Use any of the other mid-level activities.

2. Walk the length of the board holding a tray in both hands, with an empty glass on the tray.
   Variation: See first exercise.

3. Walk the length of the board holding a tray in both hands, with a glass filled with water on the tray.
   Variation: See first exercise.

4. Start down the board with the tray and glass of water, but place the glass on the board, step over the glass, and continue to the end. Turn around, walk back, pick up the glass and place it on the tray, and return to the beginning.
   Variation: See first exercise.

5. Walk the length of the board hopping over bean bags placed on it. Hop with either the right or left foot or with both feet at the same time.
   Variations:
   a. Hop backward.
   b. Hop sideways.

6. Walk the length of the board and return, balancing the bean bag on head.
   Variations:
   a. Walk backward.
   b. Walk sideways.

7. Walk the length of the board while using the bean bag to play catch with the leader.

8. Walk the length of the board, bouncing a rubber ball on alternate steps.
   Variations:
   a. Bounce the ball on the floor to the right.
   b. Bounce the ball on the floor to the left.
   c. Bounce the ball with the leader.

9. Two students walk the length of parallel walking boards and throw a bean bag back and forth.
   Variation: Bounce a ball back and forth.
10. Move in various ways along the board to dance music for one minute.
11. Be a clown on the board for one minute.
12. Move like an animal or a bird (such as a bear, tiger, elephant, monkey, giraffe, dog, cat, snake, crab, rabbit, horse, wolf, goat, ostrich, chicken, duck, turkey, goose, or robin) back and forth along the board. Other students try to guess which creature is being acted out.
    Variation: Move like an animal or a bird to music.

Balance Boards

Closely akin to the walking board is the balance board. This is usually a board approximately 14 inches square that is balanced on a 4″ × 8″ block of wood that is 2 inches high. The balance platform should have a mark at the exact center. The placement of the feet can also be marked.

As the child's balancing skill is developed, the height of the block of wood can be gradually increased until it is 4 inches high. The base board can also have rockers added on each side, as in Photo 14.3. A balance board can be improvised with a 3- to 4-foot length of shelving resting on top of a length of two-by-four board, as in Photo 14.4.

The object is to stand on the board and balance it so that it doesn't tip to either side. When the feet are placed equidistant from the center and the board is balanced, the two sides of the body are in balance, and thus the two hemispheres are in balance. The farther apart the feet are from each other, the greater the dynamics of the balancing mechanism. Balance board activities will visibly improve writing and reading skills. Thinking skills (occurring concurrently but not so visibly) will also improve.

In the beginning, the improvement in skills may last only two or three minutes, but the carry-over will gradually increase with practice. After

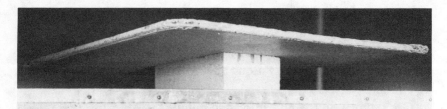

PHOTO 14.2. BASIC BALANCE BOARD. A block of wood (4″ × 8″ × 2″ high) is attached with an embedded screw to the exact center of a 14″ × 14″ platform. The height of the block of wood can be increased to 3″ and then to 4″ as the children's skill increases.

PHOTO 14.3. BALANCE BOARD WITH ROCKERS

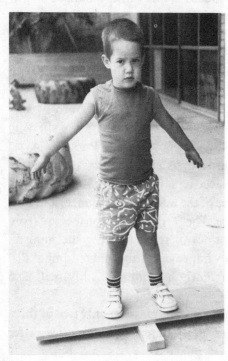

PHOTO 14.4. BALANCE BOARD IMPROVISED WITH PINE SHELVING. A 36″ length of 12″ shelving is placed across a length of two-by-four board.

much practice, the new internalization of balance and sensory integration may have a lasting effect.

Children should master each of the following exercises before going on to the next one.

ᘒ Introductory Balance Board Exercises ᔎ

1. Stand on the board with both feet exactly in the center. Balance the board.
2. Stand on the board with each foot 2 inches from the center. Balance the board.
3. Stand on the board with each foot 3 inches from the center. Balance the board.
4. Stand on the board with each foot 4 inches from the center. Balance the board.
5. Stand on the board with each foot 4 inches from the center. Balance board while touching knees with hands.
6. Same as previous exercise, touching ankles or toes.

PHOTO 14.5. USING BALANCE BOARDS AND WALKING BOARDS

7. Stand on the board with each foot 4 inches from the center. Balance board while stooping.
8. Stand on the board with each foot 2 inches from the center. Balance board while blindfolded.
9. Stand on the board with each foot 4 inches from the center. Balance board while throwing a beanbag or a ball back and forth to the leader or to another student.
10. Same as above, but each person playing catch is on a balance board.
11. While balancing on board, hold arms straight up, thus not using them to help achieve balance.

Exercises for Balance Board with Rocker

The previous exercises can be combined with the following exercises.

1. Stand so that the board can be rocked forward and backward while finding balance.
2. Stand so that the board can be rocked from side to side while finding balance.
3. Stand so that feet are at a diagonal, facing a corner of the balance board, while finding balance.

Exercises to Improve Reading, Writing, and Spelling

1. Balance on the board with each foot 2–4 inches from the center while reading aloud for 3 minutes.
2. Balance on the board with each foot 2–4 inches from the center while studying spelling words.
3. Balance on the board with each foot 2–4 inches from the center while practicing writing on a clipboard that someone is holding.
4. Balance on a board while studying.
5. Stand on the board in a comfortable balance position. Hum "America" or any favorite song. Then read aloud 30 seconds. Hum song again. Read aloud 30 seconds again. Keep repeating, switching from right (humming) to left (reading) dominance.

6. Balance on board while drawing circles around an *X* in the middle of the paper (as in Arm Dancing, pgs. 182–86) on a clipboard before doing academic activities.

Imagination Balance

Children are standing on the floor for this activity.

Leader: Close your eyes and imagine that you are standing on a balance board. You use your arms and your shoulders to balance it so well that the board is perfectly still. Feel the right side of your body as it balances with the left side. Squeeze your right fist. Tell it to hold its balance. Squeeze your left fist. Tell it to hold its balance. Now, still balancing on the board, very carefully turn yourself around, pivoting on your feet so you don't lose your balance. Very carefully turn back the way you came until you are in your original position.

You're still balancing on the board. Keep it steady. Keep your eyes closed.

Now stretch your arms out to each side. Bend over to the right until the fingertips on your right hand touch the board. Stand up straight. Now bend over to the left until the fingertips on your left hand touch the board. Next, stand up straight and stretch as tall as you can. Keep on stretching—higher . . . and higher . . . and higher. Now, very carefully keeping the balance board straight, reach your hands way up high—higher . . . and higher . . . and higher until you can touch the ceiling.

> Look at me, look at me,
> I'm as tall as I can be.
> I'm reaching so very high.
> Very soon I'll touch the sky.

Still keeping your balance on the board, please bring your hands down to your sides. Step off the balance board. Slowly . . . slowly . . . open your eyes.

🌿 Sky Journey 🌙

Children are seated on floor or rug for this activity.

Leader: With your eyes gently closed, think about how it feels when you are on the balance board and how you use all the parts of your body to balance the board. Now we're going to have another kind of experience. Keeping your eyes closed and just thinking about this in your head, I want you to imagine that you are standing on a balance board. It is very high off the ground, and as you stand on it, it gets higher and higher. And you stretch yourself way up straight so that you can be higher and higher, too. Now the board is so high that you can look down and see all the world below. You are so very high that you are really up in the sky.

You take a giant step off the board, lean your body forward with your arms stretched out behind you, and off you go—floating through the sky. It's cool and blue and free. You float on and on. There are so many things to see.

Now I'm going to be very quiet. And you're going to be very quiet. In your mind I want you to keep floating in the sky. Notice what else is in the sky. What colors do you see? What do you hear? . . . Floating *(softly)* . . . Floating *(whispering)* . . . *(long pause)* . . . Floating . . .

Now you're back at the balance board. Step on it. It takes you down, down, down . . . whizzzzzzz . . . bang! You're down on the ground. You open your eyes, look all around you, and know that it feels good to be back.

FOLLOW-UP QUESTIONS

- What did you like best about floating?
- How did the parts of your body feel when you were floating?
- What colors did you see?
- What sounds did you hear?
- Were there any smells?

- Here is a sheet of paper on which I have put many shades of blue. (Hold up a sheet that you have prepared with chalk, crayon, watercolors, colored pencils, and pieces of color cut out of magazines.) If the sky was blue, which shade of blue was it?
- Was the sky empty or did you see different things?
- If you saw things in the sky, what were they?

Night Sky Journey

Leader: Now that you know how to float through the sky, I want you to close your eyes again. This time it is night. You are floating all over as you were before, but you can't see the sun. As you float around, think about what you can see. Just keep floating . . . *(long pause)* . . . and floating . . . *(long pause)* . . . and floating . . . *(silence).*

Now gently come back into the room. Take a deep breath. Let it out slowly. . . . Another. . . . And another. . . . Open your eyes. Take another deep breath. And smile.

FOLLOW-UP QUESTIONS

- How was that different than floating in the daytime?
- What color was the sky this time?
- What did you see while you were floating?
- Was it warm or cold?
- Which was better, floating in the daytime or floating at night?
- Would you rather be a balloon floating in the air or a beautiful leaf?
- Would you rather be a star or the moon? Why?
- Would you rather be the grass or the flowers in the park?

CHAPTER 15

Kinesthetic Awareness and Body Image

DURING THEIR DEVELOPMENTAL YEARS, children are busy learning all about the various parts of their bodies, what they can do to use them, and how to use them (Chapter 4). While learning about what the body can do outwardly, they are also learning what body activities and sensations feel like inwardly. Kinesthetic awareness is important to the development of a wholesome body image, sensory motor skills, and a strong laterality.

Body Parts: Being Me

Young children should be able to respond to direction about these body parts in the exercises that follow.

arms	legs	elbows
wrists	knees	ankles
fingers	toes	head
ears	cheeks	eyebrows
eyes	forehead	nose
mouth	chin	neck
shoulders	chest	waist
hips	stomach	middle of the back
buttocks (or "seat" for younger children)	thighs (for older children)	

✒ Where Am I? ✎

This version of "Simon Says" can help you identify whether children are aware of their body parts and whether they take in verbal directions or depend solely on visual cues.

Leader: Put your hands on top of your head.

(Leader does this.)

Put your hands on your cheeks.

(Leader does this.)

Put your hands on your hips.

(Leader does this.)

Put your hands on your toes.

(Leader puts hands on top of head.)

Continue in this pattern, naming other parts of the body and doing the "wrong" movement every fourth or fifth direction.

✒ The Parts of Me ✎

Have the children sit in a circle with legs out in front in a V shape. Walk around to each child and gently massage the back of the neck and shoulders for 15–30 seconds. Now have them lie down, their legs staying in position and arms out to the side.

Leader: Close your eyes and pretend you are lying on the hot sand at the beach, with the sun shining down on you. Feel the little grains of sand against your back. Stretch one arm way out tight as though you want to make it as long as possible so it can get more sun on it. Now lift the arm off the sand and shake it gently until all the sand falls off. Now roll the arm around and around, feeling your shoulder move as you do it. Now let it fall loosely to the ground.

(Repeat this sequence with the other arm.)

Now do the same thing with your legs. First stretch one leg way out tight. Stretch and stretch. Feel the hot sun shining down on it. Feel the grains of sand clinging to it. Now lift your leg and shake it gently so that the sand will drop off. Now roll your leg around and around until all parts of it are loose. Now let it drop by itself loosely to the ground.

(Repeat this sequence with the other leg.)

Now feel your torso touching the sand. Rub your back deep into it. Stretch yourself way out so that your torso is as tight as it can be. Now let it go back loosely to its own way of being. Just let your whole body relax while you feel the sun shining down on your body.

Songs for Kinesthetic Awareness

STRETCH AND STRETCH AND STRETCH YOUR ARM
(Tune: "Mary Had a Little Lamb")

Stretch and stretch and stretch your arm,
Stretch your arm,
Stretch your arm.
Stretch and stretch and stretch your arm,
Stretch it way out tight.

Stretch and stretch your other arm,
Your other arm,
Your other arm.
Stretch and stretch your other arm,
Until it feels just right.

Shake and shake and shake your arm,
Shake your arm,
Shake your arm.
Shake and shake and shake your arm,
Shake it hard this way.

Shake and shake the other arm,
The other arm,
The other arm.
Shake and shake the other arm,
Shake it hard today.

Roll and roll and roll your arm,
Roll your arm,
Roll your arm.
Roll and roll and roll your arm,
Roll it 'round and 'round.

Now you roll the other arm,
The other arm,
The other arm.
Now you roll the other arm,
Then drop it to the ground.

Repeat the entire process, substituting *leg* for *arm*.

I TAKE MY LITTLE ARMS
(*Tune:* "I Take My Little Hands and Go Clap, Clap, Clap")

I take my little arms and stretch them way, way out.
I take my little legs and kick them all about.
I take my little head and move it 'round and 'round.
I move it 'round and 'round.

I take my little waist and bend it way, way down.
I take my little hips and shake them all over town.
I take my little back and hunch it way in tight.
I straighten it back just right.

I take my little feet and go jumpity, jump, jump.
I take my little knees together bumpity, bump, bump.
I touch down to my knees and go a-pat-a-pat-a-pat.
A-pat-pat just like that.

I take my little tummy and hold it tight, tight, tight.
I take a great big breath and breathe it out just right.

I wiggle, wiggle, wiggle, wiggle, wiggle all around.
And now I'm sitting down.

Parts of a Friend

Children stand opposite each other in pairs. When directions are given, they touch their friend rather than themselves. Have the children follow this chant.

I see your hand and go clap, clap.
And on your head I go pat, pat.
I touch one knee and go slap, slap.
And then I turn around.

I give a hug and squeeze and squeeze.
I touch your nose right where you sneeze.
I pat your cheek with an if-you-please.
And then I turn around.

PHOTO 15.1. PARTS OF A FRIEND

My elbow touches you on your side.
We hold our hands and open wide.
I touch your toes with a lot of pride.
And then I turn around.

VARIATIONS:

In the following, the "touch" continues to be to the other person. One or more touches can be combined.

1. Touch hand to knee.
2. Touch chin to shoulder.
3. Touch knee to hip.
4. Touch ear to elbow.
5. Touch head to back.
6. Touch toes to back of knee.
7. Touch nose to back of hand.
8. Continue with other combinations of one part of body to another.
9. Repeat with three children in a group.
10. Repeat with four children in a group.

Two Sides of Me

Children are lying on the floor for this exercise.

Leader: Imagine that you have two separate sides of your body. There is a wooden board dividing the two halves. They are totally apart from each other. One side of your body cannot feel the other side, because they are not connected.

Maybe you can imagine the color of the board that is dividing you in half. Is it red? Green? Yellow? Blue? Orange? Black? White? Purple? Striped? Polka-dotted? Is it two colors? Three? Think about it. But don't tell me. Just think inside your head.

Now I want you to think just about your right side. Make it tight and tense. Squeeze your right fist and make it tight and tense. Squeeze your right arm and your right leg and make it very tight and hard. Squeeze all of the right side of your body hard. Hold it as tight as you can. Now, let it go loose. Let it all relax.

Make the other side *(the left side)* very tight and tense. Squeeze your fist and your arm and your leg on that side very tight and hard as you did on the other side. Squeeze your whole body on that side. Hold it as tight as you can. Now let it go loose. Let it all relax.

How does that feel to be in two parts? Don't tell me about it. Just think about how different that feels.

Now hold one arm *(your right arm)* way up straight in the air. Wiggle it back and forth. Wiggle the fingers on that hand. Make a fist. Open it and spread your fingers way out. Now, wiggle them again. Now ve-ry qui-et-ly and ve-ry slow-ly I want you to reach that hand over to the other side of your body and touch the other hand *(the left hand)*, which is just lying quietly by your side. Now give that hand a gentle pinch. Now touch your hand to your hip. Give your hip a little pat. Which side felt that pat the most? Which side felt the pinch the most? Does it still hurt?

Now put your hand back on the side that it came from. Give your leg on that side a little wiggle. Now lift it way up high and make it go around and around. Shake it hard. Now let it drop down on the floor. Lift it and drop it. Lift it and drop it. Now wiggle your ankle around and around. Now move that leg across to the other side of your body and touch your other foot with that foot. Press them hard against each other. Which foot can you feel the most? Now put your leg back. Move your arm over to the other side and scratch your knee, then bring it back to its own side. Did the other side feel the scratch? Did the fingers doing the scratching feel anything?

(Repeat all of the above, activating the left side of the body.)

VARIATIONS:

1. One side is wiggly while the other is quiet.
2. One side is bumpy while the other is smooth.
3. One side is rubbery while the other is hard.
4. One side is silly while the other is serious.
5. One side is crooked while the other is straight.
6. One side is watery while the other is ice.
7. One side is peanut butter while the other is jelly.
8. One side is smooth while the other is rough.
9. One side is pink while the other is blue.
10. One side is big while the other is little.

The children stand to do the following variations.

11. One side kicks while the other side stamps; reverse.
12. One side swings the arm while the other side makes a fist; reverse.
13. One side snaps two fingers while the other side slaps a knee; reverse.
14. One side holds the arm straight up while the other arm jiggles around; reverse.
15. One foot taps while the other foot slides; reverse.
16. One hand writes while the other hand taps its fingers; reverse.
17. One side jiggles while the other side relaxes; reverse.
18. One side is stiff while the other side is loose; reverse.
19. One side hugs itself while the other bends its arm open and closed; reverse.
20. One side pats its leg while the other side makes its hand go around and around on the stomach; reverse.
21. Let the children think of other variations.

Bringing the Two Sides Back Together

This game will help the children feel "whole" once more.

Leader: Now, I want you to close your eyes. See the two halves of your body running in all different places. Bring them back together. Take out the board in the middle. Now you are all one again.

CLAP AND SLAP
(*Tune:* "I Take My Little Hands and Go Clap, Clap, Clap")

I take my own two feet and go tap, tap, tap.
I shuffle back and forth and go slap, slap, slap.
I tap with my two heels and go pit, pit, pat.
And I know that this is me.

I take my own two hands and go clap, clap, clap.
I put them on my knees and go slap, slap, slap.
I put them on my head and go pat, pat, pat.
Who I am is fun to be.

I wrap my arms around and go hug, hug, hug.
I stamp both of my feet and go chug, chug, chug.
I pull on both my hands and go tug, tug, tug.
I am here as you can see.

ART ACTIVITY

Supply 12" × 18" sheets of construction paper and crayons or markers. Ask the children, "How did it feel to be divided in half?" Then tell them to draw a picture of how they think they looked.

The Invisible Person

Leader: You are walking down the street. All of a sudden you stop. You look all around and everything begins to get very quiet. Suddenly, you look down at your arms and they are beginning to get invisible. You look at your legs and they are even more invisible. You look down at your feet and—that's right—they are invisible. By now, your whole body is invisible. You can walk quietly all around the room and no one can see you. You can even make funny faces because no one can see what kind of faces you are making.

> You can't see me, you can't see me.
> I'm invisible to you, as you can see.
> I'm here and there and everywhere.
> And I'm as happy as I can be.

All of a sudden you begin to get back into your skin and your muscles and your bones. Slowly, you begin to fill up all over. Now your clothes are showing, your hair is on top of your head where it belongs, and everyone can see who you are. And you know, of course, that who you are is a very wonderful somebody to be.

Repeat "Clap and Slap" (pg. 208).

FOLLOW-UP QUESTIONS

- How did it feel to be invisible?
- How did it feel when I told you your hair was back on top of your head?
- What would you do if your hair was purple?
- What other colors could your hair be?
- Which did you like best, being invisible or being two halves of a person?
- What is it like to be able to make funny faces and have no one see you?
- Do you ever do that when you're not invisible? Why?
- How does it feel when you are little and grownups are bigger than you?
- How does it feel to watch grownups do something and they don't know that you are watching?
- Do they act the same when they don't know you are watching as they do when they know you are watching?
- Is it better to be a child or a grownup? Why?

Select a recording of baroque music to play during this activity (see suggestions on page 186). Dim the lights if possible, and in general set the stage for quietness. Present a variety of paper, crayons, chalk, markers, and paints, along with scissors and paste. Allow the children to select their own media and to draw for 20 minutes. Give children the following instructions:

> Remember how you felt when you were pretending to be invisible? Now I want you to make a picture or a painting of how you felt. You may use any of the papers I put out and you may use any of the other materials I put out. This is a silent project. You may not talk while you are doing this.

Bubbles and Hard-boiled Eggs: Being Something Else

One of the traditional delights of childhood is blowing bubbles. Another is the freedom to enjoy the marvelous world of fantasy. Combining these two activities gives us an opportunity to boost children's self-esteem with feelings of great beauty, lightness, transparency, and shimmering reflections. Contrasting bubbles with hard-boiled eggs helps children sort out similarities and differences.

Bubble Recipe

Prepare bubble mixture as follows:

1. Add 1 package of unflavored gelatin to 1 quart of hot water. Mix well.
2. Add ½ cup dishwashing soap (Joy or Dawn) to 1 gallon of water. Shake well.
3. Mix the above two liquids together for bubble mixture.

VARIATION:

Substitute ¼ cup glycerin for the gelatin and hot water and add to soap. Mix well.

Make available a variety of bubble-blowing tools. The possibilities include commercial bubble blowers, wide straws, tubes from household paper goods, small cans opened at both ends, various sizes of circles made from fairly stiff small-gauge wire (such as wire coat hangers), lengths of string (from 2 feet to 8 feet) "stiffened" and tied into circles with straws, household funnels, potato mashers, wire eggbeaters, outer rings of Mason jar lids, and rims of metal sieves with the mesh removed.

Free Blow

Place materials on a table outdoors. Place bubble mixture in small containers. Have children experiment with blowing bubbles in their own ways, using any of the materials you have set out. Following are some of the things they might do.

PHOTO 15.2. BUBBLE BLOWING

DOUBLE BUBBLES

Hold two straws together to make double bubbles.

MORE BUBBLES

Add straws, one at a time, to increase the number of bubbles. The straws may be fastened together with two rubber bands or with two bands of tape—one at the top and one near the bottom.

GIANT BUBBLES

Two or more persons hold a string ring taut and dip it into a large pan of bubble solution. The pan should be on the ground. As the string is brought upward, a large bubble should form.

BUBBLE STACK

Blow a bubble near the ground (preferably grass) so it can land gently without bursting. Blow another bubble close enough so it will land on top of the other. Continue with as many as you can stack without bursting them.

BUBBLE RUN

Everyone puts some mixture on a bubble wand and runs in unison, trailing bubbles behind them.

BUBBLE MATH

Blow bubbles gently so that several cling together. Note that all of the connecting angles are 120-degree angles.

Bubble Story

Children are seated in a comfortable grouping.

> Once upon a time there was a child named Jay. That's right, Jay, just like the letter of the alphabet. Jay was a very happy boy. He ran in the sunshine, he rolled on the grass,

and he climbed on top of a big rock and looked at the world all around him. One day the sky grew very cloudy. A wind began to blow. A storm was coming. He heard thunder. And then it began to rain. Jay ran as fast as he could. He came to his house and he ran inside. Now he was very sad.

Jay's mother asked, "Why are you so sad?" Jay said, "It was sunny and I was so happy. Now everything is dark and gloomy. That's why I'm sad." His mother said, "It's all right to be sad. But you can be happy for the trees and the grass and the flowers, because the rain will help them to grow and stay beautiful." Then she said, "I know something we can make grow right now. Come into the kitchen and we can make some rainbows." Jay went into the kitchen with his mother. She mixed some soap and water and a little glycerin and put it in a bottle. She told Jay to shake it up. Then she poured some into a cup. She made a wire circle out of a coat hanger. It had a long handle on it. Jay put the circle into the cup of bubble blower, and then he blew gently on it. A bubble began to grow. Jay and his mother saw the pretty colors in the bubble. They saw red and blue and lavender and yellow and green. Jay shouted, "It's just like a rainbow!" And he was happy again. He was so happy that he kept blowing on the bubble. It got a little bigger, and then a little bigger yet, and soon it was so big that it filled up the entire kitchen. In fact, it was so big and took up so much room that before you could blink your eyes, Jay was inside the bubble.

I wonder how he got in there? Do you wonder how he got in there?

Close your eyes and imagine that you are Jay.

See yourself in the kitchen blowing this giant bubble. See it getting bigger . . . and bigger . . . and bigger. . . . Now it is so big that there is no room for you in the kitchen. But as it squeezes you against the wall, all of a sudden you are inside the bubble. What can you see? Is it warm or cold? Is the bubble slippery to walk on, or are you able to take one step at a time? Is it wet or dry? What do the colors look like from inside? Can you see through it to the outside? You feel so safe and comfortable inside the bubble. You feel really happy because it is fun to be inside a real bubble.

All of a sudden you realize you aren't inside the bubble any more. You feel yourself floating up in the air—floating just like a bubble. As you float through the house, you pass a mirror. When you look into the mirror, you don't even see a child. You see that you have become a bubble. No wonder you feel so light. And so round. And so very beautiful.

You float through an open door and out into the garden. You float over all the colorful flowers. You float over the tops of the trees. And you float higher and higher and higher until you can see all the town down below you. As you look down, you can see where your own house is. You can see your yard and you can see your neighbor's house. You can see all the other houses. You can also see all of the people running out of their houses to look at the beautiful giant bubble floating over them. Everyone is smiling because they've never seen anything like this before. And you just keep floating higher and higher . . . and soon you are way up in the open sky. . . .

(At this point, tell everyone to open their eyes and stand up. Play soft music on a record player, and allow the children to move freely about the room.)

As you hear the music playing, you start dancing all over the sky. You dance a bubble dance, of course. And all of the colors of the rainbow shine inside and outside your transparent skin.

As you silently float and dance all about, the music stops. You become very tired. You stop dancing. You stop floating. You look all around you. And suddenly, you fall to earth. And plop! You aren't a bubble any more. You are just a child who has seen the colors of the rainbow.

FOLLOW-UP QUESTIONS

- When you were a bubble, how did your skin feel?
- Were you warm or cold? Wet or dry?
- What color were you?
- What is it like to be transparent?
- What does it feel like to float over your house and over your neighborhood? How did everything look when you were up high looking down?
- What kinds of sounds did you hear when you were a bubble?
- Do bubbles make noise?
- What is the best thing about bubbles?
- In what ways is a bubble like a balloon?
- In what ways is a bubble different from a balloon?
- Name other things that are something like a bubble. Why?
- Would you rather be soapsuds or water? Why?
- Would you rather be a bubble blower or a straw? Why?
- Would you rather be transparent or invisible? Why?

Bubble Song

ALL THE BUBBLES FLOAT AROUND
(*Tune:* "London Bridge Is Falling Down")

All the bubbles float around,
   float around, float around,
All the bubbles float around, my fair lady.

Then they plop flat on the ground,
   on the ground, on the ground,
Then they plop flat on the ground, my fair lady.

Take a sponge and wipe it up,
   wipe it up, wipe it up,
Take a sponge and wipe it up, my fair lady.

Blow another bubble now,
   bubble now, bubble now,
Blow another bubble now, my fair lady.

✧ Sequencing with Bubbles ✧

Supply 8″ × 24″ (or similar long shape) sheets of paper and crayons or felt-tip markers.

Have the children draw a picture of six bubbles in a row, starting with a tiny baby one that can hardly be seen and making each one a little bigger, ending the row with a really giant bubble. Then have the children draw a picture of six bubbles in a row, but start with a big bubble and make each one in the row get smaller and smaller.

✧ Writing About Bubbles ✧

1. Write a poem about bubbles, using the following form or making one of your own.

   A bubble is a beautiful thing to see,
   _____
   _____
   _____

2. Write a story about one of the following:
   • being a bubble
   • being transparent
   • being inside a bubble
   • the tiniest bubble
   • the fastest bubble
   • the noisiest bubble
   • the prettiest bubble
   • the lost bubble
   • the dripping bubble
   • the crooked bubble

✧ Bubble Pictures ✧

1. Draw bubbles with pastel chalks.
2. Paint bubbles with watercolors.
3. Challenge older children to paint a bubble to make it look transparent.

4. Draw a picture of a bubble house or a bubble school.
5. Draw a picture of a bubble person.

My Own Bubble

MATERIALS:

12-inch balloons blown up and tied with a length of string
Strips of newspaper
Liquid starch

Cover a balloon with strips of newspaper dipped into starch. Allow to dry well. Make small opening through which to burst balloon and pull it out. Paint the resulting "bubble" white. Add reflective rainbow colors to decorate it.

The Giant Bubble

This project uses the same techniques as "my own bubble," except the paper strips are placed over a large chicken-wire sphere (with a slightly flattened base; see Figure 15.1). Leave openings for a door and a window (or several windows, if desired). Children can work on covering this sphere over several weeks. When completed and painted, they can use the "bubble" for an alone place.

Hard-boiled Eggs

Bring in some hard-boiled eggs. Pass them around so the children can examine them by feeling their texture, their weight, their shape, and their coolness.

Leader: You already pretended you were a bubble. Now I want you to pretend you are a hard-boiled egg. I want you to move across the room from this spot *(indicate)* to this spot over here *(indicate)*. Be careful. Your shell can easily crack. You need to move very gently. Now show me how you would move if you were not hard-boiled, but just a raw egg.

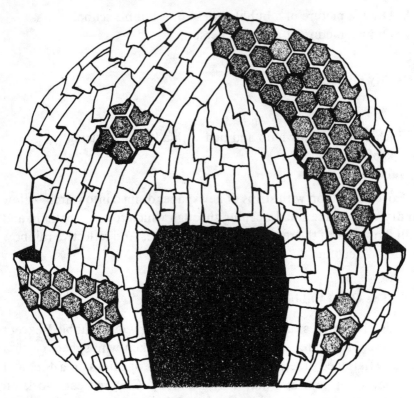

FIGURE 15.1. THE GIANT BUBBLE. Cover an 8-foot-diameter chicken-wire sphere (with a slightly flattened base) with strips of paper dipped in liquid starch. Leave openings for door and windows.

FOLLOW-UP QUESTIONS

- What was the biggest difference between moving like an egg and moving like a bubble?
- How did your skin feel?
- Did you feel heavy or light?
- What made you move?
- Which way was easier to move, being hard-boiled or raw? Why?
- Would you rather be an egg or a bubble? Why?
- Would you rather be a chicken or a bird? Why?
- Would you rather be soap or water? Why?

SCIENCE ACTIVITIES

1. Weigh a hard-boiled egg and a raw egg. Are they the same weight or different weights?
2. Roll a hard-boiled egg and a raw egg down an incline. Which goes faster? Why?
3. Shell hard-boiled eggs, and mash them with a fork until very fine. Add mayonnaise, salt, and paprika. Make an open-faced egg-salad sandwich for snack or lunch. Decorate with parsley bits, chopped olives, and pimento.
4. Break raw eggs into a bowl. Add a little water. Beat with eggbeater. Scramble in frying pan or on a griddle.

CHAPTER 16

Improving Ocular Control

WE DEPEND on our ability to control our eyes in order to acquire spatial awareness and visual information about location and direction. Developing children are learning to adjust their eyes to change focus from far to near and near to far, as needed; they are learning to track objects so that vision can flow horizontally in a smooth rather than jerky manner; and they are learning to bring their eyes to their midline without breaking their focus in order to be able to do close-up tasks such as reading, writing, or even buttoning a sweater. The ocular control required to achieve these tasks is gained through learning to control the muscles that surround and control the eyes. Practice in the use of these muscles can be gained from the following type of activities.

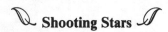 Shooting Stars

MATERIALS:

12 10-foot lengths of narrow but strong cord (obtain a type that will not unravel)
 6 empty thread spools, large wooden beads, or empty toilet tissue rolls

DIRECTIONS:

Thread two lengths of cord through the spool, bead, or tissue roll, as shown in Photos 16.1 and 16.2.

PHOTOS 16.1 AND 16.2. SHOOTING STARS

ACTIVITY:

Children work in pairs, with each hand holding one end of the two lengths of cord. By alternately bringing their hands together and moving them apart, the two children can make the spool, bead, or tissue roll move from one end of the pair of cords to the other. When the children bring their hands together, they should meet at the midline of the body.

By keeping their hands moving rhythmically, the children become involved in the ocular exercise of focusing as they follow the movement of the objects.

Children waiting their turns may stand facing the area between the two players. Thus, they will become involved in the ocular exercise of tracking as they follow the movement of the objects.

VARIATIONS:

1. Use increasingly longer cords, up to 12 feet.
2. Paint the spool, bead, or roll with two or three related colors, such as red-orange, orange, and yellow-orange, or red, orange, and yellow.
3. Paint the spool, bead, or roll with two complementary colors, such as red and green, blue and orange, or yellow and lavender.
4. Paint stripes on the spool, bead, or roll.

5. Tape a feather to the spool, bead, or roll, so that the feather extends out from it. Decorate with pipe cleaners or other items.
6. Perform this exercise to the rhythm of music.

You can use this chant to maintain a rhythm.

A-one and a-two,
A-one and a-two.
It goes to me
And it goes to you.

A-three and a-four,
A-three and a-four.
Move your hands and
Open the door.

A-five and a-six,
A-five and a-six.
Hold the string tight
To look like sticks.

A-seven and an-eight,
A-seven and an-eight.
Watch very closely so
You won't move too late.

A-nine and a-ten,
A-nine and a-ten.
Now that we're through,
We'll do it again.

Repeat with waltz music, moving arms back and forth to the rhythm. Try other types of music, experimenting with different beats and rhythms.

Pegboards

You may want to drill extra holes into a set of wooden pegboards to encourage innovative designs.

1. Make a triangle.
2. Make a circle.
3. Make a square.
4. Make a funny shape.
5. Make a crooked shape.
6. Make a wavy shape.
7. Make a long shape.
8. Make a tiny shape.
9. Make a soft shape.
10. Make a sticky shape.
11. Make a spongy shape.
12. Make a hot shape.
13. Make a stiff shape.
14. Make a watery shape.

VARIATIONS:

1. Do several of these shapes above with chalk or crayon on paper. Older children can try all 14 shapes.
2. Do several of the shapes with scissors, paste, and paper.
3. Do one or more of the shapes in six different colors.
4. Choose one of the shapes to paint as large as possible on a 36″ × 36″ sheet of paper.
5. Trace each of the shapes in the air with eyes closed.
6. Trace each of the shapes in the air with eyes open.

✏ Spot It ✏

The following activities encourage eye-hand coordination because the eye must guide the hand to the appropriate spot.

MATERIALS:

Hair curlers with hollow centers
Newspaper wands
Assorted balls, such as tennis balls, beach balls, softballs, basketballs
Assorted rings from 3 inches to 8 inches in diameter (such as embroidery hoops and bracelets)

Beanbags of assorted sizes and weights (can be made with stuffed
    socks)
Toothpicks
Tweezers
Receptacles, such as boxes and clean wastebaskets

Place hair curlers on a tray. Place a box or other small receptacle on
a table nearby.

ACTIVITIES:

1. Direct the children to pick up a curler in each of the following
   ways:
   a. by placing finger in opening,
   b. by placing pencil in opening, and
   c. by placing end of newspaper wand in opening.
2. Form teams to compete to be the first to get the curlers from the
   tray into the receptacle.
3. Same as previous activity, getting the curlers out of the box and
   back onto the tray.
4. Repeat these activities, using newspaper wands to pick up rings in
   place of curlers.
5. Create a relay course:
   a. Curler to pick up with newspaper wand and place in a nearby
      box.
   b. Ring to pick up with paper wand and place in box.
   c. Ball to hit with wand and guide into a designated area.
   d. Beanbag to pick up with tweezers and place in box.
   e. Toothpicks to pick up with tweezers and place in box.
   f. Expand course as desired with additional relay stations that
      call on focusing skills.

VARIATIONS:

1. Do any of these activities using only right eye and right hand.
2. Do any of them using only left eye and left hand.
3. Do any of them using both eyes and both hands in unison.
4. Do any of them to recorded music.

5. Have a balance board at each station, so that each activity is performed while balancing on board.
6. Have a series of large cards on which you have drawn the various items to be picked up or hit with the paper wand. Have children choose a card and carry out the activity depicted on it. When completed, they put the card back so that someone else can pick it, and they choose another card. Continue until all cards have been chosen.

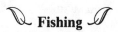 Fishing

Make poles out of string tied to the end of a newspaper wand. Use a small magnet for hooks.

Have the children pick up fish cut out of tagboard to which paper clips have been fastened.

VARIATIONS:

1. Number fish, and pick up in numerical order.
2. Alphabetize fish, and pick them up in alphabetical order.
3. Substitute large paper clips for magnets, loosening one end to form a hook. Paper clips on "fish" need to be bent up so that there is space for hook to slip in.

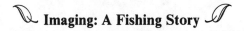 Imaging: A Fishing Story

Children are seated on floor.

Leader: Everyone close your eyes and take a very deep breath. Let it all out. Now take another deep breath. Let it all out. Now slowly take 20 little tiny breaths while I count to 20. 1-2-3-4-5-6-7-8-9-10-11-12-13-14-15-16-17-18-19-20. Now take one more deep breath and let it all out. Now just listen to your heart breathe. And pretend that you are sitting in a boat way out in the middle of a big lake. Feel the boat as it rocks gently to and fro.

Slowly, slowly, get out your fishing pole. Put bait on the hook. That's it, fasten it to the hook. Be careful. Don't hurt yourself on the hook. Now just lean over at the edge of the boat and throw your fishing line into the water. Now just sit back in your chair and wait. Feel the warmth of the sun as it covers you with its light. Reach over and pick up the hat on the floor next to you and put it on to keep the sun out of your eyes and off the top of your head. Now just close your eyes and wait. It feels so good to be out on the water in the clear air with the sun bathing you in its light. You wait . . . and wait . . . and wait.

Oh-oh! There is a pull on your fish line. You stand up, pull in the line, and there, at the end of the line, is this cute giant goldfish just winking its eye at you. You take the goldfish off the hook and throw it back into the water. And then you turn the boat around and guide it to the shore. You get out and tell your friends about the giant goldfish you caught and how it winked at you. But no one believes you. They say, "There are no goldfish in that lake." But you know better. And you have a big smile on your face as you open your eyes and come back into the school.

FOLLOW-UP QUESTIONS

- What kind of boat were you in?
- Was it made of wood, plastic, or metal?
- What color was the boat?
- What made the boat move?
- What color was the water?
- Was the water cold, cool, warm, or hot?
- What made the boat rock?
- How did you feel when it was rocking?
- If you looked across the lake, what did you see on the other side?
- What kind of hat did you pick up to put on your head?
- What was the hat made of?
- What color was the hat?
- Were you surprised when the fish winked at you?

- If you were to name the fish, what would you call it?
- Are you more like a goldfish or a whale? Why?
- Are you more like a car or a boat? Why?
- How did you feel when no one believed you saw a giant goldfish?
- Would you like to go fishing again? (If the answer to this question is affirmative, repeat the exercise, but pretend to have it take place at night. Discuss the difference.)

ART ACTIVITY: FISHING MURAL

Place a large paper on the floor to make a mural. Have some children paint in the sky. Have other children paint in the water. Have everyone design and cut out a giant goldfish, with or without a winking eye, and paste it on the mural. Have everyone design and cut out a boat and paste it on the mural.

FISH SONGS

A-BOATING WE WILL GO
(*Tune:* "A-Hunting We Will Go")

Oh, a-boating we will go, a-boating we will go.
We'll go so far, we'll catch a star,
And then we'll let it go.

Oh, a-fishing we will go, a-fishing we will go.
We'll catch a fish, and give it a kiss,
And then we'll let it go.

Oh, to the ocean we will go, to the ocean we will go.
We'll see the whales and goldfish tails
And then back home we'll go.

MY BOAT WENT OUT TO THE OCEAN
(*Tune:* "My Bonnie Lies Over the Ocean")

My own boat went out to the ocean;
My own boat went out to the sea.
I saw what I thought was a goldfish;
He wanted to come home with me.
Go back, go back, go back little fish to the sea, to the sea.
Go back, go back, you know you can't come with me.

Far-Near

On the blackboard, draw a large circle, a triangle, a square, a rectangle, a diamond, an oval, and two or three free-form shapes. Give each child a piece of paper on which you have drawn ten of each shape.

Point to one of the shapes on the blackboard with a pointer, and have the children put a dot of the same shape on their paper. Begin the activity very slowly and then speed up midway through it.

VARIATION:

Have shapes spread across the entire length of the room. If necessary, put some of the shapes on sheets of paper rather than on the blackboard, or put all the shapes on a strip of paper the length of the wall. Proceed as above, but move your pointer horizontally back and forth from shapes at one end of the wall to shapes at the other end. Children will be tracking the pointer.

Scribble Pictures

To the rhythm of recorded music, children make a large scribble design on a large sheet of newsprint or other paper, using a dark crayon. With lighter crayons, they then color each space in the design.

VARIATIONS:

1. Use related colors, such as orange, yellow, and yellow-green; blue, violet, and green; red, red-orange, orange, and yellow; blue-green, blue, violet, and red-violet (magenta); blue-green, green, yellow-green, and yellow.
2. Use a different color for each space. If spaces are left, use a different color for each space a second time.
3. Use colors that are opposites on the color wheel: red and green, blue and orange, yellow and violet, red-orange and blue-green, yellow-orange and blue-violet, or yellow-green and red-violet. Use only one pair to get a psychedelic effect. Use gray and black for spaces that are left.

4. Color spaces with paint and a fine brush. Use only one color but add increasing amounts of white and of black to have a different shade or tint in each space.

5. Color spaces with broad-tip marking pens.

6. Color spaces with colored chalk.

7. Use marking pens for the scribble design and crayons for shading.

8. Use chalk for the scribble design and crayons for shading.

9. Make scribble designs with eyes closed. Play very short segments of well-known folk songs. Have children change colors for each segment. When finished, open eyes and try to guess which color represented which song. This activity gives children a better understanding of what their eyes do and how important vision is.

10. Same as 9, but give directions for the kind of design to make with each song. For example, with this song, make wavy lines; with this song, make circles; and with this song, make triangles.

11. Instead of scribble designs, make designs with a ruler, crisscrossing lines from edge to edge. Because of the fine angles formed by the crossed lines, this design lends itself well to filling in the spaces with watercolors. Use a fine-tipped brush; show children how to hold the point as they apply the paint to the paper.

12. Use fine-pointed markers for outlining each space.

13. Make the design by tracing circular patterns to make an overlapping series of circles until entire page is covered. Fill in spaces with different colors. Use any of the previously suggested art media.

14. Have children make a design by printing their names. Letters should be as large as possible and can overlap one another. Fill in the spaces between the parts of the letters.

15. Cut out the shapes of any of the designs and reapply them with paste on a contrasting background.

16. Cut out the shapes of any of the designs and reapply them in any pattern on a larger piece of paper. Have children outline each shape with black crayon after it has been pasted on.

CHAPTER 17

Rhythmic Awareness

FROM THE BEGINNING of life, individuals function according to a variety of internal rhythms and tempos. We all have built-in circadian rhythms that largely determine our daily patterns of action and rest or sleep, generally on a 24-hour schedule. We develop not only rhythms of hunger and elimination, of which we are usually aware, but many other bodily rhythms as well. We develop built-in rhythms of blood pressure, respiration, hemoglobin levels, and amino acid levels, among others. We even develop rhythms of skin temperature, with the temperature on the left side of the body generally being higher during sleep and that on the right side generally being higher during wakeful and active periods. Our moods also function in a rhythmic pattern, of which we may or may not be aware. There are monthly and seasonal and annual rhythms in our lives, as evidenced by the well-known "spring fever" syndrome and the fall enthusiasm experienced by many people.

The very rapid rhythms of our brain waves, as seen on encephalograms, show changes in fractions of a second, and make our heartbeat seem very slow by comparison. Although we are usually most aware of the rhythm of our heartbeat and our breathing, all the body rhythms are so closely interwoven that what happens with one will affect in some way what happens with all of the others and influence our general well-being and ability to function effectively.

Much of the rhythm of activity that we develop is influenced by our culture. Children, who are born with their own rates of metabolism and hormone levels, frequently have rhythms that do not mesh with family life. They have to eat when the family eats, rest when

230

they are told to do so, go to school and be at their "prime" when the culture dictates for them to do so, whether it is the best time of the day for them or not. These manipulations of natural cycles and rhythms result in many of the conflicts that arise between adults and children. If any of the built-in rhythms are disturbed, the entire body is disturbed, resulting in behavior changes, from mild restlessness (mild disturbances) to physical disabilities (stronger disturbances) such as asthma and cerebral palsy.

One of the best ways we can help children to cope with this problem and to make necessary adjustments to the changing environments and expectations of others as they go through life is to help them develop a strong rhythmic awareness. As children progress through their developmental years, they are faced with an ever-increasing complexity of sensorimotor tasks, an ever-increasing challenge of coordination requirements, and an ever-increasing necessity to synchronize all thoughts and actions. The activities that follow are geared toward enhancing rhythmic awareness, with its accompanying temporal awareness.

Nursery Rhymes and Songs

Mother Goose rhymes and nursery songs, along with patty-cake, are still valid for toddlers and preschoolers. The rhythms of these verses and songs are so universal that they are easily assimilated by most children. Psychologically, there has been some disapproval of their content. By the same token, from a psychological point of view, they help "play out" many of the common worries and fears of young children. From these traditional rhymes, it is easy to progress to more modern songs and rhymes.

Creative Movement

Creative movement was first introduced to the world of preschool education by co-author Clare Cherry in 1968 (Cherry, 1971, rev. ed.). Her purpose then, as it is today, was to give children an opportunity to re-experience all of the developmental movements of infancy and toddlerhood, along with experiences leading to the development of more mature sensorimotor and perceptual motor skills. One of the primary thrusts of the original Creative Movement for the Developing Child program was the accompaniment for most activities by a steady, even beat in order to coordinate with the steady physiological rhythms controlled by the brain. The tambourine is a good instrument to use because its light weight allows the teacher to be involved with the children while providing rhythmic accompaniment. The tambourine does not preclude the use of other instruments, but it is excellent for that vast body of teachers who claim to be nonmusicians.

Chanting and Clapping

Guided clapping games provide many opportunities to explore movement patterns and the practice of sensorimotor integration skills. Clapping activities, which allow movement across the midline, can begin simply and progress to levels of sophistication that will stretch the skills of the children. Two strategies are involved. First, those movements in which one part of the body contacts the other to the beat of the music, called body rhythm, allow for tactile input and internalization of the beat. Second, those movements that do not result in contact of body parts allow for kinesthetic expression to the beat.

Rhythmic Patterns for Toddlers and Preschoolers

Beginning rhythmic games for very young children can take in all of the natural movements observed in normally developing children at play. These include wiggling, squirming, crawling, creeping, walking, bouncing, hopping, twirling, spinning, scooting, jumping, bending, sliding, shuffling, rocking, shaking, turning, swaying, balancing, kicking, rolling, and combinations of any of these, such as galloping and skipping. They also include hand and arm movements, such as swinging, touching, clapping, slapping, reaching, stretching, drooping, swimming, boxing, pulling, tugging, lifting, waving, scrubbing, shaking, grasping, grabbing, throwing, catching, and all kinds of finger games. Leg and foot movements include kicking, tapping, stomping, wiggling, shaking, swinging, and combinations of any of these.

Programs that incorporate all these movements over a period of time and that repeat them over and over again help to unite the psychological need for rhythmic movement and the cognitive need for rhythmic awareness (tempo and duration, pg. 74; coordination, pgs. 66–68; sequencing, pgs. 242–43).

Once children have had sufficient experience responding to a steady beat and they are able to move in a coordinated manner appropriate to their particular age or stage of development, rhythmic patterns can be introduced.

Rhythm Steps

Cut a carpet into 8- to 12-inch squares. Place squares on each side of a center line, spaced a child's stride apart.

Have the child master each of the following rhythm step patterns before going on to the next.

PATTERNS:

1. Normal walking pattern: left foot, right foot.
2. Hop-hop and step: two hops on one side and one step on the other.
3. Step-step and hop: two steps and a hop on the other side.
4. Repeat 2 and 3, using the other foot for the hops.
5. Hop-hop, hop-hop: two hops on each side.
6. Hop with both feet.
7. Hop-hop, step, step, hop-hop, step, step: two hops on left side, one step on right, one step on left; two hops on right side, one step on left, one step on right.
8. Step, wide step, step, wide step: move carpet squares on right side farther apart. Then reverse, returning right-hand squares to normal spacing and moving left-hand squares farther apart.
9. Step, small step, step, small step: move carpet squares on right side closer together. Then reverse, returning right-hand squares to normal spacing and moving left-hand squares closer together.

1. Clap hands with every move.
2. Recite the alphabet with each step.
3. Count with each step.
4. Do any of these in slow motion.
5. Do any of these in speeded-up time.
6. Do any of these to rhythm of recorded music.

Marching

Have ready a number of recordings of marches of various rhythms. With chalk, tape, or rope, create a variety of patterns all around the classroom. Have the children march to the music, following one of the patterns on the floor.

VARIATIONS:

1. March with high steps.
2. March with exaggerated swinging of arms.
3. Twist upper torso back and forth while marching.
4. March cross-legged.
5. March sideways.
6. March backward.

Name Clapping

A good way to introduce the concept of rhythmic patterns is to clap children's names. For example, *Mary Jones* would be *Ma-ree Jones*, incorporating two short beats and one long. *Tom Smithson* would be clapped as *Tom Smith-son*, one long and two short. Because there are usually several ways to clap a name, children can experiment to find the rhythm that suits them best.

Song Clapping

Name clapping can lead to song clapping, or clapping along while singing a song. First, the claps—like the beginning tambourine accompaniments—are done with a steady beat, beating out the tempo of the song. Gradually, children can learn to beat out the rhythmic pattern. The following exercises will help children achieve a mature level of this skill, and they will be able to create their own songs and patterns.

Rhythmic Activities for Elementary-School Children

It is important that rhythmic activities be continued for elementary-school children. They should be encouraged to move to a wide variety of rhythms and combinations of beats, however, rather than to a steady, even beat. They can play musical games in which they do different types of movements, such as skipping, jumping, hopping, and galloping, to various rhythms. They should be able to move their body parts to a series of changing rhythms. The two goals of rhythmic activities are (1) to help children become aware of their own unique body-rhythms and their ability to control the way they respond to rhythmic stimuli and (2) to help them develop acute auditory awareness that can be transferred to keener listening skills in all areas of life.

Pre-rhythmic Understanding

1. Discuss the various bodily rhythms that are a part of our daily lives.
2. Discuss the cultural and societal rhythms of various activities, such as going to school, test periods, daily school schedules, recess, innings during baseball games, quarters during soccer and basketball, meals, homework time, bath time, bedtime, haircuts, and vacations.
3. Go for a rhythm walk and observe the various phenomena in the natural world that function in a predictable rhythm, such as the sun and plants.

Musical Instruments

Elementary-school children enjoy making and using musical instruments to heighten their rhythmic awareness and skills. There are many craft books that show how to make simple instruments, but be sure to choose those that can provide good rhythmic sound.

Shakers can be made by putting beans or gravel in plastic bottles. One unique shaker that can be used three ways can be made by putting a few beans, dry peas, or small stones in an empty plastic egg carton and sealing it with tape. You can (1) shake this shaker back and forth and up and down, (2) beat a rhythm with a stick on its smooth top—like a drum, and (3) move a stick (6-inch length of 1-inch-diameter doweling) back and forth across the egg-holder bumps on the underside of the box.

Marching, with and without musical instruments, is a great way to introduce children to group rhythmic activity (see pg. 234). Be sure to use a variety of marches, selecting those with different types of rhythms.

Parachutes

The following activities are suggested in *Parachute Play*, by Liz and Dick Wilmes (Building Blocks, 1985).

A parachute can be used to develop a strong sense of rhythmic awareness. Children can shake it, wave it, make it go up, make it go down. They can make it go up and run to the center and back out again before it comes down. Or one child can run to the middle while the chute is up, do a specified action, and then run back out again before it comes down.

Children can learn to snap the parachute and jerk it and to pull it taut and let it go loose. They can wave it gently to slow music or shake it quickly to fast music. They can roll a beach ball on top of it, gently from one side to another, or jerkily so that it falls off. Scarves or soft rubber balls can be bounced around on top of the parachute. So can a piece of rope that the children make wiggle like a worm by wiggling the chute. Cotton balls can be pretend popcorn on the chute.

The Mirror Game

Allow children to freely create their own arm movement dances to recorded dance music, moving to the rhythm. After some practice, have the children pair off. Each pair chooses one to be A and one to be

PHOTO 17.1. THE MIRROR GAME

B. Have the children face each other and continue the arm dancing. This time, however, A takes the lead and B mirrors A's movement (see Photo 17.1). After one or two minutes, stop the music. Start over so that B is the leader and A is the mirror. As the children become experienced at mirroring, they can begin moving their entire bodies, but they should still remain within a very small area.

VARIATION:

Have two or three children be the mirror, all mimicking exactly what the leader is doing.

Hand Clapping

Have the children sit in a group in front of you. Let them sing several songs with you. Begin body rhythm by clapping hands to the songs. Then play a record, and have them follow you in clapping variations to the music. Repeat each new pattern until most of the children seem to master it.

Begin with slow records in 2/4 or 4/4 time. Gradually increase the complexity of the music as the children become more skilled. Complete one record before moving to another.

If some children have difficulty keeping up with the majority, this is a cue for you to do some problem solving and to explore whether there are any physical or developmental problems.

PATTERNS:

1. Walk around the world: clap hands on knees to music, then progress up the body, clapping up sides, over head, down sides, and back to knees.
2. Clap once on knees and once in front of face.
3. Clap twice on knees and once in front of face.
4. Clap once on knees on first beat and cross hands (without touching) in front of face on next beat.
5. Clap twice on knees and twice in front of face.
6. Clap twice on knees and cross hands twice in front of face.
7. Repeat 6 but switch crossing hands.
8. Clap once on knees and thrust fists outward on next beat. Arms may go up slightly, at a 45° angle.
9. Clap twice on knees and thrust fists outward on next two beats. Arms may go up slightly, at a 45° angle.
10. Clap twice on knees on first beat and clap twice on opposite shoulders (crossing arms) on next beat.
11. Clap on knees on first beat and cross arms to clap on opposite knees on next beat.
12. Clap twice on knees on first beat and cross arms to clap twice on opposite knees on next beat.

Hand Clapping with a Partner

Have children turn and face a partner. With their partners, they will demonstrate the following sequence of clapping patterns. Because each step is at least twice as complex as the one before it, take the children only as far as they can go successfully. Their skills will grow over time.

Use a slow record with a distinctive beat at first. Finish the record before changing patterns.

PATTERNS:

1. Each child claps once on own knees and once on partner's hands.
2. Each child claps twice on both knees to the first beat and twice on partner's hands to the next beat.
3. Each child claps once on both knees, then once with the right hand to partner's right hand, then once on both knees, and then once with the left hand to partner's left hand.
4. Each child claps twice on both knees to the first beat, then twice with right hand to partner's right hand on the second beat, then twice on both knees to third beat, and then twice with the left hand to the partner's left hand to the fourth beat.
5. Each child claps twice on both knees to the first beat, then twice with hands in front of body to second beat, then twice to each of the next two beats with both of partner's hands.
6. Each child claps twice on both knees to the first beat, then twice with hands in front of body on second beat, then twice with the right hand to partner's right hand to the third beat, and then twice with the left hand to partner's left hand to the fourth beat.
7. Allow each pair to determine its own beat patterns to specific records. Keep these records in the music center for children to use at other times.

Body Percussion

Ask the children what other ways the body can be used to make sounds. Demonstrate rubbing, patting, clicking fingers, clapping arms against body, and so on.

For these activities, use the same recordings that you did for "Hand Clapping with a Partner" because the children are familiar with them.

ACTIVITIES:

1. Do some of the clapping patterns with accompanying feet movements.
2. Make sounds to accompany music, using hands and arms without clapping.
3. Make sounds to accompany music, using mouth only, but not using words.

4. Dance freely around the room to music, clapping beats.
5. Dance freely around the room to music, using other parts of the body to make sounds.
6. Dance freely around the room to music, using only the mouth to make accompanying sounds.

 Rap Songs

Chant a sample rap song such as this one:

> Here we stand / just kicking up sand.
> We're ready to rap / and ready to clap.
> As we rave and rant, / pick up the chant
> With a stomp and a clap. / Don't be a sap.

Then have the children make up their own songs by adding three lines to each of the following lines.

1. My name is Koko. / Thing-a-ma-loco,
2. I came from afar / in a broken-down car,
3. I grew a tree / as tall as could be,
4. I painted a bug / in the middle of the rug,
5. The rain was red / and yellow he said,
6. The orange had a need / for an apple seed,
7. A dinosaur today / said "I want to play,"
8. I don't want trouble/ to burst my bubble,
9. The sun shines down / on Too-Tow-La-Town,
10. The sun forgot / to get real hot,
11. I'm all alone. / My friend went home,
12. I felt a worm. / It made me squirm,
13. My feet got sore / on the sticky floor,
14. I heard the ice / melting twice,

VARIATIONS:

1. Have children make up their own topics.
2. Have one child do the first line, someone else do the second, another the third, and yet another the fourth.

3. Two children can work together, with each doing every other line.
4. Have each child make up a rap of four to six lines. Others can make up different last lines. Compare them.
5. Make up a new rap from the last line of someone else's rap.

FOLLOW-UP ACTIVITIES

1. **Book of raps:** Make a booklet of the raps that the children create. Title each one with a feeling, such as happy, sad, scared, worried, or confused.
2. **Art activity:** Illustrate the various raps on sheets of paper or in a book format.
3. **Rhythmic movement:** Create a dance to go with your rap.
4. **Imagination:** Take the subject of one rap and create a story.
5. **Playacting:** Take the above story and create a play out of it. All the characters speak only in rap style.
6. **Fantasy:** Create fantasy costumes to go with roles in the play.

References

Cherry, Clare. [1968] 1971. *Creative Movement for the Developing Child,* rev. ed. Belmont, CA: Fearon/David S. Lake Publishers.
Wilmes, Liz, and Dick Wilmes. 1985. *Parachute Play.* Elgin, IL: Building Blocks.

CHAPTER 18

Sequencing Skills

PUTTING INFORMATION into an orderly sequence is a left-hemisphere processing function. During the developmental years, as children acquire motor skills, they learn that one particular movement precedes another. Even in learning to crawl, creep, and walk, this awareness of sequence is being internalized. Soon children learn to recognize the rhythm of the day; particular sequences of events are repeated and, therefore, come to be anticipated. When there is a slight change in a particular sequence, children may feel their "rhythm" of action has been interfered with, and even infants will display discomfort.

We learn to measure time by sequence. When we do one thing, we expect another to follow at a certain time. We learn to recognize our body rhythms and remember time according to many of our bodily functions. When we are involved in an activity that requires us to remember a great many facts or details, time may seem to drag. When we are involved in a pleasurable activity, time may seem to pass quickly. But whether time drags or passes quickly, our memory of the activity will be related to the sequence of events rather than to the length of time it took.

Sequencing is a left-hemisphere process. Some people find sequencing difficult. They remember things, but not the order of things. They follow directions, but not in the order they were given. And remembering a sequence becomes even harder for them if there are conflicting stimuli to distract them. These people may have difficulty reading or performing other structured academic tasks that depend on following a particular sequence. Time to such people is not measurable. People with strong right-hemisphere processing skills seem to have their own sense of time and rhythm. The following activities will help children to internalize the concept of sequence. Categorizing items also helps in learning to sequence.

℞ Ordering Playthings ♪

Games that require ordering are important for the preschool child. Children can arrange any of the sets of the following items (or any other sets available at home or school) in a sequence from the smallest to the largest. Items can also be arranged according to descending or ascending width, length, or weight. Items can also be categorized according to color, style, material, or shape.

MATERIALS:

Stacking shapes
Sized pegs
Nesting blocks
Small toys in a variety of sizes
Jar lids in a variety of sizes
Plastic lids in a variety of sizes
Small boxes that can be nested inside one another
Pieces of two-by-four wood cut in different lengths
Toothpicks or straws cut in different lengths
Pencils and pens of different lengths or sizes
Spools of different sizes
Blocks of different sizes
Nuts, bolts, and screws of different sizes
Nails of different sizes
Books of different sizes

℞ Daily Sequence ♪

To introduce your students to the concept of events in a sequence, discuss with them the following sequences of familiar activities:

1. before school, school, and after school;
2. breakfast, lunch, and dinner;
3. morning, afternoon, and night;
4. early morning, morning, noon, afternoon, evening, and night; and
5. wake up, eat breakfast, come to school, play, have a snack, play, eat lunch, nap, play, hear or read a story, go home, eat dinner, take a bath, go to bed.

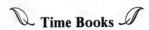 Time Books

MATERIALS:

5″ × 8″ sheets of paper

Magazines with a lot of illustrations

Have the children make a booklet for each of the daily sequences mentioned by following these steps:

1. Cut out pictures to represent the various events.
2. Paste one picture on a page—for example, one page for morning, one for afternoon, and one for night.
3. Make a cover for each booklet with a drawing and a title.
4. Staple the pages together or put them together with paper fasteners.
5. Read the books to the others in class.

Daily Plans

In preparation for the following activities, always list your daily plan and sequence of activities, with times, on the board either before your students arrive or as they watch. Discuss the day's plan with the children.

1. Provide the children with a daily plan sheet that has ten horizontal lines across the page and a vertical column on the right.

- Have children plan their day for five activities in succession. Gradually increase the number of activities they can plan ahead for.
- As they perform each activity, they can put their initials in the column by the name of that activity.
2. Have the children plan what they will do on a weekend day. Initially, plan for one day only. When this is successful, plan for two days.
3. Keep a diary of school activities. Children can be given a small notebook for this purpose. At the end of each activity's description (which may be in picture form if the children do not yet write), they can use a symbol to indicate whether it was satisfying (smiling face), dissatisfying (sad face), or in between (an X). The children may create other symbol systems.

One-Week-at-a-Time Calendar

Put up a calendar made of five sheets of paper in a row low on the bulletin board. Above each sheet place the name of one weekday. (See Photo 18.1.)

PHOTO 18.1. ONE-WEEK-AT-A-TIME CALENDAR

ACTIVITY:

1. At the beginning of each day, have children gather around the bulletin board to discuss the special activities or events that will

take place on that day. Depict one or two of these activities on the sheet of paper for that day with simple stick figures or pictures cut out of magazines and school supply catalogs.

2. At the conclusion of the day, gather around the calendar once more. Discuss what took place. Draw sketches of the primary events of the day.

3. As the week progresses, refer back to the previous days. Occasionally, you may want to plan ahead and make some sketches for the next day, or for the last day of the week, or for whenever a special event will take place. For example, if you are planning to go on a field trip on Thursday, on Monday you might depict something about that on the Thursday sheet.

4. Each week, add new daily sheets on top of the earlier ones. This gives the children an opportunity to recall an activity of a previous week.

5. Periodically review the previous weeks' activities to help the children internalize the concept of the sequencing of events.

6. First graders can arrange the sheets at the end of the month to depict the month that has just passed.

7. After some experience with the school-week calendar, Saturday and Sunday can be added. This gives additional opportunities to recall and to anticipate events, while seeing them in concrete, graphic symbols.

Telling Time

Time is a strong left-hemisphere concept. Right-hemisphere–dominant children have difficulty learning about time. The following activities can help them learn about time by manipulating real and pretend clocks.

1. Have the children each make a clock out of a paper plate. Cut a big and a little hand out of lightweight cardboard and fasten them in the center of the plate.

2. Draw clock faces and have the children match the drawing to where the hands are on the real clock.

3. Let the children take real clocks apart to see how they are made.

4. Use an alarm clock to time events for a month, or until some of the children seem to be internalizing a sense of time.

The Number Day

This activity is adapted from *Mathematics Their Way*, by Mary Barotta-Lorton (Addison-Wesley, 1976).

Put a border of adding machine tape around a bulletin board, blackboard, wall, or wherever a very long strip of tape can be conveniently located for an entire school year.

Each day put a number on the tape indicating the day of the school year. Start with 1 on the opening day of school, 2 on the second day, and so on until the final day of school. Do not count days when there is no school.

MATH ACTIVITIES

1. Put a circle around each tenth day.
2. Have a "100 party" on the 100th day. Each child can be given a plastic sandwich bag to take home to bring back filled with 100 of something—100 beans, seeds, nails, toothpicks, pieces of gravel, or 100 of anything else they can find around their homes.
3. How many circles (tenth days) were made before reaching the 100th day?

CRAFT ACTIVITIES

1. Arrange the items brought from home into a collage in ten groups of ten.
2. Arrange 100 items on a collage without grouping by tens.

Photo Album

Prepare a photo album for the class. Using an instant camera, have the children photograph events of the school year and put them in the album in the following sections:

• Section 1 will show a school day.
• Section 2 will show highlights for fall, winter, spring, summer.

- Section 3 will show comparisons of the class as a group in the fall and in the spring.
- If time and funds permit, a final section could compare each child at the beginning and the end of the school year.

✒ Telling a Story ✒

In addition to recording events through photography, have children write a story about a special event in which they participated. Stress that all stories have a specific sequence, that is, a beginning, a middle, and an ending.

ACTIVITIES:

1. When they record their stories, whether by dictation (for children too young to read) or by writing it themselves, have them first plan what the beginning, middle, and ending will be about.
2. Make an outline, showing what the beginning, middle, and ending will be about.
3. After some experience with the three-part outline, primary students can move to five parts, adding a part between the beginning and the middle, and another part between the middle and the end.

ART ACTIVITIES

1. Draw an illustration for the recorded story.
2. Draw several illustrations to show the sequence of events in the recorded story.
3. Listen to a story read out loud. Each child can draw a picture of a different part of the story. The pictures can then be displayed according to the sequence of the story. They can be made into a booklet so that children can "read" and recall the story.

✒ Following Directions ✒

Right-hemisphere–dominant children frequently have difficulty following directions in the appropriate sequence.

1. Help them develop the habit of making a list, either in words or illustrations, and checking off each item on the list as it is accomplished.
2. Help them remember the items on a list by selecting one word to be the reminder for each item. They can write just those words in the sequence of the list, or if there are only two or three, they can try memorizing them.
3. Another way to remember the items on a list is to visualize each item and its location.

CHAPTER 19

Symbolism

AS DISCUSSED in Chapter 5, the cognitive development of young children is the process of moving beyond simple physical responses to sensory stimuli toward the complex ability to use symbolism. Sensorimotor activity, as the driving force in the development of cognition, extends into symbolic expression as the child's own symbolic world expands.

Since symbolism in the form of language, imagery, and visualization begins early in life, we see its use in many aspects of children's activities and experiences. From graphic and three-dimensional art to model building and role playing, symbolism is closely woven into their lives. Musical expression unfolds in the forms of rhythm, sound, and movement. Many of the activities explored so far have included these earlier forms of symbolic expression. The following activities provide right-hemisphere and integrated experiences that merge into reading, writing, and mathematical skills, along with social skills, as more sophisticated forms of symbolic expression.

 The Musical Butterflies

MATERIALS:

Record player
Recording of *The Nutcracker Suite* or some other symphonic piece
20-foot length of butcher paper or wrapping paper (30–36 inches wide)
Felt-tip markers
Pictures of butterflies

Spread the butcher paper on the floor, and space the markers along it. As you guide the children's movement, change to another portion of the recording for a different rhythm every minute or two.

Leader: Today we're going to play with butterflies. Here are pictures of many beautiful butterflies. If you could be a butterfly, which one would you be like? What are its colors? Do you know what its name is?

(Take a few moments for everyone to identify their butterflies.)

Now pretend that your hand is that butterfly. It's sitting on the stem of a beautiful flower made by a finger on your other hand. Listen to the music *(start record player)* and let the butterfly dance to its rhythm. When the music goes slow, the butterfly will go slow, and when the music goes fast, the butterfly will go fast. Think about what the butterfly will do when the music goes high, or low, or 'round and 'round and 'round. Now close your eyes, but let the butterfly keep dancing. Here comes another butterfly from your other hand, and now the two butterflies are dancing beautifully together. *(Allow time for dancing.)* Open your eyes so that you can see how they are dancing. Now dance your butterflies over to where the paper is spread out on the floor. Pick up a marker and let that be your butterfly as it dances all over the meadow. Reach and stretch your butterfly as it explores the new space. Now here comes the other butterfly, and the two of them explore the paper together.

Now close your eyes *(room lights can also be turned off)* and feel how your butterflies keep dancing. Feel how they fly up . . . and down . . . and how they twirl all around so gracefully . . . and how they go sideways . . . and all over their space . . .

(Allow children to quietly continue dancing with eyes closed.)

Eyes are still closed . . . and dancing . . .

Open your eyes now and see where you want your butterflies to finish the dance . . .

(Stop music.)

And the butterflies flew away.

VARIATIONS:

Have the children stand and become butterflies as they dance around the room to the same music as before. Change rhythm of music periodically as above. Direct them in the following way:

Now all the butterflies are dancing to the music all over the room. The entire room is a big flower garden, and you are dancing in between and over and all around the flowers.

(As they dance, walk around and give each child a crepe paper streamer to hold in one hand. As they continue to dance, give each child a crepe paper streamer to hold in the other hand.)

Now all the butterflies look around and find a place on the ground to rest as the music comes to an end.

(Music stops at real end of recording.)

FOLLOW-UP QUESTIONS

- Can you find on your paper where the butterflies went high? Low? Sideways? Where they twirled around?
- What was your butterfly thinking about when it was flying all alone?
- Did your butterfly like it better dancing with a friend or was it better dancing all alone?
- What did the butterflies see while they were dancing?
- If your butterflies could dream, what do you think they would dream about?
- What is your favorite kind of dream? Tell us about it.

ART ACTIVITIES

1. **Butterflies in the Meadow:** Using green fingerpaint, the children pretend their hands are butterflies as they dance over a large sheet (at least 18″ × 24″) of fingerpaint paper to the music, as in the previous activity.
2. **Butterfly Walls:** Using tempera paints (mixed with white for pastel colors, except bright yellow), the children pretend their paint-

brushes are butterflies dancing all over paper taped to makeshift easel surfaces: chalkboards, windows, walls, or tables tipped on their sides. Using these surfaces gives the children a new perspective of the same motions.

3. **Butterfly Folds #1:** With an eyedropper for each color, the children squeeze tempera paints (mixed with white, as in 2, and put in small containers) onto one side of 9″ × 12″ sheets of white paper folded in half. Fold the paper in half again and rub hand over it. Open to see a butterfly.

   If you wish, you can add a few drops of white paint or one or two drops of black paint and fold paper again. Blot.

4. **Butterfly Folds #2:** With a paintbrush, children drop globs of tempera paint on large sheets of pink or yellow construction paper that have been folded and cut into butterfly-wing shapes. Fold again and rub as in 3. Open to see completed butterfly.

5. **Butterfly Mural:** On an 8- to 10-foot length of 30- to 36-inch-wide paper mounted on a wall or spread out on the floor, the children use tempera paints to paint a meadow in various shades of green. They paint a light blue sky. They create flowers out of construction paper in a variety of colors (or duplicator paper in pastel shades) and glue them onto the meadow. Flower stems are painted with dark green tempera.

   The children make butterflies for the mural by folding 4″ x 6″ pieces of construction paper and cutting out the wings (trust the children to create their own patterns). Then they place drops of tempera paint on one side of each butterfly and fold and rub. Glue the butterflies on the mural.

   VARIATIONS:

   a. Draw children, cut them out, and glue them onto the mural. Add miniature crepe paper streamers to their hands (if the children have done the butterfly dance with streamers, above).
   b. Trace children's hands onto pastel paper. Cut them out and glue them to various parts of the mural along with the butterflies.

✍ If You're Silly and You Know It ♫

Leader: I'm going to do the first verse of this silly song. Then I need each of you to make up the other things to do.

IF YOU'RE SILLY AND YOU KNOW IT
(*Tune:* "If You're Happy and You Know It")

If you're silly and you know it, act like this.

(Perform silly act.)

If you're silly and you know it, act like this.

(Repeat act.)

If you're silly and you know it, then your face will surely show it.
If you're silly and you know it, act like this.

(Repeat act.)

Continue with verses, starting with the phrases listed below. Have each child take a turn developing the action.

1. If you're a clown and you know it, act like this.
2. If you're a puppet and you know it, act like this.
3. If you're a weirdo and you know it, act like this.
4. If you're a baby and you know it, act like this.
5. If you're a bluebird and you know it, act like this.
6. If you're a scarecrow and you know it, act like this.
7. If you're a rag doll and you know it, act like this.
8. If you're a pink cow and you know it, act like this.
9. If you're a tall tree and you know it, act like this.

Continue with children making up the different things. Write down the new verses so that they can be placed in a booklet for the children to read and to use at other times.

✍ Old McDonald Had a Farm ♫

Leader: Everyone sing with me. When I point to you, tell me the name of an animal. Everyone help be that animal.

OLD McDONALD HAD A FARM

Old McDonald had a farm, ee-i-ee-i-o.
And on this farm he had a *(point to a child)* _____,
    ee-i-ee-i-o.
Here a *(sound made by the selected animal)* _____ .
    There a _____ .
Everywhere a _____ , _____ .
Old McDonald had a farm, ee-i-ee-i-o.

FOLLOW-UP ACTIVITIES

1. **The Dance on the Farm:** Play a musical selection and have everyone be the animal they selected as they "dance on the farm."

2. **McDonald's Farm:** Make a mural as in Activity 5, pg. 253, with meadow and sky. Add barn and farmhouse, animals, and the farmer and his family.

3. **McDonald's Play:** With children, create a play for McDonald's farm, with children acting out the animals they selected in the song. Someone needs to be the farmer and the farmer's family. Suggestion: It can be someone's birthday and all of the animals are invited to the party.

    VARIATIONS:

    a. Create scenery.
    b. Make costumes with an oversized mask of each animal.
    c. Present the play to other classrooms.

4. **McDonald's Puppets:** Same as 3, but present play as a puppet show. Draw figures (6–12 inches high) of each character—or cut them from magazines or discarded picture books. Mount drawings on stiff cardboard and cut out. Glue a 24-inch stick behind figure to manipulate for puppet show (see Figure 19.1).

5. **McDonald's Poem:** Have each child write a poem about McDonald's family, with an illustration on a separate piece of paper. Have poems typed up nicely on separate sheets of paper. Mount illustrations. Assemble booklet, with the illustrations facing their poems. Have several children create a cover for the booklet. Loan booklet to other classrooms for one day at a time.

ice cream sticks

FIGURE 19.1. STICK FIGURE PUPPET. Glue the face or the entire body of a person or animal onto an ice cream stick.

🎵 Musical Poetry 🎵

Have children write poems about a topic such as

- my new shoes,
- the purple cat,
- the talking daisy,
- the dancing tree,
- the chocolate clock,
- the paper boat,
- the runaway bicycle, or
- the book without words.

Then help children to make up tunes for their poems. Have the entire class join in singing each poem. Use a tape recorder so that you can refer back for each tune.

The Blue Tail Fly

1. Teach the children the first verse of the folk song "The Blue Tail Fly" or any other folk song that you feel comfortable with. Divide class into teams of four. Have each group create another verse in their own words. Allow ten minutes for this activity. Use the following example of an original verse (with traditional chorus):

> We all are here to sing a song.
> Let's sing it out and sing it strong.
> Sing real sweet or you'll know why
> You'll be bitten by the blue tail fly.

> *Chorus:*
> Jimmy crack corn and I don't care,
> Jimmy crack corn and I don't care,
> Jimmy crack corn and I don't care,
> My master's gone away.

2. Have each group sing their verse. Everyone can join in on chorus.
3. Tape-record each group as they sing their verse.
4. Compile verse into a booklet for future use.
5. Listen to tape recording. If the class chooses to do so, have each group create an additional verse. Repeat 2, 3, and 4.
6. Make an illustration for each original verse.

Season Murals

MATERIALS:

Butcher, kraft, or wrapping paper to use as background for mural
Tempera paints, construction paper, scissors, glue
Bags for collecting materials

ACTIVITY:

1. Go for a neighborhood walk, or a walk in a nearby park. If necessary, take a field trip to a park.
2. Discuss signs of the current season. What sounds do we hear? What makes those sounds? What colors are the leaves on the trees (or why are there no leaves on the trees)? What is the weather like?

How does the weather tell us what season it is? What kinds of animals do we usually see in this season?

3. Collect materials, such as leaves, twigs, seeds, and bugs, that are indicative of the season or the location. (Provide each child with a bag.)

4. On returning to the classroom, review the experience. What was seen, heard, smelled, collected? What were the signs of the particular season?

5. Create a mural of the season. Paste the collected materials on length of butcher, kraft, or wrapping paper. Add details with tempera paint and construction paper.

6. **Open House: The Seasons.** Do murals for each season as it occurs, and at the end of a year, display all the murals together. Have an open house to show off your work.

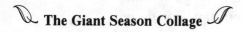 **The Giant Season Collage**

MATERIALS:

Wood or Masonite sheet, approximately 3′ × 5′ or 6′
Glue
Paint for wood or Masonite
Materials collected on season walk
Materials of the season added by leader
Other "found" objects appropriate to the season

ACTIVITY:

Assemble all the collected materials to be shared. Re-create the season or field trip site, using the collected materials and creating other scenery for the collage.

VARIATION:

Individual Collage. Create a seasonal design with collected materials from a walk or field trip glued on a 9″ × 12″ piece of wood or Masonite.

 **The Seasonal Peep Show**

Create a season collage in one end of a shoe box to make a peep show.

1. Make a background collage on a piece of cardboard cut to fit in the end of the shoe box.
2. Create a foreground collage to place flat in front of the background collage. Use tabs to make some pieces stand upright for a three-dimensional effect.
3. Make a small hole in front of the shoe box to peek through.
4. Cut a small opening near the center of the box lid. Cover the opening with cellophane or white tissue paper to let light into the box.

THE MOVIE BOX

Prepare a shoe box as above for the peep show. Cut a vertical slit in each back corner of the box. Draw signs of the season on a strip of paper 2 to 3 inches wide (such as adding machine tape). Pull the strip of paper slowly through the slit as the viewer watches the "movie."

VARIATIONS:

1. Create exciting stories and transfer them to "movie" strips.
2. Use wooden doweling as spools for winding longer strips.

INTEREST TOPICS

Create murals, individual collages, group collages, peep shows, or movies for other field trips and excursions or other topics.

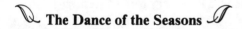

The Dance of the Seasons

MATERIALS:

A scarf, big enough to cover a child, for each child (brought from home or made of 48- to 60-inch-wide cloth cut into 48-inch lengths; use nylon jersey or other knit remnants, cotton, or other material with enough body to be able to be shaken out flat)
Recordings that are appropriate to the season being depicted

DIRECTIONS:

Each child huddles under a scarf. As the music plays, the children listen for a while and then slowly emerge and dance.

Leader: It's fall (*or winter, spring, or summer*), and you are waiting for the time to awaken.

(Music is playing.)

Suddenly you realize that you are the fall (*or winter, spring, or summer*), and you slowly rise to join into the activities of the season . . . and you dance (*using scarves any way they wish*) . . . and dance . . . and bring fall (*winter, spring, or summer*) to the whole world. . . .

(Continue for as long as the mood is appropriate.)

Night begins to fall (*turn off room lights*), and all the dancers go back under their scarves and go to sleep.

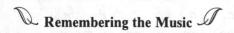 **Remembering the Music**

MATERIALS:

Mural paper
Scarves (as in Dance of the Seasons)
Recorded symphonic music

ACTIVITY:

1. Children get into a comfortable position under their scarves in a darkened room.
2. The leader suggests that this will be a very quiet listening-feeling time.
3. The music is played as the children listen.
4. When they feel they have something to contribute, they gradually come out from under their scarves, go to the mural, and paint how they "feel" or what they heard.
5. They silently go back to their scarf place and listen some more until they have something else to add.

VARIATION:

The children are each given a piece of watercolor paper and a box of watercolors and emerge from their scarves when the music is finished.

They go to their own desk and table and silently paint what they felt while listening to the music.

After completing their paintings, the children each select a word to represent their main feeling. These words are then listed on the blackboard and the class composes a group poem using the words on the list. The poem is duplicated and attached to each child's watercolor painting.

🐚 Experiencing the Alphabet ✍

Create two or three giant alphabet letters from newspaper wands made by rolling newspaper tightly and fastening the ends with tape. Leave the giant letters around the classroom for a few days and encourage the children to examine them.

Hold up a giant *A* that you have made. Ask the children if they have all seen it and touched it. If some haven't, walk around and have them touch it and hold it. After everyone has had some physical contact with the *A*, hold it up where they can see it and tell them you are going to play an imagination game with it.

PHOTO 19.1. EXPERIENCING THE ALPHABET

Leader: If I made a giant *A* on the playground out of pipes, and it was standing next to the swings, what kind of games could you play with it? What would you be able to do on the *A*?

Take all answers seriously. As the children go on, they will inspire each other. Make a mental note of all of their suggestions, so you can include them in an imaging experience similar to the following, which was created from the ideas of a group of first graders and supplemented by those of a group of third graders.

Leader: Picture the letter *A* in your mind until it is very big. See it out in the playground. It is made of pipe and it is painted red. Stand next to one of the sides and climb up to the top. Climb down the other side until you come to the crossbar of the *A*. Grab hold of the crossbar and while holding on, move one hand over the other until you get to the other side again. Jump down to the ground and spread your arms out to each side. Feel the wind as it lifts you up in the air. Lean forward so that you can drift through the window in the top part of the *A* and go through to the other side of it. The wind blows you around so that you come back through the opening. But this time you grab hold of the crossbar. You shift yourself up so that your waist is touching the bar. You bend over the bar, hanging on with your waist. You touch your feet so that your body makes an oval around the bar. You grab hold of your ankles and swing 'round and 'round and 'round. Now let go of your feet and allow the wind to blow you out in front of the *A* again, then around and up to the point at the top. At the top there is an opening in one of the pipes. Climb into that opening and slide down head first until you come to another opening near the ground. Then climb back inside the opening to climb to the top again; come out and slide down the outside of the other leg of the *A*. Now let the wind blow you back up to the bar and hold on with both hands as the wind swings you back and forth, back and forth, back and forth. Now swing yourself up and around and under and up again and around again and under and back up. Now swing a funny way. Swing a scary way. Swing a quiet way. Now swing any way you want to.

Now take one big swing around the bar, and then sit up on top of it. Look. There is a slide going from the bar down to a pool of water. You slide down into the water. That was fun. You jump very high to get up to the bar again and slide down into the water again. And again.

Now you go back to the bar, let go of it, and let the wind lift you gently off the bar and set you down on the ground next to the pool. As you watch, you see the wind blow the giant *A* way up into the clouds, and our new climbing game is gone.

VARIATIONS:

1. Use other letters of the alphabet.
2. Have children make the complete alphabet. Paint the letters. Keep them in the room for exploration activities and games.
3. Have each child hold one letter of the alphabet. Spell out words by having children get into the appropriate position according to the letter they are holding.

Experiencing Numbers

This is the same as "Experiencing the Alphabet" except that numbers are substituted for letters.

VARIATION:

Use paper wand numbers to create mathematical equations. Make three of each number and a plus, a minus, and a times sign. Have each child hold a number and get into appropriate place when called upon. Have children make up their own "equations" with the numbers they are holding.

CHAPTER 20

Metaphoric Language

METAPHORIC LANGUAGE is closely related to symbolism and imagery. It is verbal imagery, and it is especially suited to children because of its ability to unveil a delightful array of feelings and insights. Metaphoric language has been used throughout history to develop understanding. From parables and simple animal stories to more complex narratives and the wide world of poetry, metaphoric language has been used to promote understanding by comparing one thing to another more familiar thing.

Preschool children often use metaphoric language to help their own understanding. Zabeth, age 4, looked at her shoes and said, "I know. Those are beds for my feet." To help young children develop the free-flowing imagination needed to use metaphoric language deliberately, it is easiest to use activities with synonyms and similes. Synonyms are two words that mean the same thing. Similes are figures of speech in which a word or idea is compared with another word or idea that is similar in some way; a simile compares the two by using words or phrases such as *like* or *as if* or *the same as*. A metaphor, by contrast, depicts one thing in terms of another—for example, "the curtain of night," "all the world's a stage," or "drowning in sorrow." Similes and metaphors are types of analogies. Their use is a strong right-hemisphere function. When coupled with visual imagery, metaphoric language activities help to develop right-hemisphere skills and promote creative thinking.

264

The World Is Like a Game

Gather the children in a group. Tell them you are going to start a sentence and they are to finish it with the name of another object that they are reminded of. Create sentences similar to the following, using examples of people and things familiar to the children. (Do not correct children. Any words they use must be accepted.)

A cow is like a _____ .
A turtle is like a _____ .
Water feels like _____ .
Butter is almost the same as _____ .
A siren sounds like it is a _____ .
The color blue makes me feel like _____ .
The sound my mama makes is like a _____ .
Turkey smells like _____
Bananas taste like _____ .
Soap is like _____ .
Michael Jackson is like _____ .
Jumping rabbits are like _____ .
School is like _____ .
A tall building is like a _____ .

VARIATION:

To further stimulate the imagination, use "reminds me of."

Blue reminds me of _____ .
Red reminds me of _____ . *(Continue with other colors.)*
Loud noises remind me of _____ .
The sky at night reminds me of _____ .
Music reminds me of _____ .
Buttons remind me of _____ .
A sandwich reminds me of _____ .
The telephone reminds me of _____ .
A police officer reminds me of _____ .
Dust in the air reminds me of _____ .
A bed reminds me of _____ .

Once There Was a Game

Tell the following story. Have the children, as you point to each one, fill in the blanks. Accept whatever they offer, no matter how far-fetched it may sound.

Leader: Once there was a fox who found a _____ . The fox thought it was a _____ , but he wasn't certain how to find out. He took it to Nanny Goat to ask her. She tried to explain that it was a _____ , but he just couldn't understand.

So he went to Big Brown Cow. The cow was so big that surely she would know the answer. He asked her what it was. She thought and thought. She said, "Well, I don't know exactly what it is, but it might be a _____ ." He asked why. She said, "Because it is _____ ."

He still didn't understand, so he went to Curley Mule. Surely Curley Mule would know the answer. When he asked Curley Mule what it was, the mule said, "Well, I think it's a _____ , but I don't know its real name."

The fox was really getting aggravated. Someone had to know what it was that he had found. So he decided to go talk to Bog the Dog. Bog the Dog goes so many places by himself that he probably knows everything. But when the fox showed Bog the Dog what he had found, the dog said, "It reminds me of a _____ , but that's not what it is."

Mr. Fox finally went to Miss Wren, the hen who lived in the chicken yard. He said, "Look what I found. I've asked everyone and nobody can tell me what it is. I've been told it's a _____ and a _____ and a _____ and a _____ . Do you know what it is?" "Well," said Miss Wren the Hen, "If they all told you that is what it reminded them of, I think it must be a _____ ." "It must be," he said, "But it sure had me fooled."

◟ Scavenger Hunt ◝

Use metaphors to make up a list of items for children to find on a scavenger hunt. The following are examples.

Something like a soft crayon (chalk)
Something to listen to music (record)
Something that tells a story (book)
Something soft like a kitten (a stuffed animal or a sweater)
Something cold (something made of metal or a piece of fruit)
Something complicated (something mechanical or a difficult book)
Something for when you think you're late (a clock or a watch)
Something for when your feet are tired (a chair or a pillow)
Something to make words (typewriter, pencil and paper, pen, etc.)
Something that bends (a book cover or a piece of plastic or a wire)
Something that helps us (an adding machine or a sweater or a clock)
Something for when we want to see (a mirror or a light)

◟ The Slippery Story ◝

Tell the following story. Have the children, as you point to each one, fill in the missing words.

Leader: I picked up a slippery fish and couldn't hold on to it because it was as slippery as _____ . So I tried to hold on to one of those, but it was as slippery as _____ .

The next thing I picked up was a wiggly baby puppy. I couldn't hold on to it because it was as wiggly as _____ and as wiggly as _____ and as wiggly as _____ .

I put the puppy down and tried to put on my sweater. But it was inside out and one sleeve had gotten inside the other and it was as tangled as _____ or _____ or _____ .

I told my friend to hurry because it was time for us to go home. But he was as slow as _____ and even slower than

_____ . I said, "Hurry, hurry." But he still was so slow he reminded me of _____ or of _____ .

When I finally got home, I picked up my soft, furry kitten and it made me feel good. It was as soft as _____ or _____ . It felt like _____ and like _____ . But then it scratched me. "Ouch!" I said. "Your scratch feels like a _____ or _____ or _____ ."

After such a confusing day I finally went to bed. I snuggled down under my covers, my head on my cozy pillow, and I felt like I was _____ or maybe _____ or even _____ .

VARIATIONS:

1. Read a well-known story, inserting as often as possible the phrase "It reminded him (or her or it) of _____ ."
2. Sing a song that all the students know. Then sing the song again, substituting synonyms, similes, and metaphors for as many of the words as possible. The following example is a variation of "Mary Had a Little Lamb."

   Mary had a fleecy ball, a fleecy ball, a fleecy ball.
   Mary had a fleecy ball; its coat was white as hail.
   And everywhere that Mary went, Mary went, Mary went,
   Everywhere that Mary went, the ball was on her tail.

Analogy Pictures

MATERIALS:

Magazines of all types with many illustrations
School supplies catalogs
Scissors
Glue or paste

ACTIVITY:

The children cut out ten pictures of ten different types of things. They paste or glue the pictures below one another on a piece of poster board or heavy paper. Then they search through the magazines again to find a picture of something that is like (but not the same as) each of the first ten. Some of the ways that things can be alike are color, material, shape, use, size, origin, and texture. Here are some examples of picture pairs.

- A dish and a clock (both are circular)
- A head and a ball (both are spheres)
- A knife and a pair of scissors (both can cut)
- An automobile and a wagon (both have wheels)
- A couch and a chair (both are for sitting)
- A pen and a crayon (both mark on paper)
- A dress and a pair of shoes (both are clothing)
- A sink and a bathtub (both hold water)
- A window and a drinking glass (both are made of glass)
- The sky and a blue flower (both are blue)

VARIATION:

Children draw their own pictures.

Pair Charades

Children work with partners. Each pair acts out two kinds of people or animals that are similar in some way. The other children try to guess who the pair is. Here are some examples of pairs.

- A dog and a cat
- A man and a boy
- A car and a tricycle or bicycle
- Roller skates and a skateboard
- A typewriter and a computer
- A ball and a Frisbee
- A turtle and a snail
- A rabbit and a kangaroo
- A tree and a flower
- A bird and a butterfly

ᘒ Metaphor Riddles ᘓ

The teacher asks the following questions, encouraging the children to use their imaginations to come up with similes and metaphors for different words.

- When I close my eyes, how does hungry look?
- How does angry look? How does it feel?
- How does forget look? How does it feel?
- How does a scream look? How does it feel?
- How does cold look? How does it feel?
- How does newly washed hair look? How does it feel?
- How does listen look? How does it feel?
- How does quiet look? How does it feel?
- How does fun look? How does it feel?
- How does yesterday look? How does it feel?
- How does horrible look? How does it feel?
- How does ugly look? How does it feel?
- How does lost look? How does it feel?
- How does painful look? How does it feel?
- How does a heartbeat feel? How does it look?
- How does tickle feel? How does it look?
- How does beginning feel? How does it look?
- How does sleeping feel? How does it look?
- How does the smell of freshly cut grass feel?
- How does the sound of a bell feel?

ᘒ The Treasure Hunt ᘓ

This is an activity for older children. Prepare directions and a map for looking for hidden treasure. The map can be a diagram of areas around the school, but the directions (examples follow) must all be similes or metaphors leading the children to written clues.

1. Found pinned to the side of the green-haired lady. (tree)
2. Found taped to one of the arms of welcome. (door)

3. Found underneath the dependable guardian of litter. (wastebasket)
4. Found taped to the side of the leaves of knowledge. (bookcase)
5. Found pinned to a friend of information. (bulletin board)
6. Found under the corner of the woven earth. (rug)
7. Found on top of sturdy bulldog protecting teacher's belongings. (desk)
8. Found in box next to captured water. (drinking fountain)
9. Found taped to bottom rung of living puzzle. (jungle gym)
10. Found taped next to the piano key of clean darkness. (light switch)

SECTION IV

Academic Learning Activities

CHAPTER 21

Academic Learning for
Right-Hemisphere Processors

TRADITIONAL EDUCATIONAL PROGRAMS are heavily geared toward learning through left-hemisphere processes—as discussed in the opening pages of this book. For most children who are right-handed and who have a left-hemisphere function dominance, such programs work well because they rely heavily on auditory skills and auditory directions. But these traditional programs often neglect children who need visual or kinesthetic input in order to register ideas and directions.

The activities described in this book can benefit left-hemisphere-dominant children (both right- and left-handed) by increasing their motor-skill level and opening up many right-hemisphere processing functions, thus enabling them to perform left-hemisphere tasks with greater depth and with more creativity and original thinking.

These activities are essential, however, for right-hemisphere-oriented children because they need to be helped to use their unique skills in order to function successfully in a left-hemisphere–oriented environment. The activities in Section III, which emphasize overall motor development, coordination, and right-hemisphere processes, will build their self-esteem because they will be more adept at them than left-hemisphere–dominant children. But the traditional work of the classroom will remain difficult for many right-hemisphere-dominant children unless it is presented with aspects of right-hemisphere processes that can bring understanding to them.

Even before they start school, all children develop their own strategies for solving problems, according to their own experience and their own brain -processing dominance. Right-hemisphere processors, however, are often mislabelled as being learning-disabled. In fact, they are merely "people who learn differently." If you remember that as a young child you added by counting on your fingers, you are remembering a right-hemisphere process. Recognizing faces, skillfully arranging the furniture in a room, designing a quilt, creating a garden bench, and turning doodles into funny little pictures—these are all right-hemisphere tasks requiring right-hemisphere processing functions.

Remembering your own experiences with right-hemisphere activities and recalling how their effect lasts with you should make the task of presenting children with right-hemisphere processing experiences much easier.

Sensorimotor Integration

When planning any activity for children, whether they are left-hemisphere or right-hemisphere dominant, be sure you take into account their individual levels of development. Be sure they have had the opportunity to develop the coordination between their sensory and motor systems by experiences such as those described in Section III and a wide variety of other multisensory experiences.

If necessary, go back to basic developmental movement exercises in Chapters 9–15 and even those in Cherry's *Creative Movement for the Developing Child* (1971), which reviews movements that normally developing children gain control of during the first few years of life and that they continue to develop between the ages of 8 and 11.

Strategies for Teaching

The methods described in this section are not meant to replace left-hemisphere teaching methods. Rather, they are meant to provide an insight into the kinds of activities that utilize the full potential of both hemispheres for all children. These methods are especially appropriate, however, for the learning styles of right-hemisphere-dominant children, most of whom have difficulty with auditory teaching methods. We strongly recommend including the following strategies in all teaching activities in order to reach right-hemisphere-dominant children.

1. **Bridging:** relating the activity to something that the child has already had experience with at home or elsewhere.
2. **Focusing:** introducing the reading material or activity by discussing what it is about, what will be done, and what the results will be. This may include studying the illustrations, reading the last page or paragraph, and previewing the lessons from a number of viewpoints.
3. **Using visual aids:** using the actual object or drawings, sketches, diagrams, charts, photographs, or other types of illustrations or replicas of the object to be read about, or discussed.
4. **Vocabulary building:** talking about short incidents and using some of the new or difficult vocabulary words to be found in the lesson.
5. **Tactual experiences:** providing opportunities for touching items and using materials related to the concept being taught.
6. **Real-life application:** providing a tie between the concept and real-life experiences.
7. **Imaging and Visualization:** guiding students in visualizing a condition, situation, or person that is part of the coming lesson; guiding students in imagining or fantasizing a scene, condition, or situation in which they are either the observer or the central player.
8. **Origination:** inspiring and motivating students to originate new uses, ideas, methods, or conditions related to the central topic.
9. **Soliciting feedback:** questioning, responding, or reinforcing any of the processes mentioned with individual feedback.
10. **Reviewing:** providing feedback and a summation of these processes.
11. **Transference:** when they are ready, assist children in transferring learned concepts to linear problems.

Methodology

The methodology used should be experiential, functional, and manipulative. Use concrete materials as often as possible instead of ditto sheets and workbook papers. Giving children concrete tasks with things they can touch, pick up, and move feeds into their tactile system and thus reinforces sensorimotor input.

Allow enough time for children to explore tasks at their own pace. Remember that right-hemisphere–dominant children do not process time well. They accomplish more when allowed to create their own time-space.

Tasks should be inquiry-based, so each child can pursue learning the concept being presented at his or her own pace.

This methodology is responsive to the inner world of the individual. As Clare Cherry has written (1976, pg. x), "The experience comes first with its accompanying sensations and reactions. Self-evaluation and struggle for understanding come next. Evaluation with and clarification by the help of others follow."

Reference

Cherry, Clare. 1976. *Creative Play for the Developing Child*. Belmont, CA: Fearon/David S. Lake.

CHAPTER 22

Mathematics for Right-Hemisphere Processors

MANY OF US, and many of today's schoolchildren, have had negative experiences with mathematics, resulting in a mental block that inhibits even simple calculations. Finding a way to prevent this block for young children, especially those who are right-hemisphere dominant, is a challenge. Right-hemisphere processing functions, with all the intrinsic motivation inherent in that hemisphere, may be just such a way.

The following activities are by no means meant to become your program for mathematics. Rather, they are presented to give you an idea of how to adapt other programs and of the kinds of things to look for in new programs in order to reach the strongly right-hemisphere-dominant child.

Manipulation and Touch

Learning experiences that involve manipulation are beneficial to all students. But they are especially appropriate for those who have difficulty learning in a linear, two-dimensional way. Through physical exploration of the environment—science and cooking projects, block building, the pouring of liquids, and games that require the physical arrangement of sets by counting, measuring, sorting, and classifying— right-hemisphere people can develop their own symbol systems that will help them to more easily comprehend such concepts as quantity, size, dimension, volume, and direction. These concepts will later become formalized as algebra, geometry, trigonometry, calculus, and statistics.

Spatial Awareness

The understanding of mathematical concepts has its beginnings in the extensive exploration of space and of the items within that space as accomplished in the activities in Chapter 12. These types of activities are of a developmental nature for preschool children, who are at a stage when they learn best through right-hemisphere activities. But these activities are also valid for primary-grade children who are having difficulty in understanding mathematical concepts due to strong right-hemisphere dominance. These children develop spatial concepts more easily than children with strong left-hemisphere dominance. Thus, strategies should be developed to use the three-dimensional space, shapes, and the space within shapes as much as possible in teaching other mathematical concepts, rather than depending solely on ditto sheets and workbook pages.

Following are ideas for teaching activities about shapes.

BRIDGING:

- Ask what the shape reminds them of.
- Point out similarities to the children that you recognize.
- Find similar shapes in the classroom or on a walk.
- Ask children to look for similar shapes at home. Bring small items from home for a shape display.
- Have children "walk" the shape.
- Have children lie on the floor and work together to create the shape.

FOCUSING:

- Discuss the coming lesson and tell what shapes are involved.
- Create a vocabulary list of words about the shapes under discussion.
- Tell what shapes the lesson will be about.
- Tell what you expect the children to learn from the lesson.
- Tell how you will know whether or not they have learned it.

USING VISUAL AIDS:

- Create a bulletin board display with the shapes children are studying.
- Have children prepare and post materials.

- Have children go through magazines to find items of the same shapes as those they are studying.
- Build three-dimensional forms of the shape, using rolled newspaper wands (see p. 261), toothpicks, ice cream sticks, tongue depressors, or other items.
- Make a shape book, with one page for each shape on which children glue or paste cutouts, pictures, or their own drawings of the shape.
- Use a paper cutout of a shape children are studying as background for a painting.

VOCABULARY BUILDING:

- In the shape booklet, paste a cutout of the printed word that names the shape on each page.
- Label objects in the classroom with the name of their shape; for example, label a wall clock "Circle," a bulletin board "Rectangle," a box "Square," and a picture of a face "Oval."
- Label the shapes on the bulletin board.

TACTUAL EXPERIENCES:

- Touch objects of specific shapes while blindfolded. Guess shape.
- Create shapes out of clay.
- Form shapes in wet sand.

IMAGING:

- Refer to pages 174–75 for shape experiences in imagery.
- Make up imaginary stories involving a shape. Either have the children take on that shape in their fantasy, or tell a story in which they are totally involved with that shape.

VISUALIZATION:

- Refer again to pages 172–76 for shape experiences.
- Have children close their eyes and visualize the shape.
- Have them keep their eyes closed as they outline the shape.
- Have them visualize other things that you suggest that have the same shape.

ORIGINATION:

- Make people out of an assortment of cut-out shapes.
- Make houses the same way.
- Create the furniture for the houses out of cut-out shapes.
- Create a poem about each shape.
- Create a play about shapes.

SOLICITING FEEDBACK:

- Discuss with children individually what they know about shapes.
- Have each child tell the class about one particular shape.

REVIEWING:

- Review for class all of the steps that have been taken in studying a shape or a series of shapes.
- Present a shape exhibit.

Although the right-hemisphere activities for teaching shapes have been presented in a particular order here, that order is not as important as the inclusion of these activities in your lesson plans. The emphasis must be on the tactual and experiential aspects of the material being taught, because right-hemisphere processors develop their conceptual understandings through these methods.

VARIATION:

Adapt the suggestions for teaching shapes to a lesson about lines—straight, curved, and parallel lines and right angles. More experienced students might study acute angles and the angles of intersections.

Some questions for students to discuss and explore might include the following:

- Where are the lines found?
- How are they used in real life?
- How can they be used in creating designs?
- How can they be used in designing buildings? Toys? Clothing?

Introduce simple geometry at this point.

Sorting and Classifying

Bridging: Discuss items in real life that need to be sorted. How does your mother or father know which clothes to wash? When you go to the beach or on a trip, how do you decide what to take with you? When your mother or father brings groceries home, are they all put in the refrigerator? Why not?

Focusing: Explain the Sorting and Classifying Game (directions follow) so the children know what to expect.

Using visual aids: Take photos with an instant camera of some of the sortings.

Vocabulary building: List the objects being sorted. As various concepts are introduced, add them to the list.

Tactual experiences: The Sorting and Classifying Game is a tactual experience.

Imaging: Create an imagery game involving sorting. For example, the children can imagine they are being sorted by the color of their hair or eyes.

Visualization: With each new type of sorting, have the children close their eyes and get a visual picture of what has happened.

Origination: Give each child an egg carton. Provide a variety of small collage objects to be sorted and placed into the egg carton cups according to category. Have each child select one of each object to glue onto an individual collage.

Soliciting feedback: When all the sorting activities are well under way, start soliciting feedback. Repeat as activities become more complex.

Reviewing: Periodically review for the children everything that has been done so far in the sorting project activities.

Sorting and Classifying Game

MATERIALS:

2 pieces of clothesline rope or string cut into 8-foot lengths
1 chart for recording results of game

ACTIVITY:

1. Place ropes in circular forms on floor.
2. Have everyone take off their shoes and place them in one area.
3. Have children sort the shoes in each of the following ways, one way at a time:
   - those that tie and those that don't tie
   - those that have words on the outside and those that don't have words on the outside
   - those that are one color and those that are two or more colors
   - those that tie and are only one color and those that tie and are more than one color (make a third circle for those that do not meet these criteria)
4. Count the number of shoes in each instance. Show the numbers on a simple chart.

VARIATIONS:

1. Sort shoes according to those that tie and those that have Velcro. Arrange the two circles so that there is an overlapping area for shoes that have both attributes.
2. Play similar sorting games with blocks, Legos, nails, screws, lunch pails, stones and leaves collected on outdoor walks, and other items.
3. Replace the large circles used by the whole class with individual small circles at each child's table or desk.
4. Sort by two, and later three, attributes (such as color, shape, size).

Measurement

Bridging: Discuss what types of things in the children's experience need to be measured, such as height, weight, shoe size, and gallons of gasoline their parents buy at the service station for the family car.

Focusing: Explain the following lesson, describing what will be done, what you hope they will learn, and how you will know if they learned it.

Visual aids: Prepare a display table of all kinds of measuring tools. Have the children cut out pictures from magazines of things that need to be measured. Take instant photographs of some of the measuring activities. Create charts and graphs of measuring activities.

Tactual experience: The measuring activities are tactual experiences.

Imaging: Create a fantasy in which the children are measuring the world.

Visualization: Visualize the difference between various measurements.

Origination: Included in the description of measuring activities.

Soliciting feedback: Ask questions about feelings experienced. Ask questions about specific parts of the activities.

Reviewing: Summarize what the class has done regarding measurements.

Transference: Give simple equations, such as 1 foot plus 1 foot equals how many feet? Teach simple measurement equivalencies, such as 3 feet equals one yard.

Measurement Activities

1. Give students each a piece of 8½″ × 11″ paper. Have them measure the paper with a variety of items. For example, how many dominoes will fit across the paper the short way? How many fit the

long way? Other items that can be used for measuring are small rubber erasers, blackboard erasers, chalk, new crayons, paper clips, bottle caps, and finger widths.

2. As children become more aware of measurements, have them measure the room with various items.
   - Count how many bricks go along the length of a brick wall.
   - Count how many floor tiles go across the room.
   - How many 12-inch ruler lengths go across the room?
   - How many yardstick lengths go across the room?
   - How many shoe lengths go across the room?
   - Measure with other items the children think of, such as lunch pails, construction paper, books, chairs, or people lying prone on the floor.
   - Finally, measure with a measuring tape. Record the results in the notebook.
3. Create a model of the room with blocks, supplemented by pictures that the children draw.
4. Create a two-dimensional map of the room.

Practical Uses of Numbers

Develop appropriate experiential teaching strategies (as described in Chapter 21) for the following activities.

Numbers in Daily Life

1. Give the children each a notebook in which to record their counts of items such as the following:
   - supplies and equipment, such as chairs, desks, scissors, and boxes of crayons
   - people in the room
   - noses, hands, and fingers in the room
2. Have the class make a chart with each child's age, height, and weight.

3. Have the class write daily data, such as
   - the temperature (you might use an indoor-outdoor thermometer),
   - the date, and
   - the daily schedule (mark actual times next to projected times).

⟟ Food Prices ⟐

Bring in the food advertisements from the newspaper. Have the children look for one item in each of the advertisements. Compare the prices. Repeat for other items.

Make a list of items with the best prices, and have the children take the list home. Send a note along suggesting that some of the items be purchased so that the children can realize the usefulness of knowing numbers for comparison shopping.

⟟ Games ⟐

1. Play card games and other kinds of games that require recognizing numbers.
2. Show the children how to keep score.
3. Play dominoes. Have the children make their own dominoes on cardboard, which you have cut in an appropriate size.
4. Make single dominoes (only one number represented). Let children use them to figure out mathematical equations.
5. Play bingo games.
6. Play other games in which children can keep score.

Visual Aids for Numbers

Develop appropriate experiential teaching strategies (as described in Chapter 21) for the following activities.

Number Art

Have children select one number, and then make a design with it following these steps.

1. Make the number very large on a piece of 9" x 12" paper.
2. Make the same number again, crisscrossing the first number.
3. Fill in some of the empty spaces with the same number, either alone or overlapping another drawing of the same number.
4. Use crayons, watercolors, or felt-tip markers to color in the design.

Repeat these steps for the other numbers between 1 and 9 until each child has a paper for each number. Assemble each child's number designs into a number book.

VARIATIONS:

1. Use several different numbers in one design.
2. Photocopy one design by each child.
3. Have the children find and cut out one or two intact numbers from their design.

The Number People

Divide the class into nine groups. Assign each group a number. Have each group make enough foot-high drawings of its number for each member to wear. The children will pin the numbers onto themselves and wear them for the morning.

Refer to the children by their number as often as possible. Make up reasons to call on them. Repeat this activity for two weeks so each child has an opportunity to be each number.

VARIATIONS:

1. "Numbers" can arrange themselves in sequence, equations, or other ways in keeping with their classroom activities.
2. Play a "freeze" game, having the children move around the room to music until you say "freeze." Everyone freezes into position.

Then each child pairs up with the closest child. What do they add up to?

Repeat with groups of three, and then four, up to whatever limit your group can handle.

Charts and Graphs

Develop appropriate experiential teaching strategies (as described in Chapter 21) for the following activity.

MATERIALS:

A variety of graph paper with small, medium, and large squares
Poster board
T-squares for long lines
Transparent plastic rulers
Books with different types of graphs and charts (bar graphs are the easiest type for children to comprehend)

ACTIVITY:

Divide class into 10 groups. Assign each group to create one of the following graphs or charts:

1. Daily and hourly temperatures
2. Everyone's height and weight
3. Length of everyone's feet
4. Typical daily schedule of classroom activities
5. Kinds of food children bring for lunch (or what they had for breakfast at home)
6. Television programs watched at home
7. Number of pages read in half an hour
8. Number of children in class each day
9. Number of days of attendance so far
10. Number of weekends since the beginning of school

Have children create their own ideas of things to graph.

Cooking and Baking

Cooking projects are an excellent means of helping children apply principles of measurements to real-life experiences. Use recipes that yield individual servings, so each child can go through the total process. Many principles of science and good nutrition can also be coupled with cooking and baking.

Develop appropriate experiential teaching strategies (as described in Chapter 21) for cooking and baking activities. The following are general guidelines for classroom cooking projects.

1. Divide the recipe into amounts for individual servings. Thus, if a recipe yields 12 biscuits, divide each ingredient amount by 12.
2. Create cards for each ingredient to show the amount needed for a single serving. For children who cannot read yet, use drawings.
3. Place the ingredients in the order they will be used, with the appropriate card behind each one. Some teachers make little holders for each ingredient card.
4. Have each child create the recipe and then record it in his or her recipe book.

   VARIATIONS:

1. Older children can record the full-size recipe in their books by multiplying the individual-serving amounts by the number of servings.

PHOTO 22.1. COOKING IN THE CLASSROOM

2. Each child can create two or three dishes.
3. Set up a "store" so children from other classes can purchase the foods your class creates. This mock store lends itself to practicing a variety of mathematical concepts.

An Experiential Lesson in Basic Arithmetic

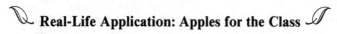

Real-Life Application: Apples for the Class

Children will more fully internalize basic mathematical concepts if they can use them immediately in real-life situations.

The following activity requires money to buy apples and a nearby store where apples can be bought. Because this may not be available for many schools, the teacher can supply a box of graham crackers to distribute and divide in place of the apples. A mock grocery store could be set up for "purchase" of the graham crackers. Another alternative is for each child to bring an apple from home to contribute to a supply for a mock market. Or several parents may each be willing to contribute a pound of apples. Whether done with apples, crackers, or some other food item, the value of the activity is in the planning, the counting of actual pennies, and the distribution of equal amounts of the food to each child.

PLANNING TO BUY APPLES FOR THE CLASS

1. Discuss trips to stores children have made with their parents.
2. Discuss the possibility of walking to a nearby store (if there is one) to purchase apples for everyone in the room.
3. How many apples will be needed?
4. How much do apples cost?
5. Bring one pound of apples to class and use them to discuss how many make up a pound.
6. How much money does each person need to buy just one apple? (Have enough pennies on hand to make up the pound cost. Have children divide the pennies until they have "sets" to equal the number of apples in a pound. Then count the pennies in each set.)

If you have more pennies than are needed, how much change will there be? (Again, figure this out by actual penny count.)
7. How many apples fit into a bag?
8. How many bags will be needed?
9. How much space on a shelf will be needed to store the apples until they are used? (Mark the space one bag takes. Add equal spaces for each bag.)

PLANNING HOW TO SERVE THE APPLES

1. Have a class discussion to decide whether to cut the apples in halves.
2. Plasticine can be formed into spheres to simulate apples. These can be halved, and, for children who are more mature, they can be quartered.
   - How many pieces will each person have if each quarter is cut in half?
   - How many pieces will there be if two persons put their apples together? (Count the pieces of Plasticine.)
3. There are four knives. How many apples can we cut at the same time? Explain why.

Continue similar activities according to the ages and skills of the children in the class.

PURCHASING THE APPLES

Armed with the information they have gleaned from the planning activities, the children next make an excursion to a market, if there is one nearby.

1. Give each child a share of the total money needed, counting as it is given.
2. Put all shares together in one coin purse, counting each contribution.
3. Record all contributions on a chart that lists the name of each child.
4. Make the excursion, with everyone helping to select the best apples, a package of paper plates, and a package of napkins. One previously selected child obtains a grocery basket. Another pre-

viously selected child wheels the basket to the checkout counter. A third previously selected child gives the money and accepts the change, if any. Previously selected children carry the purchases to the school, and others carry the bags into the school building. Still others can carry the bags into the classrooms.

SERVING AND EATING THE APPLES

1. How many paper plates will be needed?
2. How many napkins will be needed?
3. Why do we need the same number of napkins as we have plates?
4. How long did it take to eat the apples? We started eating the apples at _____ o'clock. We were all finished at _____ o'clock. We can count the minute marks to see how long it took to eat the apples.

Transference from Apples to Basic Math

One experience with apples will not by itself teach the concepts involved. But many such experiences with concrete objects will help the children internalize those concepts. Several of the steps in any of the activities should be repeated.

To begin transferring the concept of fractions, you might begin with a folding exercise:

1. Give each child a sheet of paper to fold in half. How many halves are there? Ask them to color one half only.
2. Fold the paper again the opposite way. How many sections will there be? Open the paper and count. There should be four equal sections. Color one-fourth of the paper.
3. Cut the sections into four parts.

Slowly begin to transfer the concepts about fractions to two dimensions with the following steps:

1. Draw a picture of a circle.
2. Use a ruler to divide it in two equal halves.

3. Use a ruler to divide it in quarters.
4. Show how to write the fractions ½ and ¼.
5. Add ½ and ½ together. Discuss the answer.
6. Add ¼ and ¼ together. Discuss the answer.

WORD PROBLEMS

Tell a story about going to the store to buy apples. You need apples for 20 children. You know that eight apples fit into a bag. How many bags do you need?

1. Have children close their eyes and visualize the 20 children.
2. Have them keep their eyes closed and see a bag with eight apples in it. Is that enough for 20 children? Have them visualize a second bag. Is that enough? Now add a third bag. Is that enough?
3. Have them draw eight apples in a row. These are the apples from one bag. Draw another row of eight apples for the second bag. Draw another row for the third bag. Count all of the apples. Discuss the results.

ARITHMETIC

Because these children have already had the concrete experiences with the apples, this project is within the realm of their understanding.

1. Addition: Add 8 + 8. (If they are having difficulty, tell them to close their eyes again and see two bags of apples. How many apples are there in each bag? How many in two bags?)
2. Addition: Add 16 + 8. First add 8 and 6. What happens to the 1 in the answer?
3. Subtraction: You only need 20 apples. Subtract 20 from 24. How many apples are left over? (Have children close their eyes and see 4 apples.)

Continue interweaving concrete experiences and simple equations, according to the age of the children. These experiences supplement the traditional curriculum. For those who are having difficulty understanding the traditional curriculum, these types of activities can help.

Note, too, that for children having difficulty with arithmetic, the number of problems on one page should be limited to four; a greater number appears to be too formidable.

Other Experiential Mathematics Projects

1. Learn to use the abacus for calculations.
2. Make scale drawings using graph paper.
3. Use contrasting colored chalk in setting up arithmetic problems on the blackboard—for example, use one color for the dividend, another for the divisor, a third for the answer, and perhaps a fourth for the remainder. Children can copy problems using color codes to help them follow each step.
4. Use graph paper with quarter-inch squares to learn how to write arithmetic problems with numbers in appropriate columns.
5. Learn to make scale drawings by measuring the actual size of an object.
6. Use sets of small objects, such as some of the smaller ones used in the sorting activity (Variation 2, pg. 284), and arrange them in groups of ten to add to 100 and to learn subtraction.
7. Count the number of pieces in a box of dry cereal. How many boxes will make 1,000 pieces? 10,000 pieces? 100,000? 1,000,000? Select a cereal whose piece size is appropriate for the skill level and age of the class.
8. Learn roman numerals by making designs with them.
9. Use arithmetic board games and lotto games.
10. Use real wind-up clocks to learn to tell time.
11. Make posters, measuring spaces needed for each letter and each word.

CHAPTER 23

Language Arts for
Right-Hemisphere Processors

SINCE LANGUAGE is definitely the province of the left brain hemisphere, many right-hemisphere–dominant children have difficulty learning to read and subsequently with other written language arts. Too often children are penalized throughout school because they are slow readers. The secret for success for these children is to capitalize on the knowledge that everyone has a unique way of learning. Through your observations and careful analysis, try to find which way fits each child best. The assessments in Chapter 6 and 7 can be of some help.

Introducing Reading

The following system of introducing reading to children has been used successfully by one of the authors for many years. It is a pre-phonics method and draws on the ability of the right-hemisphere–dominant person to recognize shapes and forms. The problem lies in relating those shapes and forms to something that is meaningful and that can be utilized in a purposeful way.

The concepts being taught are (1) that every letter symbolizes a sound and (2) that words are made of sounds put together. Right-hemisphere–dominant people are weak in areas of sound differences, have a poor memory for phonetic sounds, and have difficulty memorizing letter names. Because they also have poor sequencing skills, putting sounds together is also a difficult task for them.

The goal of this activity is to help children internalize the sounds of each letter so that they can recognize letters as readily as they recognize colors or shapes, in which they are usually very skilled.

How to Make a Word

MATERIALS:

Six different cut-out alphabets, both lower and upper case, in a variety of sizes from half an inch to 3 inches and in a variety of materials, such as sandpaper mounted on cardboard, styrofoam (if not too large), and varicolored felt. The important thing is that the alphabets be different in size and thickness, and have some tactile quality if possible. Smooth letters can be roughened up with a metal file, with glue coverings, or with sand glued on, for example. Capital and lower-case letters are mixed indiscriminately and used in no particular order.

Newspapers and magazines

Colored marking pens with fine points

Writing tablet

ACTIVITY:

1. Select the letters *C, L, A, P* and *c, l, a, p* from the alphabets and mix them together. Spread them out on a flat surface. (You can start with any simple word that is meaningful to young children.)
2. Explain to the child that each of these letters has its own sound. Tell the *sound* for each. Don't say the name of the letter, and don't lengthen the sound with "uh." For example, pick up a *c* and say, "This is a /k/." Make only the first sound in the word *clap*; don't say "cee" (or "kay") or "cuh." In the same way, pick up the letters *l, a,* and *p*. Make only the sounds of the letters: /l/ (not "ell"), /a/ (not "ay" or "ah"), and /p/ (the sound of air being forced through the lips, not "pee" or "puh").
3. Work on one letter at a time. From the pile, select a *c* and say "This is a /k/." Repeat ten times (or more, if necessary). Put the letters back in the pile.
4. Say to the child, "Give me a /k/." Repeat ten times (or more, if necessary).
5. Repeat 3 and 4 for each of the other letters. When the wrong letter is given to you—for example, an *a* instead of a *p*—ask for that

letter next. This is a self-correcting strategy. Usually the child will realize the mistake and correct it.

Repeat until the child has no hesitation in handing you the letter asked for, just as though you had said instead, "Give me the red crayon."

6. Have the child ask you for the letters.

7. Have the child circle all the *c*'s in one advertisement in the newspaper. Then have the child circle each of the other three letters, using a different colored marker for each.

8. Place the letters of the word you have selected in a sack and have the child find by touch the ones you ask for. Say, "Find me a /k/; find me an /l/" and so on until all the letters are out of the sack.

9. Have the child write each letter on the note pad.

10. Outline large versions of your letters for the child to cut out.

11. Repeat all the steps above for two 20-minute periods every day for seven days. You'll need considerable innovation to keep the game going with interest. Change your location. Change the kinds of written material on which the child searches for letters. Change the pens to pencils or ink pens. Never correct the child for an error.

12. *Reading day.* Show the child that if you put a *c* and an *l* and an *a* and a *p* in that order, it makes a word: *clap.* Say, "That is how we make words."

13. *Second week.* Teach /b/ (not "bee" or "buh"), /e/ (short *e* as in *net*, not "ee"), /m/ (not "em" or "muh"), /s/ (not "ess"), and /t/ (not "tee" or "tuh"). In other words, be sure you are teaching just the sound the letter makes in a word, not the name of the letter or the letter plus "uh."

Review the four letters from the first week. Combine them with this week's letters to make new words, such as *bat, bet, cat, cap, lap, mat, pat, best, last, past.*

By now the child should understand the principle that letters stand for sounds, and that sounds together make words. If the child does not, go back to Step 1 and start over. There is no use proceeding unless the concept is learned. It may take three weeks to establish the foundation that we have outlined for the first week.

14. *The next week.* Once the child understands that letters stand for sounds, introduce the rest of the sounds in the alphabet, two or three a day: /ā/ (long *a*), /s/ (represented by *s* and sometimes *c*), /d/, /ē/ (long *e* and also sometimes represented by *y*),/f/, /g/ (hard *g* as in *get*), /h/, /i/ (short *i*), /ī/ (long *i*), /j/ (both *j* and soft *g*), /k/ (represented by both *k* and *q*), /n/, /o/ (short *o*), /ō/ (long *o*), /r/, /u/ (short *u*), /ū/ (long *u*), /v/, /w/, /x/, /y/ (as in *year*), and /z/.

Play "Give me a ____" and "Find a ____" until no errors are made. Continue other activities with the individual sounds, such as marking the letters in advertisements, writing letters, and cutting them out.

15. Practice singing the alphabet song using the sounds rather than the names of the letters.

Flash Cards for Learning Words

Because right-hemisphere–dominant people respond readily to the gestalt of a thing—its wholeness—you can capitalize on that skill by using flash cards. Those who simply cannot learn to make words from letters by the method described above may learn more readily by memorizing the outline of entire words with flash cards. We have known excellent readers who learned only by the "sight" method, and though they did not start syllabifying until the third grade, they did excellent work in reading and spelling through memory. Following are some suggestions for helping right-hemisphere children learn to read through the flash card system of recognizing complete words rather than the components that make up those words.

✎ Outline Flash Cards ✒

MATERIALS:

Blank 3″ × 5″ file cards   File box
Felt-tip markers

ACTIVITY:

When a child learns a word, write in on a flash card. The letters should be very definite; you might even use a different color for each letter. Then outline the word so that its overall shape is evident. When using capitals, the outline is more difficult, but it is helpful to learn words in both capital and lower-case letters. For example, with *CLAP* the outline goes straight around the word except for an indentation between the *L* and the *A*. Place each new word in the file box.

Experience Flash Cards

Children are motivated to read words that are meaningful to them. Following are some ways to build each child's file of flash cards with personally meaningful words.

MATERIALS:

Blank 3″ × 5″ file cards
File box
Alphabetical 3″ × 5″ file guides
Felt-tip markers
2″ × 6″ strips of paper for labels

ACTIVITIES:

1. Write each child's favorites—such as foods, toys, colors—and names of family members on flash cards and add them to the child's file box.
2. Label objects in the classroom—such as door, window, drawer, bookcase, book, blackboard, chair, desk, chalk tray, floor, wastebasket, and paper—using upper- and lower-case letters. Add these words to each child's file box.
3. Make flash cards from each child's own stories about favorite or special events with family or at school, such as neighborhood walks, field trips, art projects, class parties, learning new games or songs, hearing a story, or playing with a friend.

    Begin by having the child draw a picture of the activity or one aspect of it. Then discuss the activity. Ask the child to close his or her eyes and try to visualize it, try to relive it. Ask how it felt to be doing the activity. Would it be good to repeat it? Why? What was the best thing about it? The worst thing?

Then have the child dictate a story about the drawing. Read the story back to the child. Make a flash card for each word in the story. Have the child file each word according to its first letter.

From time to time, take all the flash cards out of the box and have the child practice reading them.

VARIATIONS:

1. Have the child dictate a label for the drawing (when able to do so, the child can make the label). Labels can be extended, when the child is ready, to two sentences and then to a story with a beginning, a middle, and an end.
2. Each child can use the words in his or her file to write stories about new experiences and add new words to the file box as necessary.
3. Make the stories into booklets that others can read, thus giving additional meaning to the concept of reading in relation to writing and actual experience.

Rhyming Flash Cards

This activity is particularly useful for right-hemisphere–dominant children because they often have difficulty hearing rhyming sounds.

MATERIALS:

Blank 3″ × 5″ cards
Child's collection of flash cards
Felt-tip markers

ACTIVITY:

For each word in the file box, make another card with a word that rhymes, such as *book-cook, my-why, ball-fall, dad-sad.* Thus the child now has twice the number of useable words. The child should practice these words aloud frequently.

These words can be used in writing short poems.

1. Make flash cards for opposites of the words in the child's file box, such as *dad-mom, sad-happy*.
2. Words can also be added to the file box by making plurals of the words in it, such as *book-books, ball-balls*.

Reading Poetry

Right-hemisphere children often have difficulty in sequencing and in establishing complex rhythms. They respond well to basic rhythmic beats, such as in rapping (see pg. 240). Their reading is often jerky and halting. One way to help establish reading more rhythmically is to read rhythmic poetry. The Dr. Seuss rhyming books—such as *Cat in the Hat* for beginners and *One Fish, Two Fish, Red Fish, Blue Fish* and *If I Ran the Zoo* for older children—are excellent for this type of activity.

The following steps are useful:

1. Read the poem or story aloud, exaggerating the sing-song nature of the rhymes.
2. Read it again, leaving the last rhyming word of each verse blank. Have children fill in the word, either individually or in unison.
3. Read the poem again, this time having children fill in phrases, such as the last line of a verse, rather than individual words. Encourage them to continue in the same sing-song manner you have been demonstrating.
4. Repeat the same poems several days in a row, until the rhythm is well established.
5. Go on to another poem or story.

VARIATIONS:

1. Tape-record children when it is their turn to read. Having them listen to their rhythm pattern (or lack of it) sometimes helps to improve it.
2. Tape record yourself reading the poem in a very rhythmic manner. Have individual children listen to the tape and read along with it.

Phrase Reading

In order to improve sequencing skills, be sure to do activities such as those in Chapter 18. Because of their difficulty in sequencing, right-hemisphere children may learn to read words, but cannot put them together in sequential order with ease. They can be helped to do so by learning to do phrase reading.

ACTIVITIES:

1. Make a vertical list of the words on their flash cards. Long words can be written on two or more lines so that only four or five letters are on one line. Children should practice reading these vertical lists so that they become accustomed to reading "at a glance."
2. Making lists of numbers is also good practice. Start out with a list of four numbers. Increase to five, then six, and finally seven. Children read these without shifting eyes horizontally, only vertically.
3. When children acquire facility with the lists of single words and numbers, start making lists of two-word phrases, such as *and then, pretty soon, too bad, good thing, one time, so that, run fast,* and *eat lunch.*
4. When they achieve facility with two-word phrases, increase to three-word phrases, such as *in the morning, do it again, come back later, help me out, close the door, go this way, pick it up,* and *put it down.*
5. Transfer the phrase reading to books. Mark sentences into phrases, for example, "The cat/wanted to/get back/into the house./ Mrs. Jones/didn't want/ to let/the cat/ come in." Soon the phrases can be expanded: "The cat/ wanted to get/ back into the house./ Mrs. Jones/didn't want to let/ the cat come in."

VARIATIONS:

1. Practice the same kind of reading aloud using simple nursery tales. The children's familiarity with the plot and the characters can put them at ease so they can be relaxed in their reading and concentrate on adopting a rhythmic flow.

2. Have the children read limericks aloud. Because of their unique rhythm-rhyme pattern, they are beneficial in establishing a rhythm to reading out loud. Limericks are usually humorous, thus much appreciated by right-hemisphere children. Many good limerick books are available, but children especially like the work of Edward Lear, because of its humor.

Audio-Visual Aids

When introducing a new story or other reading matter, have as many supplementary audio-visual aids on hand as possible. These can include

pictures and photographs,	charts,
slides,	demonstrations,
movies,	models, and
videotapes,	puppets.
recordings,	

After a new topic has been introduced, ask the children to bring in additional visual aids to supplement those you have supplied.

Functional Reading

Rote reading is a waste of time for right-hemisphere children. Keying in to their special ways of processing thoughts can make reading a meaningful experience, put them at greater ease so that the reading requires a minimum of tension, and prevent total failure because they already know generally what the reading is about.

Right-hemisphere–dominant children want things to be functional. They need to be able to relate reading material to other types of experiences, such as previously heard stories or some type of real-life function. Reading, for them, needs to be something they can manipulate, even if the manipulation is just in their minds. Bridging and focusing (see pg. 277) are functional approaches.

Bridging Strategies

Relating a forthcoming story or other reading material to functions that the children are already familiar with leads to increased interest and comprehension. For example, if the story the child is going to read is about some lost person or animal, discuss with the children the concept of being lost. What about things that are lost? Were any of them ever "lost"? How do people feel when they lose something? If the story is about a family, talk about different kinds of families. Talk about single-parent families, about step-families and stepparents, about grandparents, and about other relatives that help make up an extended family. If the story is about something that happened in a school, talk about other schools. Why do we have schools? Does everyone go to school? How do people feel about going to school?

Focusing Strategies

Familiarity with a story makes it easier to read. Before the children start to read a new story, talk about the following aspects of it as a means of focusing.

1. **Picture interpretation:**
   a. What illustrations are used for the story?
   b. Who are the people in the pictures? How do you think they walk? (Have the children demonstrate.) How do you think they talk? (Have the children demonstrate.) What kind of house do they live in? (Have the children close their eyes and visualize the kinds of houses that might be in the story.)
   c. Is there anything in the pictures that tells us what the story is about?
   d. What kind of day is it? What is the weather like? What time is it?
2. **Visualization:** Have the children close their eyes and imagine themselves in one of the illustrations.
3. **Summary:** Give the main idea of the story, summarize the plot, and then have the children give you feedback on what the story is about.
4. **Skimming:** Skim through the story with the children, reading some of the key sentences.

5. **Vocabulary:**
   a. Make a list of a few key words in the story. Don't list every new word—just a few important ones that will help key the children to the plot.
   b. Spell each key word out loud. Have the class spell them with you.
   c. Have the children close their eyes and visualize each word after spelling it.
   d. Write the key words on index cards. Play "Give me the _____" by asking children to hand you specific words. Do not correct a child for giving you the wrong card; simply ask for that card next. Most children will self-correct and realize they have just given you the card with that word on it.
6. **Underlining:** Underline the key words in the text.
7. **Previewing:** You might want to read the story out loud first, or just part of it. One successful technique with mystery stories is to read the beginning aloud until it gets to an interesting bit of action and have the children continue from there.
8. **Ending:** Another successful technique is to read the last chapter out loud, thus giving the children a holistic view of where the story is going.
9. **Verifying:** Have the children read the story with the idea of verifying the facts you have already told them about.

Follow-up Activities

1. **New discoveries:** Ask what happened in the story that you forgot to tell them.
2. **Playacting:** If a story has several characters, you can preview it or review it by playacting. As you read the story, have various children act out assigned roles. This technique works especially well with children who appear to have auditory problems. An alternative is to have the children pretend they are on the radio, so they can read the words right out of the book.
3. **Puppets:**
   a. Stick puppets. An easy way to make a puppet is to draw a picture of the character, cut it out, and glue it to an ice cream

stick (see pg. 256). Children hold the puppets in their hands during the show.

b. Finger puppets. Another easy-to-make puppet is the finger puppet. Draw a picture of the character as for a stick puppet, but make it no more than 3 inches high. Glue it on a ¾-inch band of paper that can be slipped over a finger (see Figure 23.1).

c. Hand puppets. Use a cotton sock to devise a hand puppet, decorating it with buttons, bottle caps, sequins, crayons, yarn, and other small objects.

d. Paper bag puppets. There are several books on the market with patterns for making puppets out of paper bags; see, for example, *Bagging It with Puppets,* by Gloria Mehrens and Karen Wick (Fearon Teacher Aids/ David S. Lake Publishers, 1988).

4. **Pantomime:** Play charades. Have various children act out characters that are in the story to be read or already read. Other children guess what characters are being acted out.

5. **Peep shows:** Make a peep show about an episode in the story. (Refer to pgs. 258–59 for instructions on making peep shows.)

6. **Shadow box:** A shadow box depicting a scene in the story can be made by constructing a scene to stand on the narrow rim of a shoe-box lid—with the lid itself forming the background.

7. **Masks:** Create masks representing the various characters in the story.

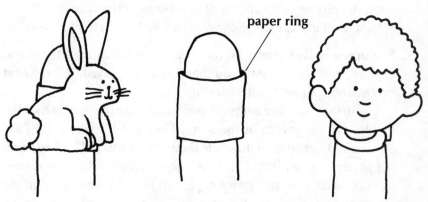

paper ring

FIGURE 23.1. FINGER PUPPET. Glue a face or figure to a paper ring that fits over the finger.

8. **Models:** Provide children with Plasticine from which they can model some of the characters in the story. These can be used for a tabletop display depicting a scene in the story.

9. **Shadow show:** Hang a sheet in a doorway. Have one side (where the actors are) dark with a gooseneck-type lamp shining on the actors, throwing their shadows on the sheet. Cardboard cutouts can be used for props needed to enact the story. A reader tells (or reads) the story while the actors' shadows create the action.

10. **Expanding:** Help children expand the story by asking such questions as

    - What do you think might have happened the next day?
    - What do you think might have happened the next week?
    - What do you think _____ (a character in the story) decided to do next? Tell about it.

    Or make changes in the story by questions such as

    - What if it had rained while all that was happening?
    - What if in the middle of (what was happening) a giant elephant walked into the room?
    - What if everyone in the story became invisible? What do you think would happen then?
    - When the story was almost over, what if an earthquake (or a tornado) happened and all of the buildings started shaking?
    - How would the story be different if it happened in _____ (name a nearby city or some country the class has been studying)?
    - How would you change the story to make it better?

11. **Feelings and Reactions:** To increase understanding of the story, discuss the feelings the various characters displayed. Why? What brings about those kinds of feelings?

    To further increase comprehension, discuss the reaction of the children to the events in the story. How did it make them feel? What did they think about while they were reading? Do they think the person who wrote the story is a good writer? Why or why not?

    Make a chart of the various types of feelings mentioned in the story.

Or make a simple graph titled "Feelings about (title of story)." Use graph paper, with one square representing one person's opinion. Columns can be headed "Liked it very much," "Liked it a little," "Didn't like it very much," "Disliked it very much." Starting from a base line at the bottom, have children fill in squares in whatever column applies to their individual feelings.

Even slow readers who are guided toward the type of functional activities listed above will become interested, avid readers.

Stories of Personal Interest

Basal readers are often boring to right-hemisphere–dominant children who happen to be slow readers and who have had negative experiences in struggling with these readers. These children, like gifted readers, should be allowed much opportunity to select the type of reading material that is most interesting to them or the stories in a particular basal reader that appear to be of interest—as if they were reading a magazine. They should be encouraged to go to the library and select books that are about a subject or type of character especially interesting to them. When allowed to select their own books, they will often do so not only on the basis of interest but also on the basis of illustrations.

They can then be guided toward doing their own "focusing"—tell them to look at the illustrations, read the table of contents, pick out some of the key characters, and even read the last chapter. This type of orientation to the book will help them keep their focus if the reading becomes difficult. By getting an idea ahead of time where the book is going, the reader can approach it from a holistic viewpoint, which is comfortable for right-brain–dominant people, who are then less apt to get off the track of the story when momentarily disrupted by some outside stimuli, such as a question by another person, the sound of a car honking its horn, or even a clock ticking or someone coughing in the room. Many right-brain–dominant people have poor auditory figure-ground discrimination. It is often difficult for them to screen out the unimportant background sounds from foreground sounds, or to screen out all sounds when trying to concentrate on the difficult task (to them) of reading. The reader should be encouraged, if necessary, to again go to the last chapter, or even the next-to-last one, to refocus the entire book.

Writing the Alphabet

During all the time the children are learning to read and spell, they are presumably also learning to write the alphabet. Right-brain-dominant children, because of their preference for the gestalt, can learn best by writing the whole letter rather than by breaking it up into strokes. Traditional manuscript writing (printing), which most children are taught in the primary grades, is very geometrical and depends on putting strokes together to form the whole letter. We prefer D'Nealian lettering for beginning writers (a series of books is available in the *Scott, Foresman D'Nealian Handwriting Program*). The poem in Photo 23.1 (pg. 317) is an example of D'Nealian lettering, written by the kindergarten teacher. This writing is more easily transferable to cursive writing because it uses one continuous line to form each letter. It also allows more leeway in the formation of the letters because they are not geometrically shaped.

Other techniques that can be used to help children "write" include tracing letters, walking the shapes of letters, coloring in the shapes of letters, acting them out in body movement, making collages that follow the shapes of letters (using rice, beans, colored fish-tank gravel, etc.).

One especially interesting technique that utilizes the right-hemisphere function of seeing the whole of an object is the formation of letters from strips of soft, flexible wire. Provide the children with 4-inch-long pieces of wire. (Have several wire cutters on hand to cut shorter pieces as needed.) Have the children form letters out of the wire.

Functional Writing

Reading and writing should be fun. Children should be encouraged to write about the things that interest them. Beginning writers need many opportunities to use their new skill functionally—in more ways than just writing their names and the date on their work and filling in blanks in workbooks. All of their writing tasks should be functional and in some way related to direct experience.

Not only are right-brain–dominant children very imaginative, but they are also skilled at relating things to direct experience. They should be encouraged to write about their families, homes, playthings, friends, trips, relatives, and other subjects with which they have had direct experience.

Bulletin Board Signs

Have the children make the signs for your bulletin boards. Allow them to create the entire bulletin board, with instructions to make signs for them. These signs do not have to be large-lettered, "adult-quality" ones; rather, they should be directly representative of the children's level of skill. Their efforts will improve the quality of their work as they see acceptance of the results of those efforts.

Here are some hints to help your students make signs:

- Provide an alphabet chart for guidelines for whatever method of writing is being taught.
- Provide sentence strips or other appropriate paper with the appropriate media.
- Teach the children to make models first by writing the needed words on a piece of paper and making sure they are spelled correctly.
- If the sign is done in a nonerasable medium, have the children mark out the words with a light pencil first.
- Help them align the letters by drawing extra horizontal lines on the sentence strips.
- Show appreciation for their efforts. Avoid doctoring their work to make it more adult-oriented.

Labels

Just as you have the children make signs for the bulletin board, have them make the labels for objects in the room. This activity can be used to expand their vocabulary.

- Provide an alphabet chart for guidelines for whatever method of writing is being used.
- Provide the needed cardboard strips for the labels, with the appropriate markers for writing.
- Allow the children to decide what should be labelled.

Book Reports with a Structure

As a natural follow-up to their newly acquired reading skills, have beginning writers report on stories that they have heard or read. One common technique is to have children illustrate one aspect or detail of the story and to write about it.

Help them to write at least three sentences so the book report will have a beginning, a middle, and an end. By using this structure in their first simple "picture reports," they will learn the importance of always structuring their writing, whether it be a paragraph or a term paper.

As their skill increases, they can write two sentences for each part, and then a paragraph for each part.

COLOR CODING

Because right-brain–dominant children respond well to color, have the class decide on a color code for the beginning, the middle, and the end. Use these crayon or pencil colors to write under the book report illustrations. Not only does this use of color help the children organize their thoughts, but it also results in a colorful display of completed work. Another bonus is that the colors can be utilized to help explain to parents the process of using the three parts, so that they can help guide their children in future homework assignments when thoughts need to be organized in story form.

For extremely right-brain–dominant children, we suggest this method of color coding for longer paragraph and story writing as well. Allow each child to decide when the extra boost of color coding is no longer needed.

Letter Writing

Another functional method of helping children to use their newly acquired writing skill is correspondence. Letters, too, require a beginning, a middle, and an end. They, too, can be written according to color codes. Here are some ideas for functional letters:

- A letter to parents reporting on a school event
- A letter to parents reporting on a school activity that has taken place, such as a particular lesson, a walk, a new game, an art project, or anything else related to the curriculum or to recess time
- A letter to parents thanking them for preparing their lunch and reporting on how good it was
- A letter to the school principal to thank him or her for some new addition or supplies
- Letters of thanks during gift-giving seasons

℞ Notes ✍

Closely related to letters are personal notes. Encourage children to write notes to one another. Have a class mailbox for depositing notes so that they don't have to be passed surreptitiously during lessons.

℞ News Bulletin ✍

Establish a class newspaper on a bulletin board where items reported by children are posted. These items may include class events, announcements about children's birthdays, or even news events the children may have heard about on radio, television, or in adult discussions. When posting a news item written by a child, show your regard for it by mounting it on a colorful background sheet of paper rather than directly on the bulletin board.

℞ Newspaper and Interviews ✍

Items from the news bulletin can be typed for the children to make a newspaper. This leads them to a new type of writing: interviews. Have selected children interview other teachers and school administrators about subjects of interest to the entire school community. Intersperse these interviews with items about class events, birthdays, other dates of interest, and cartoons made by the classroom artists.

Class Booklets

Put together many class booklets with recordings by all the children about a particular school lesson or event.

Class Diary

Have one child be class secretary for the day and record the events that happened in class that day. Compile all of these daily records into a booklet. Important feedback for the entire class can take place when the diary is reviewed—every time the list of contributors starts over again. The diary will be of special interest to parents and other visitors.

Beginning Creative Writing

One of the important rules for creative writing is to stress ideas, vocabulary, and imagination. Leave spelling lessons for spelling lessons. Many right-brain–dominant children will create wonderfully imaginative stories yet have many misspelled words. Evaluate their papers on the basis of their creative ideas and the development of the story. Ignore the spelling errors. Very often when you give a paper to the author several days later, he or she will be able to find most of the spelling errors and make corrections.

Story Starters

Right-hemisphere–dominant children will use their imaginations to write creative stories, but sometimes they need a "story starter." This could be an incomplete sentence, such as the following:

- It is good to plan for a rainy day. For a rainy day, I will need . . .
- My friend is coming to my house to visit. We will . . .
- If I had to prepare dinner for my family, I would make a list to shop for . . .
- If today were my birthday, I would like . . .

Here is an example by a first grader in response to the unfinished sentence "To go to the beach, you need . . ."

> *. . . a towel, umbrella, sunblock, suntan lotion, and a bathing suit. This summer I hope to have fun and go swimming. I get to play lots of games and tell stories and play house.* (RENEE, age 6)

Older children are often helped by topics suggested as "story starters." Here are some examples:

- a worm's view
- hidden treasure
- being scared
- if I were the Loch Ness monster
- the hyena (or other animal)
- the day everything froze
- lost in the desert (or woods or city)
- the upside-down house
- the lonely tree
- the pig that could talk
- the camera that laughed out loud

My Own Poetry

Writing poetry is an excellent way to increase children's confidence and facility with creative writing. Start out by reading a great deal of poetry out loud to the class (as suggested on pg. 303) and discussing what you have read.

An excellent book is *Wishes, Lies, and Dreams*, by Kenneth Koch. He suggests that "children often need help in starting to feel free and imaginative about a particular theme. Examples give them courage." He suggests first making up poems as a group, with children volunteering lines, which can then be jumbled up and put together in other than the original order. Seeing this done as a class can help children write on their own. Some of the "starter" ideas suggested by Koch are

- I wish (highly recommended for group poems)
- Lies (in which the child writes a lie on each line)
- Colors (in which children write thoughts a particular color brings to mind)
- Comparisons

Other ideas are

- Laughter
- When it's dark at night
- On a sunny day
- At the park

Here is a poem about school by 7-year-old Joshua.

> I see kids working.
> I hear kids talking.
> I smell erasers.
> I taste my lunch.
> I feel tables.
> I know I'm at school.

Here is a poem about books by 7-year-old Jared.

> I like to write books,
> Funny books!
> Scary books!
> Books with a little boo!
> Books with creepy, creepy things within.

Here is a poem about love by Adrian, age 8.

> Love is a pretty day and happy day. Just like Valentine's Day.
> Love is a nice morning.
> Love is a key to two hearts broken.
> Love is a red rose.
> Love is a porcelain heart.
> Love is a person crying.
> Love is like people's hearts going.
> Love is like people trying not to cry.

PHOTO 23.1. CLASS POEM.
This poem was created by a
class of 18 kindergarten
children. Each child
contributed one line. The
teacher used D'Nealian
writing to copy the poem
onto a poster.

Vocabulary-building Exercises and Games

Writing can be practiced through the playing of games such as these.

How Many Words Do I Know?

Children are each given a piece of paper on which, during a given time, they write down as many words as they know.

Rhymes

Children are given one word at a time, and during a given time they write down all the words they can think of that rhyme with the given word.

℘ Opposites ℘

Children are given a list of words, and during a given time they write down the opposite (antonym) of each word. Have children create sentences that incorporate a list of opposites.

℘ Verbs ℘

Give children the following list to complete within a given time. Then have the children use their verbs in another sentence.

A child can _____ .
A baby can _____ .
A cat can _____ .
A dog can _____ .
A horse can _____ .
A ball can _____ .
An airplane can _____ .
A bird can _____ .
I can make a pencil _____ .

℘ Anagrams ℘

Within a given time, have children create new words out of the following words:

- *bent* (be, ten, Ben, net)
- *heat* (he, at, tea, the, hat)
- *under* (red, Ned, run)
- *about* (but, tub, bat, tab)
- *step* (pet, pest)
- *Monday* (day, mad, no, do, Dan, man)
- *friend* (fire, ride, find, fed, Fred, red, Ned, den)

As they become familiar with the technique, use longer words.

🖎 Name Words ✍

Have children write their names vertically and after each letter, write a descriptive word. Here are examples by Charlie and Evan, ages 6½.

E lephant
V ery nice
A nimal
N oisy

C ar
H op
R abbit
A round
L ove Mom
I love
the E nd

Class Books

Writings by children should be collected and saved for class books. Jennifer, a second-grade teacher, has her students reprint their poetry on sheets of colored paper. They make book covers by selecting a sheet of paper from a wallpaper sample book. These are pasted onto cardboard covers and laminated. The inside pages are either stapled or fastened with paper fasteners. The first and last pages are taped to the inside of the cover, which keeps the book sturdy through repeated handlings.

Reference

Koch, Kenneth, et al. 1980. *Wishes, Lies, and Dreams: Teaching Children to Write Poetry*. New York: Harper & Row.

CHAPTER 24

Science for Right-Hemisphere Processors

RIGHT-HEMISPHERE-DOMINANT CHILDREN generally are interested in all the possibilities of a situation. Thus, given the motivation and an environment that allows them to explore freely, they frequently do well in scientific exploration, though they may be weak in reporting exactly what they have done or how they have done it.

But if the strategies of involvement listed in Chapter 21 are used, the study of science can provide many opportunities for right-hemisphere-dominant children to excel. It is important that you match your teaching strategies to their unique styles of learning. You can capitalize on their curiosity, which is motivation from within and which has its origins in the right hemisphere. By demonstrating curiosity, you can provide a model that the children will naturally copy. Such statements as "I wonder where . . . " or "I wonder why that is . . . " or "I wonder what is happening . . . " will produce a parallel "wondering" in the children. Teachers who ask questions that take the children to the next level of thinking tend to enhance the drive to know. Such questions as, What else is happening? and What special sound does it make? extend children's skills for observation and increase their ability to monitor their world in a more detailed way.

The following are some of the science topics that can enhance the accomplishments of the right-hemisphere–dominant child:

- The seasons
- The animal world
- The plant world

- The sensory system of our body
- The body
- The planetary system
- The ocean and its seashore
- Matter and energy, including light, heat, electricity, and magnetism
- Air, water, and weather
- The exploration of outer space

Some of the goals of any science activity should include

- Making hypotheses and estimates
- Testing the hypothesis by
    making comparisons,
    testing variables, and
    making observations
- Recording observations
- Originating new approaches and new ideas—inventing

Scientific Inquiry: Making and Testing Hypotheses

The essence of scientific inquiry is forming and testing hypotheses. A hypothesis is simply a proposition based on a partial collection of information. In essence, a hypothesis is a guess—something that right-brain–dominant children are very good at. Following are two activities in which children develop and test hypotheses.

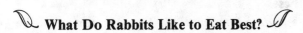

What Do Rabbits Like to Eat Best?

A teacher asked a group of 25 first graders, "What do rabbits like to eat?" Nine hands went up immediately, but six of those children were simply guessing. Some guesses were more informed than others—but all were merely inferences. These inferences were simple hypotheses and were based on some information that the children had about rabbits (either real or cartoon characters) or about animals in general. How could they test the validity of their hypotheses?

This unit should begin with bridging activities. Discuss with the children the types of foods they eat, their preferences, where the food is obtained, and other related topics. You might develop a unit on "The Foods We Eat" before doing this one.

1. **Making Hypotheses**

    Ask the question, "What do rabbits like to eat?" Probably, a lot of the answers will be "carrots"—based on Bugs Bunny cartoons. Ask, "I wonder what else they eat?" to stimulate additional answers.

    Write each answer, no matter how far-fetched, on a list on the blackboard. Then ask, "I wonder how we can find out if the answers are correct?"

2. **Planning How to Test the Hypotheses**

    Let the children brainstorm strategies, capitalizing on both right- and left-hemisphere skills. Because children will suggest a number of different hypotheses and solutions, this approach allows them to develop strategies for finding answers in a variety of ways and for satisfying their curiosity.

    Suggestions may include bringing a rabbit into the classroom, visiting the zoo or a pet shop that has rabbits, or visiting someone who raises rabbits, reading books about rabbits, and going out and "catching" a rabbit. Of all these suggestions, the most valuable is to bring a rabbit into the classroom. This allows the children to experiment with different foods and in the process develop skills in testing hypotheses. In the following activity, a guinea pig, gerbil, or white mouse can be studied instead of the rabbit, if any of these are easier for you to obtain.

3. **Testing the Hypotheses**

    a. *Making and recording observations.* To determine what the rabbit eats, have the children feed the rabbit a different kind of food each day (but be sure that none of the foods will be harmful to the rabbit). Have them weigh and measure (1 cup, 1 carrot, etc.) the portion of each food, observe whether the rabbit likes the food, and record the data on a chart with the following headings:

Date   Time Fed   Kind of Food   Portion   Weight   Ate Food   Didn't Eat Food.

    b. *Making and recording comparisons.* Next, to determine what foods the rabbit prefers, have the children put portions of two kinds of food the rabbit eats in the cage at the same time and observe which the rabbit eats first. Repeat the process with two different foods each day until all the foods that the rabbit eats have been tested. Record the data on a chart with the following headings:

Date	Time Fed	Food #1	Food #2	Food Preferred	
		Portion Weight	Portion Weight	#1	#2

c. *Process of elimination.* Repeat the process of offering two foods each day but use only the preferred foods. Record the observations in the same way to form a new, shorter list. Repeat the process again with the new list and continue this process of elimination until one overall preference is apparent.

This process of elimination is a strategy that the children will internalize and be able to call on to test other hypotheses in the future. It will also give them the important experience of staying with a task over a long period of time.

FOLLOW-UP ACTIVITIES

To extend this project, appoint committees to study each one of the following questions and report to the class.

- Where do rabbits live in the wild?
- What animals eat rabbits?
- Do people eat rabbit?
- What colors do rabbits come in? Are they always the same color?

RABBIT POEM

Write a poem about a rabbit. Start it out with this line:

I saw a little rabbit looking at me

_____

_____

_____

RABBIT PLAYACTING

Read *Peter Rabbit* while children act out the various parts.

RABBIT SONG

LITTLE RABBITS
(*Tune:* "Frère Jacques")

Little rabbits, little rabbits,
Hiding now, hiding now,
Come and get your good food.
I think you'll think it's very good.
Get it now. Get it now.

Little rabbits, little rabbits,
I see you. I see you.
Come and be my friend now.
Come and I'll show you how,
As I pet you, as I pet you.

Have children write additional verses to the same tune.

What Makes a Bean Sprout Grow Best?

Have the children create a list of hypotheses about what a bean sprout needs to grow. This list might include

- water,
- air,
- light,
- a particular kind of soil,
- fertilizer, and
- being talked to.

To test the hypotheses, you will need the following materials:

- lima beans
- measuring cup
- 1-quart fruit jars or similar glass containers (if space is a problem, use pint jars or jelly glasses)
- sand
- potting soil

• clay (from a creek bed, or pottery clay from an art shop)
• fertilizer or plant food

If children suggest other growing mediums, such as humus, vermiculite, or gravel, you might add those, too.

Next, the children can test the hypotheses step by step.

Step 1: Give each child a plastic glass. Have them fill their glasses with water and add a lima bean. Observe growth over a week and record the length on a simple chart every two or three days. The chart should show the date and the length of the sprout.

Step 2: Divide the class into groups, with one group for each kind of soil being tested. Each group has two jars, which they fill three-quarters full with soil. Have them add the appropriate amount of fertilizer to each jar. Have them plant two or three lima beans (because some may not grow) halfway down each jar against the side so that growth can be easily observed.

For the first two days, they will just let the beans sit in the dry soil and then observe any changes. For the remainder of the week, have them add water as often as necessary to keep the soil moist (but not soggy). Then have them record the growth on a chart that shows the date of each observation, the type of soil, whether it was fertilized or not, and the length of the sprout. The children then can compare their sprouts to see which soil worked best and whether fertilizer promoted growth.

Step 3: Once the class has discovered which growing medium is most effective, they can experiment with light. Give each group a clean jar, which they fill with the best soil (and fertilizer, if that proved to help growth). Each group will water as in Step 2. One group can keep their bean in the sunlight for the entire week. Another group can keep their bean in the dark for the entire week. A third group can bring their bean out of the dark after two or three days. A fourth group might keep their bean under a grow-light that is left on day and night. Have each group record the growth of the bean on a chart that shows the date of each observation, the length of time it received light, and the amount of growth.

Step 4: Create a master chart to show the optimum conditions for the growth of bean sprouts.

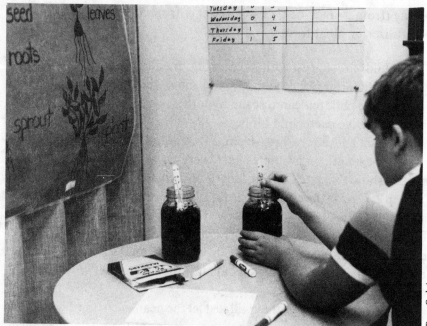

	Tuesday				
	Wednesday	0	4		
	Thursday	1	4		
	Friday	1	5		

PHOTO 24.1. TESTING HYPOTHESES ABOUT WHAT MAKES BEAN SPROUTS GROW

Doug Godwin

VARIATIONS:

1. Add another glass or jar to any of the steps mentioned to experiment with the effect of talking to the beans.
2. Simultaneously test other kinds of beans and seeds.

FOLLOW-UP ACTIVITIES

1. Using the materials that have proven to be optimal for growing beans, children can prepare a planter box to grow flowers or small vegetables, such as radishes and carrots.
2. Plant an outdoor garden if space is available.

ART ACTIVITIES

1. Draw beans, showing how the roots sprout out from the bean.
2. Introduce negative space drawing. Place a jar of beans against a 24″ × 36″ cardboard background. Ask children to draw *only* the cardboard, not the jars. Assist them by pointing out that they see

only part of the cardboard and that is the part they are asked to draw. Repeat the project, using two jars, then three.

3. Introduce still-life drawing by having children draw a jar with beans growing in it. If they have done the negative space project, this will not seem so difficult because they have already drawn the outline of the jar.

As in any art project, there is no wrong way. Each child's perception of the still life, each child's eye-hand coordination, and each child's ability to use the right hemisphere will be different. Thus, each picture will be different and acceptable.

Electromechanical Explorations

This is a rather complex science activity that could be spread out over an entire school quarter or semester. It will provide many opportunities for children to ask questions to which you can answer, "I don't know. Let's see how we can find out." Not only will this encourage research and exploration, which you do with the children, but it will also be a valid demonstration of the importance of honesty in day-to-day dealings with children. The joy of discovering answers together will enhance both your teaching experience and the children's learning experience.

You may prefer to assign this activity to a group of strongly right-hemisphere–dominant children to work on during free periods or while other students are doing more intensive left-hemisphere tasks that these children are unable to attend to. As they explore electrical energy and become knowledgeable about it, they can introduce their findings to the rest of the class. Such self-esteem–building experiences are very important for those students who are not doing well with left-hemisphere tasks. Success in right-hemisphere tasks will encourage them to concentrate to the best of their ability during the left-hemisphere classroom activities.

Use your local electronics supply store salesperson as a consultant to get a basic introduction to the type of activities that follow, unless you have already had this type of experience.

MATERIALS:

Erector Set, which includes a 6-volt motor with a pulley (you might be able to borrow one from a child)

6-volt lantern battery

10 pieces of light gauge wire, 2 feet long (strip ½ inch of insulation from each end of each piece)

5 pieces of light gauge wire, 6 inches long (string ½ inch of insulation from each end of each piece)

Small 6-volt light bulb with a socket

6-volt light bulb painted black with oven paint, covered by the toe end of a black sock held on by a rubber band around the base (this can be used to demonstrate heat without light)

6-volt buzzer

6-volt bell

Small electromagnet

Switch

Electric pushbutton doorbell

Wind-up alarm clock that can be taken apart in order to use gears and other parts for "inventions" (optional)

Tinkertoys

Broken electrical toys (contributed by the children)

3″ × 5″ file cards

Small gummed labels

If you have difficulty obtaining any of the items on this list from a hardware or electrical supply store or a friend who tinkers with electronics, you might try sending a note to parents with the list of items in order to solicit contributions or loans.

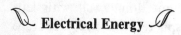

Electrical Energy

BRIDGING

- Discuss with class the uses of electricity and power in their homes and in the community. Discuss electrical toys, flashlights, and other small electrical items with which they may have had personal experience.

- Discuss the difference between supplying energy for a toy with a wind-up key and spring and supplying energy with an electrical battery.
- Read a story to the class about Benjamin Franklin and his key experiment with lightning.
- Discuss electric shocks and hazardous electrical practices.

FOCUSING

- Give the class a list of the materials that will be used. Go over each item and explain why that item is on the list and how they might be able to use it.
- Use illustrations. You might obtain some illustrations from an electronics store supply catalog.
- Have children participate in collecting the needed items.
- Have children participate in preparing the display of the items, making the labels, and otherwise preparing for the activity.
- Discuss with the class the knowledge they will have at the conclusion of the project, and in what ways they might be able to apply that knowledge in the future.
- Take plenty of time to answer questions the children may have.

MANIPULATION

1. Fasten each of the items on the materials list in a display on a piece of plywood.
2. Place the display on your "science" table and invite children to explore how the items work by connecting them to the battery.
3. Encourage the children to experiment to figure out different ways to make the connections.

Your role is to continuously ask questions. Ask them to explain what they did and ask what else can be done.

DESCRIPTIVE SYMBOLISM

1. Label each item on the display board.
2. Assign various items to committees. Each committee writes a descriptive paragraph of the item on a 3″ × 5″ card. Gather

information from an encyclopedia or from books on electricity that you have made available.

SYMBOLIC MANIPULATION

Have children diagram the items of their choice to show how those items can be hooked up to an electrical source (battery). Most left-hemisphere–dominant thinkers will probably just show one connection to the battery. Right-hemisphere explorers may show wires going all around the board, hooking up one thing to another, and another, and yet another, until they finally come to the battery. Or they may show three hook-ups or maybe only two. But their natural tendency will be to experiment with many different ways of making the connections.

After they have made their diagrams, ask the following questions:

- How does each item use electricity? (sound, heat, light, movement, magnetism)
- Which of these items will you find in your home?
- Why is it that the more items you hook together, the slower and weaker the electricity is?

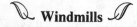 Windmills

BRIDGING

- How do we get water in our homes?
- What do people do if they don't have faucets and pipes?

FOCUSING

- Windmills are used in some parts of our country to pump water. They are used in prairie lands in the Midwest. Where else are they used?
- Discuss the use of windmills in Holland to pump water from the land to keep it dry.
- Use the encyclopedia and other reference books to find out more about the use of windmills.

- Discuss the use of windmills to make electricity.
- Outline the windmill-making project. Tell the children what is available, what they can try to do with it, and what they will have when the project is complete.

BUILDING A WINDMILL

Using the electric motor with the pulley, Tinkertoys, and rubber bands, have children experiment to figure out how to make a windmill.

FOLLOW-UP ACTIVITIES

1. *Craft:* Make pinwheels and have the children let them blow in the wind. (If you need a pattern, see *Patterns for Pinwheels, Pop-Ups, and Puppets* by Marilyn Barr, Fearon Teacher Aids/David S. Lake Publishers, 1988.)
2. *Art:* Have children design their own windmills on paper, color them, and cut them out to create a bulletin board display or a mural.
3. *Dance:* Play a waltz on the record player. Have children dance to the music, pretending to be windmills. Have children dance in pairs to make a larger windmill. Try combinations of three and four children in groups, simulating windmills as they move to the rhythm of the music.
4. *Dance-Song:*

THE WINDMILL IS TURNING ROUND AND ROUND
(*Tune:* "Pop Goes the Weasel")

The windmill is turning round and round
As the wind keeps blowing.
It makes the water move along
And keeps the flowers growing.

Turning, turning, windmill arms,
Swing around your center.
Feel the wind blow on your face
It feels as cold as winter.

Have children make up additional verses.

ℒ Crane ℐ

BRIDGING

- Prior to this activity, it would be helpful if a group of children could visit a wrecking yard to see a crane in operation. These children could then lead the class in making a crane.
- Talk about some of the taller buildings in the community or those in photographs of a large city. How did they get the material to the top part of the building to finish it?
- Talk about how we lift things.
- What about things that are too heavy for our arms to lift?
- How could a hook be used for lifting?
- How could a magnet be used for lifting?
- What else can be used for lifting?
- How do elephants lift things?

FOCUSING

- Explain the project of making a crane.
- Display a toy crane obtained from one of the children, a preschool class, a friend, or some other source.
- Discuss the availability of needed materials.
- Discuss how they will actually be able to use the crane when it is finished.

BUILDING A CRANE

Have children build a crane using the motor and electromagnet.

FOLLOW-UP ACTIVITIES

1. Bring in two pulleys and a rope into the classroom and extend the pulleys across the classroom. Transport paper (clipped on with clothespins) and other items suggested by the children.
2. Allow children to explore other ways of using the pulleys for lifting and transporting items.

⚘ Moving Car ✍

Have the more exploratory children use the Erector Set to build a car that will move by use of the electric motor. Challenge children to use as many of the electrical items as possible on the car.

⚘ Personal Inventions ✍

Have children design and invent their own electrical constructions to move or carry things.

CHAPTER 25

Social Studies for
Right-Hemisphere Processors

THROUGH SOCIAL STUDIES, children can apply their growing understanding of symbolism. Many referents can be brought into the classroom for exploration. For example, the study of people (both here and in other lands), food, clothing, music, and games all provide children with first-hand experiences of the customs and mores of various cultures. Adding the descriptive symbolism of written and spoken language, pictures, models, and media expands understanding while enhancing reading and observation skills. Allowing the children to explore through visual symbolism—by drawing pictures about their experiences, building cultural bulletin boards, making costumes, and writing related stories—maintains their role as active participants in the learning process. Each level of the sequence in turn enriches its own set of thinking skills.

In applying curriculum to the development of children, the content by itself does not determine the roles of each hemisphere in the learning process. Teaching strategies largely determine the richness of the learning experience and the development of thinking skills.

Feelings

Right-hemisphere–dominant people are frequently especially sensitive to the moods and feelings of others. They are usually very expressive and open with their feelings, but they may not understand them. Talking about feelings and exploring their own feelings and those of others can lead to better self-understanding and help build

334

self-esteem for all children, but it may be especially useful for children with strong right-hemisphere characteristics. In working with feelings and learning to understand that they are valid, the goal should be to help children learn that they can control their feelings, rather than letting their feelings control them. It is important to stress that "being in control" doesn't mean suppressing feelings and not expressing one's self. Rather, it means accepting, recognizing, and expressing one's feelings in a rational manner—in a way that is helpful rather than detrimental.

BRIDGING

Talk about the ways our lives are alike and the ways they are different. We all live in a town or city; we live at a street address, but the addresses are different; we live in different kinds of houses or apartments; we have different kinds of families; and we all eat different meals in our homes. We wear our own clothes to school; we do our schoolwork our own way; and we all have different kinds of handwriting. And we all have feelings, although we don't necessarily have the same feelings about things.

FOCUSING

- Begin discussing feelings with the following questions:
  How can we find out about our own feelings?
  How do we express our feelings?
  How can we tell what kind of mood people are in?
  How can we tell what kind of mood we are in?
- Tell the class that during the next few weeks they can all prepare their own "Feelings" book in which they can draw pictures and write poems about feelings. (All of the activities that follow can go into this book.)
- On a chart, list all the different feelings that the children can brainstorm, leaving space for additional feelings as they come up during the following activities.
- To begin discussing different types of feelings, give everyone a list with the following feelings. You can go over each one and ask, "Do we ever feel _____ ?"

sad	lonely	afraid
hungry	angry	embarrassed
serious	worried	self-conscious
curious	enthusiastic	playful
accomplished	successful	daring
surprised	joyful	trusting
helpful	friendly	smart
clever	impatient	tired
confused	at ease	silly
annoyed	sympathetic	appreciative
elated	cooperative	creative
bored	amazed	resourceful
skeptical	stingy	stimulated
generous	shy	distracted
proud	amused	isolated
responsive	thoughtful	strong
foolish	puzzled	encouraged
hateful	clumsy	graceful
bossy	secure	self-reliant
tolerant	communicative	festive
suspicious	anxious	ignored
loyal	determined	pleased
pressured	nonpressured	empathic
kind	relaxed	weak
tired	lonely	loving
disappointed	depressed	wise
frustrated	important	busy
challenged	impressed	self-assured
eager	rejected	uptight
free	threatened	satisfied
dumb	mean	

There should also be some extra spaces to add whatever words are current among the children, such as *groovy* or *"bad."*

VISUAL AIDS AND RESOURCES

- Have available pictures of people showing different kinds of feelings through facial expressions and through actions.
- Involve students in preparing a bulletin-board display using the various illustrations.
- Take instant-camera pictures of the children expressing different feelings to supplement the bulletin-board display.
- Have available magazines with pictures of people that children can use to cut out as the study progresses.

✒ Ways I Feel When I Do Things ✐

Begin by discussing the following questions:

- How can we learn to express our feelings?
- Is it better to express our feelings or to hide them from people?

Give the following list to each child. Complete the list through class discussion. State each situation and have the children verbalize their feelings. Have them write down one that they or others verbalized.

When I wake up in the morning, I feel _____ .

When I eat my breakfast, I feel _____ .

When I see my friends at school, I feel _____ .

When the bell rings to go into class, I feel _____ .

When I read a book, I feel _____ .

When I play ball, I feel _____ .

When I watch a movie, I feel _____ .

When I get into a fight, I feel _____ .

When I get home from school, I feel _____ .

When I have a birthday, I feel _____ .

When someone is sick, I feel _____ .

When I get into bed at night and get ready to fall asleep, I feel _____ .

⚞ Times That I Had Certain Feelings ⚟

Complete the following list through class discussion.

I felt very excited when _____ .

I was disappointed when _____ .

I was very frightened when _____ .

I felt proud of myself when _____ .

I was very worried when _____ .

I felt very important when _____ .

I felt annoyed when _____ .

I felt very happy when _____ .

It embarrassed me when _____ .

It made me feel very smart when _____ .

I feel nervous when _____ .

I get impatient when _____ .

Optional—these are a little more difficult:

I feel _____ when _____

_____ .

I felt _____ when _____

_____ .

I usually feel _____ when _____

_____ .

How I Express My Feelings

Complete the following list through class discussion.

When I am very angry, I usually _____.

When I am worried, I usually _____.

When I am impatient, I usually _____.

When I am very happy, I usually _____.

I laugh very hard when _____.

I cry when _____.

I pout when _____.

I smile softly when _____.

When I feel very friendly, I _____.

Expressing Anger

Begin this activity by discussing the following questions:

- What makes different people feel angry?
- How do we act when we are angry? Show us.
  1. Have children take turns demonstrating displays of anger.
  2. Divide class into pairs. Have each pair create an "act" to display two persons arguing and getting angry with each other.
  3. **Nonphysical anger.** Divide class into groups of six or eight persons each. Have each group stand in a circle. Through pantomime, the members of the group start arguing with one another. Using only gestures and body language, they "yell" and "scream" to express their anger. The rule is "No physical contact."
  4. **Physical expression of anger.** Divide the class into partners again. State that the rules of this game are to pretend anger and not to really hurt anyone.

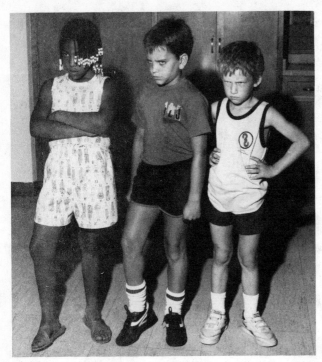

PHOTO 25.1.
EXPRESSING ANGER

Partners stand facing each other, with palms of hands against each other. They tell each other, "I hate what you did. It made me angry." They push against each other's palms to express the anger. Repeat activity with different partners.

5. **Things that make me angry.** Begin by discussing the question, What kinds of things really make you angry? After the discussion, have each student make a list, "Things That Make Me Angry."
6. Draw pictures of people who look angry.
7. Draw yourself looking very angry.

Feeling Important

Many children feel that others are important but that they themselves never are. These children need to have their self-esteem boosted by learning to recognize and acknowledge times when they do feel important or are being treated as though they are really special but do not recognize it because of their low self-esteem.

1. Complete the following, discussing each question with the entire class and sharing ideas for answers.
   • On my birthday, I feel _____ .
   • When I get new shoes, I feel _____ .
   • I feel important when _____ .
   • I also feel important when _____ .
   • I also feel important when _____ .
   • My mother (father) feels important when _____ .
   • My brother (sister) feels important when _____ .
   • A baby feels important when _____ .
   • A teacher feels important when _____ .

2. **Who's the boss?** Divide class into pairs. One person of each pair is "A" and the other is "B." All of the As sit on the floor, with the Bs standing next to them. The B is the boss and starts telling the A what to do. For example, "Put your hands on top of your head. Now fold them and put them in your lap. Smile. Blink your eyes. Say, 'You are important' to me. Salute me." Children can make up their own commands as long as no one does anything that physically hurts anyone.

   After two minutes, the roles are reversed. Then have the children discuss how they each felt when playing the role of the boss and how they each felt when being bossed.

Sadness and Gladness

Sadness is another feeling that is sometimes difficult for children to deal with, just as it is for adults. Children need to know that all people feel sad at times, that it is a legitimate feeling (like all other feelings), and that it is all right to talk about it.

1. **The saddest time of my life was. . . .** Ask children to tell about the saddest time they remember. After each person tells about his or

her saddest time, have one person go to that person and give him or her a hug and say, "I'm sorry you need to be so sad."

2. **Things that make us sad.** Discuss the question, What kinds of things make us sad? After the discussion, have each student make a list, "I Feel Sad When . . ."

3. **Things that make us glad.** Counteract the above activity by asking what kinds of things make us feel glad and completing another list, "Things that Make Me Feel Glad."

Sculptured Feelings

Create clay sculptures of faces with expressions of different feelings. Happiness, sadness, anger, fear, sleepiness, worry, and silliness are some of the easier feelings to depict. Children can add others.

The Clown

Make a clown face from a 5-inch-diameter circle painted white. Make the clown's hair by cutting orange yarn into 6-inch lengths and gluing it in bunches at the top of the clown face on both sides. Glue small pieces of Velcro in the appropriate spots for the eyebrows, eyes, nose, ears, and mouth. Have the children help you prepare a variety of mouths, eyes, noses, ears, and eyebrows to use on the clown for various expressions. Glue a small piece of Velcro on the back of each facial feature so that they can be used on the clown face. Keep these pieces in an envelope, box, or other container next to the clown face.

Have the children use the facial features to make the clown's face express various feelings.

Children may also make individual clown faces with a variety of changeable features to add to their notebook on feelings. The features can be kept in a plastic envelope or sandwich bag fastened to the back of the sheet that has the clown face on it.

Masks

Give everyone a paper plate on which to draw a face representing a particular mood or feeling. Cut holes at the child's eye level so that the plate can be used as a mask. Cut a notch at nose-level to facilitate breathing. Staple ribbons or narrow elastic on each side so that the mask can be tied onto the head. Allow children the freedom to make or select a mask whenever they have a feeling they want to express strongly to the entire class.

Sad-Happy Face

Make a sad-happy paper-plate mask that can be worn according to one's mood.

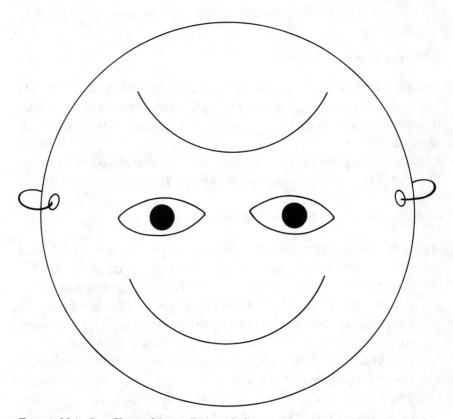

FIGURE 25.1. SAD-HAPPY MASK. Draw this face on a paper plate. Cut out eyeholes and holes for string to tie around head.

◟ Mood Painting ◞

Hang a large sheet of paper for a mural across a wall. Cover the rest of the wall and the floor under the mural with newspaper, to one foot out from the wall. Place containers of liquid tempera every 12 inches along the floor on the newspaper. Have brushes in each container. Play soft music on the record player or on a tape. Dim the lights. Have children paint feelings that are evoked by the music. Change the pace of the music periodically.

VARIATIONS:

1. Place the colors in pie plates. Use feather dusters for brushes.
2. Give each person an individual sheet of paper. Use chalk for color.
3. Set up areas for fingerpainting. Fingerpaint "moods" to music.

◟ Feelings Map ◞

This activity should be done during a quiet time of the day, possibly after a lunch period, and after children have had time to unwind from their lunch-recess activities. The lights in the room should be dimmed, if possible.

On a record player play soft music. The best music is baroque music with a 4/4 beat (by such composers as Bach, Handel, and Purcell), but any classical music will do.

Give each child a piece of drawing paper.

Leader: In the center of the paper, write the phrase "I feel" and put a circle around it. Now make little lines going out in all directions from the circle about halfway to the edge of the paper. They can be straight lines, wiggly or squiggly lines, curvy lines, dotted lines, or any other kinds of lines you want to make. Now listen to the music and start thinking about how you feel. How do you feel right now? Then start thinking about feelings you have had at different times. Write down if you were ever worried or upset or angry or happy or excited— or whatever other kinds of feelings you think of. Just write what comes to your mind while listening to the music. Let yourself think about things that have happened to you. Don't write down what happened. Just write down the feeling the music makes you remember.

This activity can be modified and repeated periodically for the expression of one particular feeling.

✒ Feelings Stories ✒

Have the children select a favorite story. Give each one a turn to read one paragraph out loud. Children read the paragraph from the book as is, except that wherever possible, the reader inserts a feeling word. For example, the sentences "It was a sunny day. The White family was getting ready to go on a picnic" could be changed to "It was a happy, sunny day. The White family was excitedly getting ready to go on a picnic."

✒ Singing about Feelings ✒

To the tune of "If You're Happy and You Know It," you can sing about all sorts of feelings. This is how it was done in *Think of Something Quiet* (Cherry, 1981, pg. 126):

IF YOU'RE ANGRY
(*Tune*: "If You're Happy and You Know It")

If you're angry and you feel it, stamp your feet.
If you're angry and you feel it, stamp your feet.
If you're angry and you feel it,
Show us all how you would show it.
If you're angry and you feel it, stamp your feet.

If you're mean and you feel it, scrunch your face. . . .
If you're silly and you feel it, dance a jig. . . .
If you're scared and you feel it, give a shriek. . . .
If you're sad and you feel it, cry boo-hoo. . . .
If you're selfish and you feel it, bow your head. . . .
If you're proud and you feel it, stand up tall. . . .

If you're tired and you feel it, give a yawn. . . .
If you're sleepy and you feel it, blink your eyes. . . .
If you're loving and you feel it, throw a kiss. . . .
If you're glad and you feel it, smile a smile. . . .
If you're excited and you feel it, give a jump. . . .
If you're relaxed and you feel it, flop around. . . .

Have the children make up verses of their own. Have them make up feelings verses to other tunes.

Being Alike and Different

Not only are feelings that children experience the same as those that others experience, but there are other things that everyone has in common.

To go with the book on feelings, have the children prepare two other books, "Myself" and "My Friends." In doing these books they can explore the ways they are alike and different from one another.

How We Are Alike

Begin a discussion by saying, "We already found out that we have the same kinds of feelings. In what other ways are we alike?" Then discuss each of the following statements, and have children fill in the blanks:

I am like everyone else because I have _____ legs and _____ arms and _____ head.

My head is like everyone else's because I have _____ eyes, and _____ ears, and _____ nose and _____ mouth with _____ lips.

I am like everyone else because I am in the _____ grade and I attend _____ school.

I am like everyone else because I have a family. In my family there are_____ , _____ , _____ , _____ , _____ , and _____ .

I am like everyone else because I have a place to live. I live at _____ .

I am like everyone else because when it is cold outdoors, I feel _____ . When it is very hot outdoors, I feel _____ . When it is winter, I wear a _____ . When it is summer, I wear _____ clothes.

I am like everyone else because I get sleepy at night and go to _____ .

I am like everyone else because when I get up in the morning, I am _____ and I eat _____ .

I am like everyone else because I get _____ so I drink water.

Continue the game with ideas from the children.

Partners Who Look Alike

Ask the children how many ways they can find someone like them to be their partner.

- Have them find a partner who is wearing something that is the same color they are wearing.
- Have them find a partner who has the same color hair they have.
- Have them find a partner who has the same color eyes they have.
- Have them find a partner who has the same kind of shoes on that they have. If none are like theirs, tell them to find someone whose shoes are the most different from theirs.

Continue the game with ideas from the children.

❧ Button Partners ✍

Prepare a box or tray with enough buttons so that there is one for everyone in the room. Have two of each kind of button.

Leader: I know a different way to find a partner. Here is a box of buttons. I want everyone to pick out one button. *(Allow children to pick one button.)* Now I want you to find the person who picked the same kind of button you did, and that person will be your partner today.

VARIATIONS:

1. Use pictures of automobiles from magazines. Have a picture for each child in class. Make sure that there are two of each kind of automobile, even though the colors may vary.
2. Use magazine pictures of automobiles of different styles and makes, but only two of each color.
3. Use magazine pictures of people at work, being sure there are two of each activity.
4. Use pictures or drawings of flowers, with two of each kind.
5. Use action verbs—such as *walk, run, jump, climb, sit, hop, spin, crawl, slide, bounce, bend, shake, roll, skip, gallop, shuffle,* and *stoop*—written on slips of paper. Make sure there are two of each word and that the total equals the number of children in the class.
6. Use pairs of seashells.
7. Use pairs of colored rocks.
8. Use other items that the children think of.

❧ Partner Friends ✍

Each time the children have a partner, have them fill out a "Partner Friend" page for their "My Friends" book.

Date _____

Today my partner is _____

because we both _____
                              (write the reason why the partner was chosen)

_____

Height _____   (In this space draw a picture
                        of your partner's face.)
Weight _____

Birthdate _____

Color hair _____

Color of eyes _____

What my partner wore to school today: _____

_____

_____

ℒ Partner Activities ⌐

Assign one partner activity each day after selecting partners.

1. **Blindfold walk**—*giving directions.* Take turns with one partner being blindfolded and the other giving directions of where to walk, when to turn, how many steps to take, when to stop, and when to go.
2. **Baby feeding**—*building trust.* Take turns feeding each other lunch. The person being fed does not use his or her hands at all.
3. **Poetry writing**—*building cooperation.* Work together to compose a poem called "A Partner Is a Friend."
4. **Pantomiming**—*partners are helpful.* Work together to create a pantomime of some situation in which one partner is helping the other.
5. **Design making**—*listening to and following directions.* Make a design on a piece of paper. Blindfold one partner and give that person a crayon. The other partner gives directions so that the blindfolded person can trace the design without looking at it.

   Prepare several designs. When the partners trade places, they trade roles but use a new design.
6. **Picture stories**—*recording data as symbols.* Partners create a story about ways that they are alike, using pictures in place of words wherever possible.
7. **Moving partners**—*movement skills.* When partners have been selected by matching action verbs (see Button Partners, Variations),

have them list as many ways as they can to do the activity that they chose. Have them demonstrate the variety of ways to the class.

8. **Partners for assignments**—*cooperation*. Have children work as partners on regular classroom assignments in other areas of study.

〰 How We Are Different ✍

Have the children next discuss ways that they are different from one another. Make a list of the ways the children think of, adding some of your own. The list you come up with will probably be similar to the one below. Discuss each feature and have the children describe or draw their own to put in their book "Myself" (see p. 346). Have on hand mirrors, microscopes, magnifying glasses, watercolors, colored pencils, felt markers, chalks, and other art material. Prepare a chart of the height and weight of all students as well as the average height and weight for the class.

1. **Hair.**

    My hair is _____
    (straight, curly, wavy)

    It looks like this under a microscope:

    This is its color:

2. **Eyes.**

    My eyes look like this:

3. **Teeth.**

    My two front teeth (or side ones if the front ones are missing) look like this:

4. **Height.**

    I am _____ feet _____ inches tall. We made a chart in our room and found out that the average height in the class is

    _____ .

    Therefore, I am _____ the
    (taller than, shorter than, the same as)
    average.

5. **Weight.**

I weigh _____ pounds and _____ ounces. We made a chart in our room and found out that the average weight in the class is _____ pounds _____ ounces. Therefore, I am _____ the average.
(the same as, lighter than, heavier than)

6. **Skin color.**

My skin is this color:

7. **Family.**

These are stick figures of the people in my family.

8. **House.**

My house is made of _____ . It looks like this:

Children Around the World

BRIDGING

Write down on 3″ × 5″ cards

- five foods that you like to eat
- five songs that you like to sing
- five games that you like to play
- five things that you like to wear

FOCUSING

Leader: We need to find out how other children around the world live. They eat and wear clothes and play and sing songs just like we do. But the food they eat, the clothes they wear, and the songs they sing are different. I wonder if the games they play are different? How do you think we can find out about these? What books will we need? Does anyone have any videotapes at home about other countries?

Explore the available resources of information about other countries, such as universities, colleges, embassies, television and radio stations, bookstores, magazines, local immigrants, and direct correspondence with their governments. Resources you provide in the classroom might include illustrations of people in various countries, *National Geographic* magazines, including an index, selections from different encyclopedia sets, books, tapes, artifacts borrowed from families of your students, and records.

CHOOSING AND STUDYING COUNTRIES

Divide the class into groups. Have each group choose the country they want to study and the methods they want to use.

1. Provide a list of countries similar to the following, modifying it according to countries for which you may already have resources available.
   • Brazil or other South American country
   • Ghana or other African country
   • Japan or other Far Eastern country
   • Norway or other Scandinavian country
   • Israel or other Near or Middle Eastern country
   • Italy or other European country
2. Have the children brainstorm ways of obtaining information. As in all brainstorming sessions, all ideas are acceptable. If the session does not provide the following ideas, you might add them.
   • Write to a school in that country.
   • Go to the library and find books with pictures.
   • Go to a public or university library and find out what tapes are available.
   • Write to the public broadcasting station to find out what documentaries are available.
   • Contact a nearby university to find students from any of the lands you are studying who may be able to come speak to the class.
   • Ask parents if they know people from any of those lands to come to speak to the class.

REPORTING

Have groups compile the information that they have gathered about the different countries and make oral reports to the class.

FOLLOW-UP ACTIVITIES

1. Have the children make preference cards for each country. On each card is a list—Food, Clothing, Games, and Activities—and two columns headed "Like" and "Dislike," where the children can check their preferences.
2. Do art and craft activities from the various countries.
3. Make costumes representing the various countries.
4. Make puppets representing characters of the various countries.
5. Create puppet shows depicting various countries.
6. Create a play, acting out a scene in the particular country.
7. Learn and perform dances from a particular country.
8. Have each group prepare a meal from one of the countries. Each child can bring money from home to help pay for the meal. Parents may also be willing to donate some of the ingredients for this project. Let parents know that the child does not have to bring (or buy) lunch on that day, and that the money will cover the cost of the meal.

   The group preparing the meal should also decorate the room, plan for entertainment, and otherwise set the mood in keeping with the customs of the country.

Reference

Cherry, Clare. 1981. *Think of Something Quiet*. Belmont, CA: Fearon/David S. Lake.

EPILOGUE

Pulling It All Together—
Three People We Want You to Know

Billy

Billy, an eighth grader, sat staring vacantly at the chalkboard, on which the teacher was busily writing an assignment. Billy had mentally retreated to where he spent most of his time during the school day—in castles chasing ghosts and dragons, in toy shops visually figuring out how the latest car models are assembled, high in the blue sky flying the latest jet plane, which he himself had designed and built, or in a Star Wars battle in which everyone looked to him to save the day. School was not that important to him. After all, it kept reminding him of all his too-frequent failures. Just last week he had taken home the second F that semester on his report card. It didn't matter that he had scored in the top 20 percent on the standardized math test. He simply could not bring himself to read through the dull homework, even though it counted for so much toward his final grade. When he did venture to do some of the homework, usually under pressure at home, he either forgot where he put it or forgot to hand it in. If he couldn't be helped to perform successfully in school, he would do so in his dreams, in which he found frequent solace.

Doreen

On Billy's left sat Doreen, watching the chalkboard with dutiful interest. She was taking in all that was being explained and paid particular attention when the assignment was announced. She recorded it carefully and noted the teacher's response to any questions others asked about the assignment. At the teacher's cue, she immediately began to work on the assignment as instructed. When in doubt about a problem or about the teacher's expectations, she would raise her hand until she was recognized, go up to the desk, and ask the teacher her questions, and then return to continue working. What was not completed in school was carefully placed in her organizer and taken home to finish.

Doreen had always been like that. She quietly did what was expected and adjusted well to most situations as long as the expectations were there. Now she was in the eighth grade and was comfortable. Teachers occasionally recognized her work, but mostly they left her alone.

Children at Risk

For Billy, the school system doesn't fit. It does not address his ways of learning, nor does it employ techniques for detecting them. His bright mind works outside the parameters for learning set down by the school. Here is a bright, loving, intelligent, imaginative youngster, ready to reach for the rainbows and conquer the world. He is slipping through the cracks of the system that is supposed to be helping him, and he is in grave danger of dropping out of school—and perhaps even out of society.

Doreen is equally at risk. She is also a bright, loving, intelligent youngster, but she has a way of blending into the background, of becoming one of the "other ten kids"—you know, the ones whose presence you can't quite remember without looking at your roll book. She is a blessing who needs little attention. The potential inside her may never be found, however, because it will never be challenged. Her dreams, her ideas, her promise most likely will remain dormant until, if she is fortunate, someone or something in her adult life will ignite the spark.

Mrs. Bartholomew: Making a Difference

Mrs. Bartholomew had been working at Johnson Elementary School for 22 years, teaching first, second, and third grades. With her seniority, she could have had her pick of classes; the bright and the beautiful gifted children could be hers for the asking. But that didn't appeal to her. She hadn't retired yet and wasn't about to while working for the school that had come to mean so much to her. It had taken too long to polish her skills, and she hadn't given up on the notion of adding a few more to her repertoire. Besides, more and more children were coming to her from high-stress situations, and she realized she could make a positive impact on their lives.

During the opening weeks of the new school year, she looked at each child thoroughly, trying to find out how he or she functioned. Mrs. Bartholomew was always surprised at how many more details about their behavior and her own that she noticed every year. She was also aware that she was noticing finer and finer details. She heard differences in tones. She was alert to the most subtle body language signals. She listened to feelings, not just to words. She noticed movements and facial expressions. She noted how each child approached new problems and how they went about pursuing and completing assigned tasks. She became aware of friendships and picked up social patterns on the playground. She found herself listening to conversations during bus duty and during lunch duty and would frequently drop what she was doing to help a hesitant child work through whatever was worrying him or her.

Soon Mrs. Bartholomew found herself flooded with a wealth of information about each of the children in her class. The two professional conferences that she attended that year had new meaning to her. She had many new questions to ask at in-service sessions. As in the past, she felt that this would perhaps be her most successful year as an educator. And it was. Not only did the children grow, but she also continued to grow and reached a new level of accomplishment. Her third-grade classroom became the center of all school activity. People visited daily to see the vibrant displays, the active children, the creative projects, the colorful array of visual stimuli that was so much a part of her environment. They loved to listen to her guided imagery exercises and to watch the involved expressions on all of the children's faces as they allowed themselves to become immersed in the symbolism of the moment. They could tell that this was a gifted teacher. This one woman alone was making a difference. Both Billy and Doreen would have flourished had they been fortunate enough to go through school having teachers like Mrs. Bartholomew.

Is the Left Brain Always Right?

Mary W., the kindergarten teacher whom we met in the opening pages of this book, heard about this fascinating classroom from some of her friends. One day she played hooky and visited Johnson Elementary School. The minute she poked her head into Mrs. Bartholomew's classroom she felt the vitality and richness of this learning environment and cried out, "I knew it! I knew it! THE LEFT BRAIN IS NOT ALWAYS RIGHT!"

Bibliography

Arnheim, Rudolf. *Art and Visual Perception: A Psychology of the Creative Eye.* Berkeley and Los Angeles: University of California Press, 1966.
———. *Visual Thinking.* Berkeley and Los Angeles: University of California Press, 1969.

Ayres, A. Jean. *Sensory Integration and Learning Disorders.* Los Angeles: Western Psychological Services, 1973.
———. *Sensory Integration and the Child.* Los Angeles: Western Psychological Services, 1979.

Barlin, Anne L. *Teaching Your Wings to Fly: The Nonspecialist's Guide to Movement Activities for Young Children.* Santa Monica, CA: Goodyear, 1979.
Belgau, Frank A., and Beverley V. Basden. *Perceptual Motor and Visual Perception Handbook of Developmental Activities for Schools, Clinics, Parents, and Preschool Programs.* Port Angeles, WA: Perception Development Research Associates, 1971.
Bergan, John R., and Ronald W. Henderson. *Child Development.* Columbus, OH: Charles Merrill, 1979.
Blakeslee, Thomas R. *The Right Brain: A New Understanding of the Unconscious Mind and Its Creative Powers.* Garden City, NY: Doubleday/Anchor, 1980.
Bogen, J. E. "Educational Aspects and Hemispheric Specialization." In *The Human Brain,* ed. M. C. Wittrock. Englewood Cliffs, NJ: Prentice-Hall, 1977.
Bower, T. G. *A Primer of Infant Development.* New York: W. H. Freeman, 1977.
Brown, K., and S. J. Cooper, eds. *Chemical Influence on Behavior.* New York: Academic Press, 1979.
Buzan, Tony. *Use Both Sides of Your Brain.* New York: Dutton, 1976.

Capon, Jack. *Basic Movement Activities.* Perceptual Motor Development Series, Book 1. Belmont, CA: Fearon/ David S. Lake Publishers, 1975.
Castillo, Gloria A. *Left-Handed Teaching: Lessons in Affective Education,* 2d ed. New York: Holt, Rinehart & Winston, 1978.
Chall, Jeanne, and Allan Mirsky, eds. *Education and the Brain: Seventy-Seventh Yearbook, Part II, of the National Society for the Study of Education.* Chicago: University of Chicago Press, 1978.

Chaney, Clara M., and Newell C. Kephart. *Motoric Aids to Perceptual Training.* Columbus, OH: Charles Merrill, 1968.

Cherry, Clare. *Creative Art for the Developing Child: A Teacher's Handbook for Early Childhood Education,* rev. ed. Belmont, CA: David S. Lake, 1972.

———. *Creative Movement for the Developing Child: A Nursery School Handbook for Non-Musicians.* Belmont, CA: David S. Lake, 1971.

———. *Creative Play for the Developing Child: Early Lifehood Education Through Play.* Belmont, CA: David S. Lake, 1976.

———. *Think of Something Quiet: A Guide for Achieving Serenity in Early Childhood Classrooms.* Belmont, CA: David S. Lake, 1981.

Cleary, Brian. *Moving Is Learning.* Montreal, Canada: McGill University, 1968.

Corballis, Michael C., and Ivan L. Beale. *The Psychology of Left and Right.* New York: Halstead Press, 1976.

Cratty, Bryant J. *Physical Expressions of Intelligence.* Englewood Cliffs, NJ: Prentice-Hall, 1972.

The Diagram Group. *The Brain: A User's Manual.* New York: Berkley Books, 1983.

Dimond, S. J., and J. G. Beaumont, eds. *Hemisphere Function of the Human Brain.* New York: Wiley, 1974.

Dixon, Terence, and Tony Buzan. *The Evolving Brain.* New York: Holt, Rinehart & Winston, 1978.

Drowatzky, John N. *Motor Learning: Principles and Practices.* Minneapolis: Burgess, 1975.

Facklam, Margery, and Howard Facklam. *The Brain: Magnificent Mind Machine.* San Diego: Harcourt Brace Jovanovich, 1982.

Feldenkrais, Moshe. *Awareness Through Movement: Health Exercises for Personal Growth.* New York: Harper & Row, 1972.

———. *Body and Mature Behavior: A Study of Anxiety, Sex, Gravitation and Learning.* New York: International Universities Press, 1970.

Ferguson, Marilyn. *The Aquarian Conspiracy: Personal and Social Transformation in the 1980s.* Los Angeles: Tarcher, 1981.

———. *The Brain Revolution.* New York: Taplinger, 1974.

Flavell, John H. *Cognitive Development.* Englewood Cliffs, NJ: Prentice-Hall, 1977.

Fox, Patricia L. "Reading as a Whole Brain Function," *The Reading Teacher,* October 1979.

Gallahue, David L. *Motor Development and Movement Experiences for Young Children.* New York: Wiley, 1976.

Gardner, Howard. *Frames of Mind: The Theory of Multiple Intelligences.* New York: Basic Books, 1983.

Gardner, Martin. *The Ambidextrous Universe: Mirror Asymmetry and Time-Reversed Worlds,* rev. ed. New York: Scribners, 1979.

Gerhardt, Lydia A. *Moving and Knowing: The Young Child Orients Himself to Space.* Englewood Cliffs, NJ: Prentice-Hall, 1973.

Gesell, Arnold. *The First Five Years of Life.* New York: Harper & Row, 1940.

Gesell, Arnold, and Frances Ilg. *The Child from Five to Ten.* New York: Harper, 1946.

Godwin, Douglas C. "Development of Symbolism in Young Children." Paper presented at the East Texas Methodist Day-School Conference, at Tyler, Texas, 1987.

Graham, George, Shirley Ann Holt-Hale, and M. Parker. *Children Moving: A Teacher's Guide to Developing a Successful Physical Education Program*, 2d ed. Palo Alto, CA: Mayfield, 1987.

Gray, Darlene, Jesse Staples, et al. *A Chance to Be Children: Curriculum Guide.* San Bernardino, CA: San Bernardino County Schools Office, Special Services, 1980.

Gregory, Richard L., ed. *Oxford Companion to the Mind.* New York: Oxford University Press, 1987.

Gregson, Bob. *The Incredible Indoor Games Book.* Belmont, CA: Fearon/David S. Lake Publishers, 1982.

———. *The Outrageous Outdoor Games Book.* Belmont, CA: Fearon/David S. Lake Publishers, 1984.

Haines, Gail K. *Brain Power: What Does It Mean to Be Smart?* New York: Watts, 1979.

Hampden-Turner, Charles. *Maps of the Mind.* New York: Macmillan/Collier, 1981.

Harnad, Stevan, ed. *Lateralization in the Nervous System.* New York: Academic Press, 1977.

Hart, Leslie A. *How the Brain Works: A New Understanding of Human Learning, Emotion and Thinking.* New York: Basic Books, 1975.

Hatcher, Caro C., and Hilda Mullin. *More Than Words: Movement Activities for Children.* Pasadena, CA: Parents-for-Movement, 1967.

Hendricks, Gay. *The Centered Teacher: Awareness Activities for Teachers and Their Students.* Englewood Cliffs, NJ: Prentice-Hall, 1981.

Hendricks, (C. Gaylord) Gay, and James Fadiman, eds. *Transpersonal Education: A Curriculum for Feeling and Being.* Englewood Cliffs, NJ: Prentice-Hall, 1976.

Hendricks, Gay, and Kathlyn Hendricks. *The Moving Center: Exploring Movement Activities for the Classroom.* Englewood Cliffs, NJ: Prentice-Hall, 1983.

Hendricks, Gay, and T. Roberts. *The Second Centering Book: More Awareness Activities for Children, Parents, and Teachers.* Englewood Cliffs, NJ: Prentice-Hall, 1977.

Hendricks, (C. G.) Gay, and Russell Wills. *The Centering Book: Awareness Activities for Children, Parents, and Teachers.* Englewood Cliffs, NJ: Prentice-Hall, 1975.

Hicks, R. E., and M. Kinsbourne. "Lateralized Concomitants of Human Handedness." *Journal of Motor Behavior* 10(1978): pgs. 83–94.

———. "On the Genesis of Human Handedness: A Review." *Journal of Motor Behavior* 8(1976): pgs. 257-66.

Jones, Richard M. *Fantasy and Feeling in Education.* New York: New York
   University Press, 1968.

Kephart, Newell C. *The Slow Learner in the Classroom*, 2d ed. Columbus, OH:
   Charles Merrill, 1971.
Koch, Kenneth, et al. *Wishes, Lies, and Dreams: Teaching Children to Write
   Poetry.* New York: Harper & Row, 1980.
Kogan, Sheila. *Step by Step: A Complete Movement Education Curriculum from
   Preschool to Sixth Grade.* Edited by Frank Alexander. Byron, CA: Front Row
   Experience, 1982.
Kolers, Paul A., and W. E. Smythe. "Images, Symbols, and Skills." *Canadian
   Journal of Psychology* 33(1979), pgs. 158-84.
Krishamurti, Jiddu. *Commentaries on Living*, Series 2. New York: Harper & Row,
   1981.
———. *Education and the Significance of Life.* New York: Harper & Row, 1981.

Landis, Beth, and Polly Carder. *The Eclectic Curriculum in American Music
   Education: Contributions of Dalcroze, Kodaly, and Orff.* Washington, DC:
   Music Educators National Conference, 1972.
Languis, Marlin, Tobie Sanders, and Steven Tipps. *Brain and Learning: Directions
   in ECE.* Washington, DC: NAEYC, 1980.
Leff, Herbert L. *Playful Perception: Choosing How to Experience Your World.*
   Burlington, VT: Waterfront Books, 1984.

MacLean, Paul D. *A Triune Concept of the Brain and Behavior.* Toronto, Canada:
   University of Toronto Press, 1973.
Maslow, Abraham. *The Farther Reaches of Human Nature.* New York:
   Viking/Penguin, 1976.
Memmler, Ruth L., and Dena Wood. *Structure and Function of the Human Body.*
   Philadelphia: Lippincott, 1977.

Numella, Renate M., and Tennes M. Rosengren. "The Brain's Routes and Maps:
   Vital Connections in Learning." *NASSP Bulletin* (April 1986).
———. "What's Happening in Students' Brains May Redefine Teaching."
   Educational Leadership 43(1986), pgs. 49-53.

Ornstein, Robert E. *The Mind Field.* New York: Grossman, 1976.
———. *The Nature of Human Consciousness: A Book of Readings.* San Francisco:
   W. H. Freeman, 1973.
———. *The Psychology of Consciousness*, 2d ed. San Diego: Harcourt Brace
   Jovanovich, 1977.
Ornstein, Robert E., and Richard F. Thompson. *The Amazing Brain.* Boston:
   Houghton Mifflin, 1984.
Ostrander, Sheila, and Lynn Schroeder. *Superlearning.* New York: Dell/Delta,
   1980.

Pearce, Joseph C. *Exploring the Crack in the Cosmic Egg*. New York: Simon & Schuster, 1974.

―――. *The Magical Child: Rediscovering Nature's Plan for Our Children*. New York: Dutton, 1977.

―――. *The Magical Child Matures*. New York: Dutton, 1985.

Piaget, Jean. *Play, Dreams, and Imitation in Childhood*. New York: Norton, 1962.

―――. *Science of Education and the Psychology of the Child*. Translated by Derek Coltman. New York: Orion Press, 1970.

Piaget, Jean, and Barbel Inhelder. *The Psychology of the Child*. New York: Basic Books, 1969.

Pribram, Karl. *Languages of the Brain*. Englewood Cliffs, NJ: Prentice-Hall, 1971.

Restak, Richard M. *The Brain: The Last Frontier*. Garden City, NY: Doubleday, 1979.

Robbins, Arthur, and Linda Sibley. *Creative Art Therapy*. New York: Brunner-Mazel, 1976.

Rogers, Carl. *Freedom to Learn*. Columbus, OH: Charles Merrill, 1969.

Russell, Peter. *The Global Brain: Speculations on the Evolutionary Leap to Planetary Consciousness*. Los Angeles: Tarcher, 1983.

Samples, Bob. *The Metaphoric Mind*. Reading, MA: Addison-Wesley, 1976.

―――. *Openmind/Wholemind*. Rolling Hills Estates, CA: Jalmar Press, 1987.

Schnitker, Max. *The Teacher's Guide to the Brain and Learning*. San Rafael, CA: Academic Therapy Publications, 1972.

Simon, Sidney. *Caring, Feeling, Touching*. Niles, IL: Argus Communications, 1976.

Singer, Jerome. *The Inner World of Daydreaming*. New York: Harper & Row, 1976.

Smith, Anthony. *The Mind*. New York: Viking, 1984.

Springer, Sally P., and Georg Deutsch. *Left Brain, Right Brain*. New York: W. H. Freeman, 1981.

Sullivan, Molly. *Feeling Strong, Feeling Free: Movement Exploration for Young Children*. Washington, DC: NAEYC, 1982.

Thomas, J. "Children's Motor Skill Development." In *Motor Skill Development During Childhood and Adolescence*, edited by J. Thomas. Minneapolis: Burgess, 1984.

Trevarthen, Colwyn. "Brain Development." In *Oxford Companion to the Mind*, pgs. 101–10. New York: Oxford University Press, 1987.

Turnbull, Colin. *The Human Cycle*. New York: Simon and Schuster, 1983.

Valett, Robert. *Humanistic Education: Developing the Total Person*. St. Louis: C. V. Mosby, 1977.

Vitale, Barbara Meister. *Free Flight*. Rolling Hills Estates, CA: Jalmar Press, 1986.

―――. *Unicorns Are Real: A Right-brained Approach to Learning*. Rolling Hills Estates, CA: Jalmar Press, 1982.

Von Oech, Roger. *A Whack on the Side of the Head: How to Unlock Your Mind for Innovation*. New York: Warner Books, 1983.

Wickstrom, Ralph L. *Fundamental Motor Patterns*, 3d ed. Philadelphia: Lea and Febiger, 1983.

Williams, Verlee L. *Teaching for the Two-sided Mind: A Guide to Right Brain-Left Brain Education*. Englewood Cliffs, NJ: Prentice-Hall, 1983.

Wilmes, Liz, and Dick Wilmes. *Parachute Play*. Elgin, IL: Building Blocks, 1985.

Wittrock, Merl, et al. *The Human Brain*. Englewood Cliffs, NJ: Prentice-Hall, 1977.

Wonder, Jacquelyn, and Priscilla Donovan. *Whole Brain Thinking*. New York: Morrow, 1984.

Zaichkowsky, Lionard D., et al. *Growth and Development: The Child in Physical Activity*. St. Louis: C. V. Mosby, 1980.

Index

The names of activities are in italics. *The page numbers of illustrations are in* boldface *type.*

Following Directions, 248–49
Food Prices, 287
Foot-eye coordination, 66, 68
Foot preference
  as assessment of hemisphericity, 109
Free Blow (bubbles), 211–12, **211**
Friends, 171–72
Frog Jumps, 158
Functional reading, 304–9

Games (for teaching numbers), 287
Giant Bubble, The, 217, **218**
Giant Season Collage, The, 258
Guided imagery, 126, 128–29. *See also*
  Imagery *and* Imaging

Hand Clapping, 237–38
Hand Clapping with a Partner, 238–39
Hand-eye coordination, 66
Hand position for writing
  as assessment of hemisphericity, 111,
  112, 113
Handedness
  as assessment of hemisphericity,
  107–9
  and dominance, 11, 72
  and laterality, 72–73
Hanging Loose, 138–40, **139**
Hard-boiled Eggs, 217–19
Hebb, D. O., 27, 79
Hemisphere, left
  Broca's area, 38, 125
  dominance, 17, 275
  functions, 13
  and language, 18, 125, 296
  and right side of body, 10, 17, 62, 73,
  111
  and sequencing, 242
Hemisphere, right
  and directionality, 170
  and feelings, 334–35
  functions, 13, 16–17, 276
  and imagination, 126, 311
  and left side of body, 10, 62, 73, 111
  and metaphoric language, 125–26,
  264
  and rhythm, 243
  and scientific exploration, 320
  and spatial awareness, 18, 124
  and symbolism, 83, 125

  and temporal awareness, 278
  use of, in early childhood, 11, 41, 83,
  90
  and writing alphabet, 310
Hemispheres of cerebral cortex. *See
  also* Dominance, hemispheric
  anatomy of, 10, 11, **35**, 36–39, **37**
  association fibers, 41, **42**, 43
  asymmetry of, 10, 12–13, 15, 17–19,
  36, 79, 89, 111
  in cerebrum, 36
  communication between, 11, 39
  and creativity, 12, 133
  frontal lobe, **35**, **37**, 38
  functions, 10–11, 13, 18–20, 38
  integration of, 12, 15, 21, 62, 75, 143
  lobes, 10, **35**, **37**–39
  motor cortex, 25, 34, **35**
  occipital lobe, **35**, **37**–39
  parietal lobe, **35**, **37**, 38
  projection fibers, 41, **42**, 43
  sensory cortex, 25, 34, **35**
  temporal lobe, 10, **37**, 38
  and vision, 37, 39
Hemisphericity, 17–19. *See also*
  Dominance, hemispheric, *and*
  Hemispheres of cerebral cortex:
  asymmetry of
Hippocampus, **40**, 44
Holonomic model of brain, 26–27
Hoops, 180
Hopping, 160
  activities, 160–65
Hopping Circle, The, 161–64
Hopping Maze, 164–65, **164**
Hopping Rope, The, 165
Hopscotch Games, 161
Hopscotch patterns, **162**
House Place, The, 175–76
How I Express My Feelings, 339
How Many Words Do I Know? 317
How to Make a Word, 297–99
How We Are Alike, 346–47
How We Are Different, 350–51
Hunt, J. McV., 78
Hypothalamus, **40**, 45

If You're Silly and You Know It, 254
Imagery, 128, 130. *See also* Imaging
  and Metaphoric language